WITHDRAWAL

TWENTY MODERN
BRITISH PLAYWRIGHTS

GARLAND REFERENCE LIBRARY
OF THE HUMANITIES
(VOL. 98)

"TWENTY MODERN BRITISH PLAYWRIGHTS
A Bibliography, 1956 to 1976 "

Kimball King

GARLAND PUBLISHING, INC. • NEW YORK & LONDON
1977

Library of Congress Cataloging in Publication Data
King, Kimball.
   Twenty modern British playwrights.

   (Garland reference library of the humanities; v. 96)
   Includes index.
   CONTENTS: John Arden.—Alan Ayckbourn.—Peter
Barnes.—Robert Bolt.—Edward Bond. [etc.]
   1. English drama—20th century—Bibliography. I. Title.
Z2014.D7K47   [PR736]   016.'822'9'1   77-83353
ISBN 0-8240-9853-6

CONTENTS

ACKNOWLEDGMENTS

I owe a great debt to the playwrights and their agents who checked my lists of primary sources to make them as inclusive and accurate as possible. In particular I wish to thank Simon Gray, John Osborne, N. F. Simpson, and Arnold Wesker for personally responding to my inquiries and for checking over my copy and making suggestions. Margaret Ramsay Ltd., who represents more than half of the playwrights named in the study, was especially helpful and made additions and corrections to my bibliographies of John Arden, Alan Ayckbourn, Peter Barnes, Robert Bolt, Edward Bond, Christopher Hampton, Ann Jellicoe, Peter Nichols, and David Storey. Emmanuel Wax, agent for Heathcote Williams, also mailed revisions to me.

In addition I would like to thank Mrs. Pattie McIntyre and the staff at Wilson Memorial Library for crucial assistance, particularly in the planning stages of my research; the Smith fund of the University of North Carolina and the Department of English for providing funds for typists, research assistants, and proofreaders; Wade Pridgen, Cynthia Adams, Mary Jean Moore, James Hoeflinger, and John Leland, all graduate students at Chapel Hill, for being excellent scholarly detectives; Mrs. Joyce Bradshaw for typing my handwritten annotations and Mrs. Muriel Dyer for typing an earlier, unannotated bibliography and my manuscript in its present form.

Kimball King
Department of English
University of North Carolina
Chapel Hill, North Carolina

INTRODUCTION

Although there are always a few gifted playwrights in any civilized country, the phenomenon of a group of dramatists working with common themes or goals is extremely rare. Such creative movements in the theatre have usually developed in a major commercial city. The Athens of Aeschylus, Sophocles, and Euripides comes immediately to mind. The neoclassical dramas of Corneille, Molière, and Racine are inextricably connected with seventeenth-century Paris. In English literature, of course, the range and power of the Renaissance drama still astound, for Shakespeare's London was also the home of Ben Jonson, Marlowe, Middleton, Rowley, Beaumont and Fletcher, Chapman, Webster, and Ford. A combination of historical and cultural forces as well as possibly inexplicable accidents of genius produced one of the world's most extensive theatre movements. The exhilarating reign of Queen Elizabeth I, the growth of humanism in the universities, the Protestant concern with the individual's obligation to examine moral issues, the spirit of renewal brought by colonization, and the rapid growth of trade and commerce may all have contributed to an intellectual climate where great art could flourish. The focus of attention was on the Globe Theatre where Shakespeare's greatest plays were performed before the building was destroyed by fire. The English stage became a mirror of Elizabethan, then Jacobean, life. It took the Puritan revolution and the subsequent closing of the theatres to terminate England's greatest dramatic period.

When eighteen years later in the Restoration the theatres reopened with cynical comedies and grandiose "heroic" dramas, the stage again exuded vitality; certainly a movement with identifiable themes and prominent playwrights could be defined, but the depth and complexity of the Renaissance productions were missing. In the years to follow, from the eighteenth to the twentieth century, certain outstanding playwrights made literary history—Sheridan, Goldsmith, Wilde, and Shaw, to name the most prominent. But none of these individualistic playwrights spearheaded a dramatic movement.

No, the English-speaking world waited until May 8, 1956, for a genuine theatre movement which would demand worldwide recognition. On that day John Osborne's *Look Back in Anger* was first performed at the Royal Court Theatre on Sloan Square. Now the Royal Court, rather than the Globe, is the symbolic home for avant-garde dramatists. Another Elizabeth is queen, although she presides over what seems to be a declining empire. The welfare state has stifled the English business instinct. Only the Irish problem links the country to her past, although curiously few of the new playwrights dwell on this controversial topic. In fact, few of these playwrights are overtly political; all are obsessed, on the contrary, with class conflict, the decline in humanistic values, the escalation of violence in civilized societies, or personal and social alienation. A movement which began as an expression of anger—frustration at England's dwindling role in world affairs, at the failed promises of socialism, at continued economic injustice—seems now to be more concerned with the *fear* of anger. The pretense of a calm rationality masks the rage of the heroes and anti-heroes of recent years.

Theatre in New York or even Paris has recently been dominated by English imports. There is no comparable theatrical movement outside of Britain—nothing with the range, energy, or sheer prodigious output. Undoubtedly the popularity of television after World War II had an impact on these writers, since so many have had television experience, in some cases doing their first writing for television. Even more important, the subsidization of art by the English Arts Council, established in 1945, had a great influence on the quality of the theatre. The English Stage Company, the National Theatre Company, and the Royal Shakespeare Company provide unexcelled opportunities for the finest actors. The superb performances of many of these plays have given additional momentum to the movement. There are

thirty or more playwrights, ranging in age from their early
twenties to late fifties, producing drama of the highest calibre.
Most likely we shall be hearing from this group for at least
another fifty years. All of these artists seem to be acquiring new
skills and maturing as thinkers. Osborne, Pinter, and Stoppard
show signs of becoming "the Greats" of their time, although
Arden, the Shaffer brothers, Christopher Hampton, Simon Gray,
Edward Bond, David Storey, and others should not be
overlooked.

For this bibliography I have chosen twenty English
playwrights, somewhat arbitrarily. My research grew out of my
own attempts to evaluate the range of New Drama. Because
many graduate and undergraduate students and colleagues
expressed an interest in obtaining critical materials related to the
movement, it seemed logical to place checklists of the major
figures in a single volume. Naturally the list of primary and
secondary materials is constantly growing, but a student should
find here a useful starting place for research. I omitted Brendan
Behan because he is essentially an Irish writer whose themes and
preoccupations differ widely from the mainstream. And Samuel
Beckett, though Irish by birth, is the leader of the French
absurdist movement. In some cases there was insufficient
scholarship available to warrant inclusion. Fine playwrights, such
as David Rudkin, Peter Terson, or John Hopkins, have not yet
been "discovered" by critics.

My major sources for groundwork are listed below. Primary
sources in the bibliography have been verified whenever possible
by the playwrights themselves or their agents. Interviews and
critical articles have been comprehensively surveyed and
annotated. It should be noted that articles only one page in length
have not been annotated. Reviews included here have been
treated more selectively since, necessarily, their quantity is
disproportionate to their value as literary research material.

Abstracts of English Studies, 1958– . Boulder, Colo.: National
Council of Teachers of English.

Annual Bibliography of English Language and Literature,
   1920– . London: Modern Humanities Research Association.

Cambridge Bibliography of English Literature, 5 vols.
   Cambridge: Cambridge University Press.

Contemporary Dramatists, ed. James Vinson. London: St.
   James Press, 1973.

Cumulative Book Index, 1928– . New York: H. W. Wilson.

Dissertation Abstracts, 1938– . Ann Arbor, Mich.: University
   Microfilms.

*Dissertations in English and American Literature; Theses
   Accepted by American, British, and German Universities,
   1865–1964*, by Lawrence F. McNamee. New York and
   London: R. R. Bowker, 1968.

Drama Criticism Index by Paul Breed and Florence Sniderman.
   Detroit: Gale Research Co., 1972.

Dramatic Index, 1909–1949. Boston, R. W. Faxon.

Essay and General Literature Index, 1900– . New York: H. W.
   Wilson.

Index to Little Magazines, 1943– . Denver: Alan Swallow.

*Index to Theses Accepted for Higher Degrees in the Universities
   of Great Britain and Ireland*, 1950– . London: ASLIB.

International Index to Periodicals, 1907– . New York: H. W.
   Wilson. From vol. 19 (April 1965–March 1966) called *Social
   Sciences and Humanities Index*.

Masters Abstracts, 1962– . Ann Arbor, Mich.: University
   Microfilms.

New York Times Index.

PMLA Bibliography.

Readers' Guide to Periodical Literature, 1900– . New York: H. W. Wilson.

Subject Index to Periodicals, 1915–1961. London: The Library Association. Continued as *British Humanities Index*, 1962– .

Theatre Dissertations, ed. Frederic M. Litto. Kent, Ohio: Kent State University Press, 1969.

The Times Index.

Year's Work in English Studies, 1919– . London: The English Association.

JOHN ARDEN

Born Barnsley, Yorkshire, October 26, 1930

John Arden is more a playwright of the countercul-
ture than Osborne and in England he is equally famous.
During the Vietnamese conflict **Serjeant Musgrave's Dance**
with its firm criticism of capitalism and war-mongering
made a notable impact in America as well as England. Arden's dramatic techniques are powerful. He imitates
Brecht, creating a kind of epic theatre. He is not as
good a poet as Brecht; his music is not so skillfully
interwoven into the total spectacle. Yet his ideas are
clearly articulated and nearly always didactic. Recently
Arden and his wife Margaretta D'Arcy have been intensely
involved with the problems of Northern Ireland. The production of an Arden play is apt to be a scene of violent
political demonstrations. It remains to be seen if his
radicalism will be a source of strength for his playwriting or whether it will divert him from the theatre. Un-
questionably he is idealistic, socially concerned, and
has an explosive style.

PRIMARY SOURCES

I. STAGE

All Fall Down. Staged Edinburgh 1955.

Armstrong's Last Goodnight: An Exercise in Diplomacy.
    London: Eyre Methuen, 1965.

_____. New York: Grove Press, 1967.

Ars Longa, Vita Brevis. Encore, 11, ii (March-April
    1964), 13-20

_____. With Margaretta D'Arcy. London: Cassell, 1965.

The Bagman; or, the Impromptu of Muswell Hill. In Two
    Autobiographical Plays.

1

_____. Scripts, 1, viii (June 1972).

The Ballygomkeen Bequest. With Margaretta D'Arcy. Scripts, 1, ix (September 1972).

The Business of Good Government: A Christmas Play. With Margaretta D'Arcy. (Produced as A Christmas Play.) London: Eyre Methuen, 1963.

_____. With Margaretta D'Arcy. (Produced as A Christmas Play.) New York: Grove Press, 1967.

Fidelio. Adaptation of a libretto by Joseph Sonnleithner and Friedrich Treitschke, music by Beethoven. Staged London. 1965.

Friday's Hiding. With Margaretta D'Arcy. In Soldier, Soldier and Other Plays.

The Happy Haven. With Margaretta D'Arcy. In Three Plays.

_____. With Margaretta D'Arcy. In New English Dramatists 4. London: Penguin, 1962.

Harold Muggins Is a Martyr. With Margaretta D'Arcy and the Cartoon Archetypal Slogan Theatre. Staged London 1968.

The Hero Rises Up: A Romantic Melodrama. With Margaretta D'Arcy. London: Eyre Methuen, 1969.

Ironhand. Adaptation of the play Goetz von Berlichingen by Goethe. London: Eyre Methuen, 1965.

The Island of the Mighty. With Margaretta D'Arcy. London: Eyre Methuen, 1971.

_____. With Margaretta D'Arcy. Plays and Players, 20, v, vi (February, March 1973).

_____. With Margaretta D'Arcy. London: Eyre Methuen, 1974. (Illustrated with drawings by the authors.)

Left-Handed Liberty: A Play about Magna Carta. London: Eyre Methuen, 1965.

_____. New York: Grove Press, 1966.

Live Like Pigs. In Three Plays.

_____. In New English Dramatists 3. London: Penguin, 1961.

2

_____. In <u>Post-War Drama</u>: <u>Extracts from Eleven Plays</u>.
Ed. John Hale. London: Faber and Faber, 1966.

The <u>Non-Stop Connolly Show</u>. Staged Dublin 1975. With
Margaretta D'Arcy.

<u>Play Without Words</u>. Staged Glasgow 1965.

The <u>Royal Pardon</u>; or <u>The Soldier Who Became an Actor</u>.
With Margaretta D'Arcy. London: Eyre Methuen,
1966.

<u>Serjeant Musgrave's Dance</u>: <u>An Unhistorical Parable</u>.
London: Eyre Methuen, 1960.

_____. <u>Plays and Players</u> 8 (September-October 1961).

_____. New York: Grove Press, 1962.

_____. Revised version. Staged London 1962.

_____. In <u>The New British Drama</u>. Ed. Henry Popkin.
New York: Grove Press, 1964.

<u>La Danse du Sergent Musgrave</u>. <u>L'Avant Scene</u>, 309 (April
1964). In French.

<u>Soldier, Soldier</u>. In <u>Soldier, Soldier and Other Plays</u>.

<u>Soldier, Soldier and Other Plays</u>. London: Eyre Methuen,
1966. (Includes <u>Wet Fish</u>, <u>When Is a Door Not a
Door?</u>, and <u>Friday's Hiding</u>.)

The <u>Soldier's Tale</u>. Adaptation of a libretto by Ramuz,
music by Stravinsky. Staged Bath, Somerset 1968.

<u>Three Plays</u>: <u>The Waters of Babylon</u>, <u>Live Like Pigs</u>, <u>The
Happy Haven</u>. London: Penguin, 1964.

_____. New York: Grove Press, 1966.

The <u>True History of Squire Jonathan and His Unfortunate
Treasure</u>. <u>Plays and Players</u>, 15 (August 1968).

_____. in <u>Two Autobiographical Plays</u>.

<u>Two Autobiographical Plays</u>: <u>The True History of Squire
Jonathan and His Unfortunate Treasure</u>, and <u>The Bag-
man; or, The Impromptu of Muswell Hill</u>. London:
Eyre Methuen, 1971.

The <u>Waters of Babylon</u>. In <u>Three Plays</u>.

<u>Wet Fish</u>. In <u>Soldier, Soldier and Other Plays</u>.

When Is a Door Not a Door? In Soldier, Soldier and Other
    Plays.

The Workhouse Donkey. Plays and Players, 10 (August-
    September 1963).

The Workhouse Donkey: A Vulgar Melodrama. London: Eyre
    Methuen, 1964.

The Workhouse Donkey. New York: Grove Press, 1967.

Wozzeck. Adaptation of a libretto by Alan Berg, based on
    the play by Büchner, music by Alan Berg. Staged
    London 1964.

II. TELEVISION

Sean O'Casey: A TV Portrait.

Soldier, Soldier, 1960.

Wet Fish, 1961.

III. RADIO PLAYS

The Bagman, 1970.

Keep Those People Moving (a nativity play for children),
    1972.

The Life of a Man, 1956.

Pearl, 1977.

IV. FICTION

"Whose Dreams." New Statesman, 14 July 1961, p. 60.
    [A poem.]

"Johnny Finn." Twentieth Century, 169 (February 1961),
    220.

V. NON-FICTION

"Brecht and the Brass Trade." The Guardian, 29 July
    1965, p. 6.

The Caretaker. New Theatre Magazine, 4 (July 1960), 29-
    30.

"Correspondence to the Editor." Encore (May-June 1959).

"Delusions of Grandeur." Twentieth Century, 169 (Febru-
     ary 1961), 200-06.

"An Embarrassment to the Tidy Mind." Ambit, 22 (1972),
     30-37.

"How to Understand Hell." Twentieth Century, 173 (Winter
     1964-65), 99-101.

"Letters to the Editors." Encore (September-October
     1964), 50-52.

"Poetry and Theatre." Times Literary Supplement, 6
     August 1964, p. 705.

"Shakespeare: To a Young Dramatist." The Guardian, 23
     April 1964, p. 11.

"Telling A True Tale." In The Encore Reader. Ed. Charles
     Marowitz. London: Eyre Methuen, 1965. Pages 125-
     29. Reprinted from Encore, 7, iii (1960), 41-43.

"Theatre People Reply to Our Inquiry [about realism]."
     World Theatre, 14, i (1965), 44-45.

"A Thoroughly Romantic View." London Magazine (July
     1960), 11-15.

"Verse in the Theatre." New Theatre Magazine, 2, iii
     (1961), 200-06.

"Vital Theatre." Encore, 6, iii (1959), 41-43. [Letter.]

VI. INTERVIEWS

Hennessy, Brendan. "John Arden." The Times Educational
     Supplement, 9 April 1971, p. 19.

Hunt, Albert. "On Comedy: John Arden Talks to Albert
     Hunt about The Workhouse Donkey." Encore, 12, v,
     (1965), 13-19.
          The playwright discusses the significance of the
     donkey, particularly as a medieval Lord of Misrule,
     symbol of annual Feast of Fools. Arden advocates a
     relaxation of censorship through which the theater
     may deal with explicit material in other than a
     serious context. His discussions of character and
     morality center around The Workhouse Donkey with
     occasional references to Brecht and Greek comedy.

Marowitz, Charles and Simon Trussler. Theatre at Work.
London: Eyre Methuen, 1967. Pages 12, 17, 34, 36-
57. (Interview with Tom Milne and Clive Goodwin,
first published in Encore in 1961, followed by replies to further questions put by Simon Trussler in
1966.)
This is a good general interview covering, among
other subjects, Arden's career as a playwright, his
writing techniques, his political themes, and his
use of prose for "conveying plot and character relationships" and poetry for heightened emotion. Arden
answers a number of specific and unrelated questions
on The Happy Haven, Serjeant Musgrave's Dance, The
Business of Good Government, The Workhouse Donkey,
Armstrong's Last Goodnight, Left-Handed Liberty, and
Ars Longa, Vita Brevis. Of his plays, he claims, "I
write . . . partly indeed to express what I know,
feel, and see, but even more to test the truth of my
knowledge, feelings and vision."

Wager, Walter, ed. The Playwrights Speak. New York:
Delacorte, 1967. Pages 244-68.
The introduction to this interview chronicles
Arden's career through the 1966 American premiere
of Musgrave's Dance. The interview itself is basi-
cally the same as the one which appeared in Tulane
Drama Review, 11, ii (1966) under the title "Who's
For a Revolution," 41-53.

_____ and Simon Trussler. "Who's for a Revolution? Two
Interviews with John Arden." Tulane Drama Review,
11, ii (1966), 41-53. [Ed. Kelly Morris.]
In the first interview by Walter Wager, Arden
discusses the situation of his playwriting, his education, where he writes and at what pace, his tastes
in European and American drama, and his relationships with other playwrights, with his neighbors,
and with television. The interview by Trussler concerns the themes and characters of several Arden
plays, including Left-Handed Liberty, Armstrong,
and Ars Longa.

SECONDARY SOURCES

I. CRITICISM

Abirached, Robert. "Le Jeune Théâtre Anglais." Nouvelle
Revue Française, 29 (February 1967), 314-21.
Arden is mentioned as a playwright who makes ef-
fective use of symbols and parables in his work.

Adler, Thomas P. "Religious Ritual in John Arden's Ser-
    jeant Musgrave's Dance." Modern Drama, 16 (1973),
    163-66.
        In response to Mary B. O'Connell's suggestion
    that Serjeant Musgrave's Dance is a folk ritual
    based on the medieval mummers play, Adler posits
    that the first dance in the play contains more spe-
    cifically religious elements and that Musgrave's
    hoisting of the skeleton and his dance around it is
    a grotesque parody of the crucifixion. Musgrave's
    failure, Adler argues, is that his plan for ven-
    geance is antithetical to the meaning of the cross.
    But the ultimate deaths of Altercliffe and Musgrave
    in the play may, in fact, be an expiation for their
    violence and "one step closer to inaugurating God's
    dance of love and peace on earth."

"Arden Professionals and Amateurs." Encore, 12, v
    (1965), 9-12. (A conversation between Albert Hunt
    and Geoffrey Reeves.)
        Albert Hunt and Geoffrey Reeves, both of whom have
    directed Arden plays, discuss techniques and prob-
    lems of interpretation with particular regard to Ars
    Longa. Hunt finds Arden "first and foremost a story
    teller," and stresses the importance of maintaining
    a view of the work as a whole despite the temptation
    to concentrate on particulars. Both directors see
    Arden as iconoclastic; Reeves advocates a reforma-
    tion of the current "professional framework," while
    Hunt asks the public to reconcile the theatre with
    everyday life.

Blau, Herbert. The Impossible Theatre. New York: Mac-
    millan, 1964. Pages 220-27.
        Blau examines Musgrave's Dance as a portrayal of
    the "divided nature of man." The play's ballad-like
    structure renders its images timeless and powerful.
    Blau discusses in detail his experience with the
    American premiere of the play, with particular at-
    tention to problems of pacing and set design.

Blindheim, Joan T. "John Arden's Use of the Stage."
    Modern Drama, 11 (1968), 306-16.
        Arden himself, has stated his concern with prac-
    tical matters, such as set decoration and the logis-
    tics of a large cast, to his architectural training.
    Blindheim examines the physical aspects of each play
    and outlines Arden's range from traditional realism
    to anti-illusionism to experimental "vital theatre."
    Sources from theatre history, particularly medièval
    and eighteenth century plays, are cited, but Blind-
    heim stresses the originality of Arden's stage tech-
    nique.

Bonford, François. "Falstaffian Characters in Two Plays
    by John Arden." Revue des Langues Vivantes
    (Bruxelles), 38 (1972), 164-74.
        Bonford sees Arden's plays as presentations of
    moral conflict embodied in antagonistic characters
    rather than Brechtian political dramas. Armstrong's
    Last Goodnight, and to some extent The Workhouse
    Donkey, are compared to Shakespeare's Henry the
    Fourth. Bonford finds similarities of conflict
    among the plays and suggests that such a study might
    reveal more clearly the structure of Arden's politi-
    cal situation and clarify his intended message.

Brandt, G. W. "Realism and Parables: From Brecht to
    Arden." In Contemporary Theatre. Ed. John Russell
    Brown and Bernard Harris. Stratford-upon-Avon
    Studies, 4. London: Arnold, 1962. Pages 33-55.
        In this pot-pourri of modern English parable
    plays, Brandt briefly discusses theme, poetic ele-
    ments and recurrent color imagery in Arden's Ser-
    jeant Musgrave's Dance.

Brown, John R. Theatre Language: A Study of Arden, Os-
    borne, Pinter and Wesker. London: Allen Lane,
    1972. Pages 190-234.
        Brown devotes a chapter to Arden's unusual com-
    binations of prosaic and poetic verbal rhythms, his
    use of music, his treatment of direct, yet evocative,
    dialogue.

Bryden, Ronald. "Deep as England." New Statesman, 17
    December 1965, p. 979.

Capriolo, Ettore. "Introduzione a Arden." Nuova Cor-
    rente, 13, xxxvii (1966), 50-58.
        This is a general introduction to Arden for
    Italian scholars which includes a brief biography,
    plot summaries and a discussion of themes and tech-
    niques.

Chiari, Joseph. Landmarks of Contemporary Drama. London:
    Herbert Jenkins, 1965. Pages 118-19.
        Chiari makes an occasional mention of Arden:
    ". . . on the strength of Serjeant Musgrave's Dance,
    it is safe to say that he shows greater possibili-
    ties of originality than most of his contemporaries."

Craig, H. A. L. "Poetry in the Theatre." New Statesman
    and Nation, 12 November 1960, pp. 734, 736.
        Poetry exists in the modern theatre according to
    Craig in the guise of prose. Beckett, Pinter, and
    Arden transform ordinary speech into an extraordi-
    nary current between character and audience. In

Serjeant Musgrave's Dance, Craig suggests, Arden has
come closer to heroic poetry than anyone in his
generation. Though neither Pinter nor Arden share
Beckett's poetic invention and discipline, their
work achieves a synthesis of body and soul, forging
the true mark of poetry in the theatre.

Day, P. W. "Individual and Society in the Early Plays of
John Arden." *Modern Drama*, 18 (1975), 239-49.
    John Russell Taylor and J. D. Hainsworth are
among the very few critics who, according to Day,
have attempted to analyze Arden's work. Day examines their interpretations before proposing his own
--that the structure of Arden's first plays is based
upon the conventional music-hall format, overlaid
with conventional plot-lines, such as comedy in-
trigue, soap opera, and thriller. Arden's strong
portrayal of social structure, according to Day,
polarizes his characters into "acceptors" and "non-
acceptors." From this conflict arise dramatic paradoxes, self-interest and social concern.

_____. "Social Commentary and Dramatic Method in the
Plays of John Arden." In *Australasian Universities
Language and Literature Association: Proceedings and
Papers of the Thirteenth Congress Held at Monash
University 12-18 August 1970*. Ed. J. R. Ellis.
Melbourne: AULLA and Monash University, 197[1].
Pages 148-50. [Abstract.]
    This paper examines scenes from *Serjeant Mus-
grave's Dance*, *Live Like Pigs*, and *The Workhouse
Donkey*, which illustrate elements common to Arden's
plays. These include an "episodic music-hall type
of scene," use of both a working and governing
class, and a poetically-expressed social reality.

Epstein, Arthur D. "John Arden's Fun House." *University
Review* (Kansas City, Mo.), 36 (1970), 243-51. [On
The Happy Haven.]
    In a close examination of Arden's *The Happy Haven*,
Epstein finds madness still to prevail at the end of
the play. The substitution of Mrs. Phineus for the
doctor as supervisor of the ward is a comic reversal;
but, moreover, it is merely a substitution of one
form of irresponsibility for another. Epstein sees
no winner in Arden's Truth Game. Rather, the playwright points "the ironic finger of truth" at all
six of his characters.

Esslin, Martin. "Brecht and the English Theatre." *Tulane
Drama Review*, 11, ii (1966), 63-70.
    Brecht, Esslin suggests, has become more a fig-
urehead for left-wing, heavily subsidized theatre,
than a substantive influence upon it. Esslin finds

9

most recent English productions of Brecht unsatisfactory, due in part to overconcern with the
"Brechtian style" and misapprehension of the texts.
John Arden is considered the "truest follower of
Brecht," both in staging and subject matter. According to Esslin, "Arden, like Brecht, is a major poet
who uses charm as a vehicle for the special poetry
of the stage."

_____. "Brecht, the Absurd, and the Future." <u>Tulane</u>
     <u>Drama Review</u>, 7, iv (1963), 43-54.
          Brechtians argue that the Theatre of the Absurd
     is ineffective as social criticism, while Ionesco,
     as spokesman for the Absurdists, maintains that art
     cannot exist merely as a vehicle for theory, but
     must constitute an individual, self-contained ex-
     pression of itself. Esslin believes that a fusion
     of these two methods could result in great strides
     for avant-garde theatre. Both stem from an acknowl-
     edgement of the stage as such, rather than preten-
     sion to reality itself.

Fletcher, John. "Arnold Wesker, John Arden, and Arthur
     Adamov." <u>Caliban</u>, 3, ii (1967), 153-56.
          Two English playwrights and a French contemporary
     are compared here from their political themes. <u>Ser-</u>
     <u>jeant Musgrave's Dance</u>, says Fletcher, despite the
     ambiguities of its protagonist, "leaves no doubt
     about where Arden's own sympathies lie. . . ."
     Arden is found to have a wider range and power of
     language than either Osborne or Wesker. The poetic
     quality of his plays, according to Fletcher, will
     insure his lasting importance in the theatre.

Gascoigne, Bamber. <u>Twentieth-Century Drama</u>. London:
     Hutchinson & Co., 1962. Pages 204-06.
          In a survey of the New Drama, Gascoigne finds
     <u>Serjeant Musgrave's Dance</u> "more deeply thoughtful
     than any other new British play and the thought is
     fully dramatized." He attributes the play's commer-
     cial failure to the undue length of time preceding
     the revelation of the true nature of the soldier's
     mission.

Gilman, Richard. "Arden's Unsteady Ground." <u>Tulane</u>
     <u>Drama Review</u>, 11, ii (1966), 54-62. Reprinted in
     <u>Modern British Dramatists</u>. Ed. John Russell Brown.
     Englewood Cliffs: Prentice Hall, 1968. Pages 104-16.
          According to Gilman, Arden is not a traditional
     "political" or "sociological" playwright because his
     world offers no clear choices of action. Arden's
     drama arises from the conflict between the individual
     and the order and power which he knows must be im-
     posed. Gilman discusses this social and political

ambiguity as expressed in <u>Left-Handed Liberty</u>, the
<u>Happy Haven</u>, <u>Live Like Pigs</u>, <u>Musgrave</u>, and <u>Armstrong's Last Goodnight</u>.

Gowda, H. H. A. "John Arden and the Avant-Garde in English Drama." <u>Literary Half-Yearly</u>, 7, i (1966), 41-51.
    Gowda believes Arden is the most appealing English playwright of the 1960s. He emphasizes Arden's didacticism and commitment to moral change.

Grishina, E. "Dzoon Arden brosaet vyzov." <u>Teatr</u>, 5 (1969), 167-69.
    Arden offers a double challenge--both to Western values and to traditional methods of stagecraft.

Hahnloser-Ingold, Margrit. <u>Das englishe Theater und Bert Brecht: Die Dramen von W. H. Auden, John Osborne, John Arden in ihrer Beziehung zum epischen Theater von Bert Brecht und gemeinsamen elisabethanischen Quellen</u>. Bern: Francke, 1970.
    This book is divided into four parts. The first offers a survey of the new British dramatists, including Arden, and the second is an analysis of Brecht's career and techniques; parts three and four demonstrate thematic and structural similarities between the German and the English playwrights.

Hainsworth, J. D. "John Arden." <u>Hibbert Journal</u>, 65 (Autumn 1966), 25-27.
    Hainsworth calls Arden the most promising of New Wave playwrights and examines the complexity of several of his "failed idealists." Arden's moral ambiguity is seen as a method of making the public more aware of certain highly complex situations, the solutions to which, Hainsworth says, could not possibly be arrived at in the theatre.

_____. "John Arden and the Absurd." <u>Review of English Literature</u> (Leeds), 7, iv (1966), 42-49.
    In response to John Russell Taylor's assertion that Arden has disregarded entirely the current "fashion" for the Theatre of the Absurd, Hainsworth posits that Arden's plays, particularly <u>The Happy Haven</u> and <u>Musgrave's Dance</u>, share important themes with Absurdist drama. Despite their "topicality," Arden's plays convey the Absurdist sense of pessimism and disillusion quite often in the typically Absurdist form of farce.

Hampton, N. "Freedom and Order in Arden's <u>Ironhand</u>." <u>Modern Drama</u>, 19 (1976), 129-33.
    <u>Ironhand</u> is evidence of a basic paradox in Arden's world. Man needs to be free, but he must also live in a society.

Hare, Carl. "Creativity and Commitment in the Contemporary British Theatre." Humanities Association Bulletin, 16, i (1965), 21-28.
    After outlining the emergence of the New Wave,
Hare discusses four of the movement's major play-
wrights--Osborne, Wesker, Arden, and Pinter--with
regard to their attitudes toward social commitment.
Osborne and Wesker are found to be most concerned
with the social involvement of their characters,
while Arden examines more closely the situation out
of which commitments inevitably arise. Pinter's
plays, antithetical to those of Wesker and Osborne,
reveal characters too perplexed and frightened by
the world to venture out toward commitment.

Hatch, Robert. "A Coming Talent Casts Its Shadow Before."
Horizon, 4, vi (1962), 91-94.
    Hatch outlines Musgrave's Dance, Live Like Pigs,
and The Happy Haven in an attempt to introduce Arden
to the American public. Musgrave, he says, would
require the "money and the professional polish of a
Broadway production," while Live Like Pigs is more
suitable to off-Broadway. He calls for prompt attention to, and production of, Arden in this country.

Hayman, Ronald. John Arden. World Dramatists Series.
New York: Ungar, 1972.
    This drama series pamphlet is an excellent start-
ing place for a study of Arden. It includes biography, a chronology, and general explication of the
works and bibliography.

Hunt, Albert. Arden: A Study of His Plays. London:
Eyre Methuen, 1974.
    Hunt states the thesis of his book: "that the
revolutionary content of Arden's plays make stylistic demands that are outside the normal range of the
established theatre." The author provides an analysis of Arden's major works, and traces the playwright's increasing political commitment.

_____. "Arden's Stagecraft." Encore, 12, v (1965), 9-12.
Reprinted in Modern British Dramatists. Ed. John
Russell Brown. Englewood Cliffs: Prentice-Hall,
1968. Pages 98-102.
    According to Hunt, to see Arden as a naturalist
is to miss his point entirely. Arden's characters
are presented for compassion and contemplation
rather than for emotional appeal. Close identification with character by the spectator precludes the
overview from which the moral evaluation of a character arises. Hunt argues that by emphasizing the
unreality of his characters through use of masks or
other devices Arden allows them to comment upon

their own roles. Thus, Arden belongs in the popular
tradition of pantomime, in which constant awareness
of unreality transcends the traditional theatrical
requisite of belief.

_____. "Around Us . . . Things Are There." Encore, 8,
vi (1961), 24-32.
Modern British drama, claims Hunt, is a "poetry
of physical reality." He examines several naturalistic plays and films, with special attention to the
directorial techniques of Lindsay Anderson and his
experience with Arden's work. Serjeant Musgrave's
Dance is treated as an example of "materialist
poetry."

Jacquot, Jean. "Présentation de John Arden." In Le
théâtre moderne, II: Depuis la deuxième guerre
mondiale. Ed. Jean Jacquot. Paris: Eds. du
Centre National de la Recherche Scientifique, 1967.
Pages 133-56.
Jacquot notes that in Arden's ten year career he
has combined the popular English tradition with international theatrical innovations. His actors are
known for their special rapport with audiences. Beginning with The Waters of Babylon, Jacquot surveys
Arden's contribution. The playwright's central interest is man's government and the working out of
the social contract. Arden is a compassionate reformer who loves man despite his obvious imperfec-
tions.

Jones, David and Trevor Nunn. "Letter to the Editor,"
The Times, 5 December 1972, p. 17e. [Concerning The
Island of the Mighty.]

Jordan, Robert J. "Serjeant Musgrave's Problem." Modern
Drama, 13 (1970), 54-62.
The organization of Musgrave's Dance around the
conflict of duty and personal conviction, violence
and pacificism, aligns it with the Victorian and
Edwardian "problem play" tradition. Jordan cites
Musgrave's adherence to an "impersonal mechanical"
duty as the play's central issue, and thus inter-
prets the future of that system as at least a partial moral statement on Arden's part, an attribute
of his work which most critics have ignored or de-
nied. Jordan, however, concedes that the play ultimately fails to reconcile the conflict of personal
interest and general ideal.

Kitchin, Laurence. "Realism in the English Mid Century
Drama." World Theatre, 14, i (1965), 17-26.
Kitchin mentions Arden as one of the realists of
the 50s British dramatic generation who closed the

gap between theatre and life through their concern
with realistic dialect, stage setting, the lower
classes, and defiance of authority and convention.

Klotz, Günther. "Ein irisches Vermächtnis: The Bally-
gombeen Bequest von John Arden und Margaret D'Arcy."
Zeitschrift für Anglistik und Amerikanislik (East
Berlin), 22 (1974), 419-24.
    Klotz discusses the play which John Arden and
his wife Margaretta D'Arcy have written together as
an exploration of Anglo-Irish tensions. Klotz surveys the new drama briefly, summarizes Arden's
career, and praises the play.

Lacey, Paul A. "Two for the Revolution." Religious
Theatre, 6 (Summer 1968), 30-38.
    A comparison of Musgrave's Dance and Kenneth
Brown's The Brig reveals that these two seemingly
dissimilar plays are built upon a single theme:
"the devotion to violence even as a way to end violence" within a power structure. Lacey examines the
plays and their characters for ways in which man
"domesticates" violence, particularly through ritual
and discipline. Such structures he finds ultimately
to be vicious circles.

Lumley, Frederick. New Trends in Twentieth Century
Drama. London: Barrie and Rockliff, 1967. Pages
260-66.
    In this overview of Arden's work, Lumley finds
him ultimately bewildering. Musgrave's Dance is
seen as a "strange, complex and unsatisfactory play,"
as are The Workhouse Donkey, The Happy Haven, and
Left-Handed Liberty. Lumley finds Armstrong's Last
Goodnight Arden's only successful work to date.

Marowitz, Charles. "The Workhouse Donkey." In The Encore Reader. Ed. Charles Marowitz. London: Eyre
Methuen, 1965. Pages 238-41. Reprinted from Encore,
September 1963.
    This favorable review finds most other Arden
criticism inadequate. Critical circles, and the
public as well, says Marowitz, have been unwilling
to allow Arden the wide range of subject matter and
style which his peculiar talent demands at present.
The Workhouse Donkey is found to be intelligent,
funny, generous, and "meaningfully complex."

Marsh, P. "Easter at Liberty Hall: the Ardens' Non-Stop
Connolly Show." Theatre Quarterly, 5 (December
1975), 133-41.
    This is "a detailed report on the contents of the
six constituent plays (of Arden's and D'Arcy's Non-
Stop Connelly Show), their rehearsal, and their

14

reception." Marsh criticizes the lack of focus in the plays and the dense political debates which make them difficult to understand.

Matthews, Honor. The Primal Curse. New York: Schocken Books, 1967. Pages 190-94.
    Serjeant Musgrave's Dance, suggests Matthews, stems directly from Elizabethan Revenge drama, as practiced by Kyd, et al. Particular attention is given here to the episode of Musgrave's revelation of Billy Hicks' skeleton. Both the form and content of the scene are compared to certain Elizabethan conventions.

McMillan, Grant E. "The Bargee in Serjeant Musgrave's Dance." Educational Theatre Journal, 25 (1973), 500-03.
    McMillan feels that most critics have failed to see, and thus to examine, the profound pessimism of Serjeant Musgrave's Dance. Though he agrees with Mary O'Connell's suggestion that the play is a "contemporary folk ritual," he takes issue with her analysis of the play's cyclical implications. McMillan sees the Bargee as a reminder of the possible absurdity of natural cycles. Because the Bargee, like Milton's Satan, has chosen evil for his good, peace is unlikely to be achieved in the Dance and the cycle is unlikely to have meaning.

Messenger, Ann P. "John Arden's Essential Vision: Tragical-Historical-Political." Quarterly Journal of Speech, 58 (1972), 307-12.
    Messenger attempts here to find a common thread in Arden's canon to date. His tragic heroes, she says, never win our entire sympathy, for Arden never commits himself fully to an ideal. Rather, his plays portray a tragic conflict in which victory, freedom, and order occur as fleeting interludes.

Mills, John. "Love and Anarchy in Serjeant Musgrave's Dance." Drama Survey (Minneapolis), 7 (1969), 45-51.
    In reply to Malcolm Page's assertion that Musgrave's Dance challenges the motives of pacifists, Mills suggests that the play concerns itself more with anarchy. Annie in the pub scene serves for Mills as a symbol of "all there is" in the play's barren and tragic landscape; her life exists outside the confines of authority as an expression, however squalid, of individual determination.

Milne, Tom. "Cruelty, Cruelty." Encore, 11, ii (1964), 9-12.
    The trouble with "experimental theatre," suggests Milne, "is that the more successful the experiment,

the less experimental it seems." He finds the
"Theatre of Cruelty's" current program old-hat with
the exception of Arden's Ars Longa, Vita Brevis. At-
tributing most recent innovation to playwrights
alone, Milne calls for a rethinking by actors,
directors, and audience as well.

_____. "The Hidden Face of Violence." Encore, 7, i,
(1960), 14-20. Reprinted in Modern British Dramatists. Ed. John Russell Brown. Englewood Cliffs:
Prentice-Hall, 1968. Pages 38-46. Also reprinted
in The Encore Reader. Ed. Charles Marowitz. London: Eyre Methuen, 1965. Pages 122-23.
     Whiting's Saint's Day, Pinter's The Birthday
Party, and Arden's Serjeant Musgrave's Dance posits
Milne, are analyses of violence in the way that Mrs.
Warren's Profession and Ghosts are analyses of their
milieu's sexual malaise. "Each of these plays," he
says, "creates its own distinctive world . . . with
a mood and logic of urgency, directness and excitement." Each demands a high degree of emotional and
intellectual participation by the audience.

_____. "Producing Arden: an Interview with William
Gaskill." Encore, 12, v (1965), 37-44.
     Milne discusses with director William Gaskill the
generally unfavorable reaction of critics to Arden's
plays, particularly Armstrong's Last Goodnight.
Gaskill cites Arden's rich language and his use of
violence as a particular challenge to the director.
He compares Arden's language to Shakespeare's in
that both convey an extraordinary sense of "social
environment, and the texture of people's lives." As
a consequence, Arden overwrites and Gaskill sees
this as a unique trait in contemporary drama.

_____. "A Study of John Arden's Plays." New Left Review,
7 (January-February 1961), 21-23.
     Milne defends Arden's plays, claiming that they
are poorly received because (1) they challenge,
rather than corroborate the audience's prejudices
and (2) they do not explicitly state their message
but require instead concentrated imaginative involvement. Milne also discusses the primacy of
character over theme in Live Like Pigs, The Waters
of Babylon, and Serjeant Musgrave's Dance.

Morris, Rekha R. "John Arden's Significant Failure."
Literary Criterion (University of Mysore, India), 9,
ii (1970), 28-40.
     Arden is seen as a playwright who has received
more unfavorable criticism than praise, who has
explored unpopular topics, and has employed some
controversial techniques. Nevertheless, his daring,

16

his idealism, his wide range of interests command
respect.

Nightingale, Benedict. "The Theatre of Bewilderment."
The Guardian, 6 July 1965, p. 7.

O'Connell, M. B. "Ritual Elements in John Arden's Serjeant Musgrave's Dance." Modern Drama, 13 (1971),
356-59.
    According to O'Connell, Arden has modeled this
"contemporary folk ritual" upon the Mummers Play of
Plough Monday, in which folk characters enact a
drama consisting of three parts--Presentation, Dis-
pute and Quest. In the Middle Ages ritual dances
allowed for a realignment with moral and religious
order. O'Connell sees the modern version as a ritu-
alization of the contemporary attitudes toward violence and social structure.

Page, Malcolm. "The Motives of Pacifists: John Arden's
Serjeant Musgrave's Dance. Drama Survey (Minneapolis), 6 (1967), 66-73.
    Page interprets what has generally been regarded
as Arden's moral ambiguity as a theme of the plays--
that pacifists have had little impact precisely because they are uncertain of their own objectives and
do not clearly assess their social and political
milieu. The failure of Musgrave's pacificism is attributed to his own lack of understanding rather
than to the encompassing social structure.

_____. "Some Sources of Arden's Serjeant Musgrave's
Dance." Moderna Språk (Stockholm), 67 (1973), 332-
41.
    Page has consulted Arden himself on this topic
and attributes much of the play's plot to a recent
Cyprus incident, an American film, The Raid, Arden's
own experience, and his television play, Soldier,
Soldier. This article reveals in detail Arden's
"fleshing out" of Musgrave's story on a technical
framework derived from Brecht and the Elizabethans.

_____ and V. Evans. "Approaches to John Arden's Squire
Jonathan." Modern Drama, 13 (1971), 360-65.
    After chronicling what they term Arden's "repu-
diation of professional theater of the West End of
London in the last few years," Page and Evans examine Squire Jonathan as an inversion of fairytale and
myth. Jonathan, though of royal descent, is unat-
tractive; his damsel is called an "elephant"; and
their happy union is never achieved. Page and Evans
suggest parallels of imagery with Yeats and Lawrence
and touch upon a possible political theme, but ultimately find these aspects of the play inconsequential.

Prickett, Stephen. "Three Modern English Plays." Philologica Pragensia, 10 (1967), 12-21.
    Prickett maintains that Jellicoe's The Knack,
Arden's Musgrave's Dance and Pinter's The Caretaker
are all dramatic departures from naturalism which
nevertheless owe their effects to the naturalism
with which they are juxtaposed. Jellicoe's "savage
sexual farce" is ultimately an archetypal myth, a
fairy tale where the puny weakling wins the girl
from the villain. Arden's play is both the most
naturalistic yet the closest to being a parable,
where mankind must choose between the rose (ideal
beauty) or the apple (sensuous human beauty). Pinter
manages to make both the naturalistic world and the
mythic world exist simultaneously. He is influenced
by Beckett whereas Jellicoe and Arden owe a debt to
Brecht.

Reeves, Geoffrey. "John Arden et le théâtre populaire en
Angleterre." In Le theatre moderne, II: Depuis la
deuxième guerre mondiale. Ed. Jean Jacquot. Paris:
Eds. du Centre Nationale de la Recherche Scientifique, 1967. Pages 157-61.
    Like the Jacquot article which precedes it in the
same volume, this article takes a favorable view of
Arden's achievement. Reeves believes Arden is unpopular in some circles because he challenges many
basic premises of Western society and forces audiences to be self-critical.

Rush, David. "Grief, but Good Order." Moderna Språk
(Stockholm), 58 (1964), 452-58.
    Rush examines the appeal of Serjeant Musgrave's
Dance in its written form. He is most concerned
with Musgrave's motives and with the Brechtian "dis-
tancing" of subject matter, through which the audience may better achieve objectivity. This objectivity, along with Arden's rather traditional story-
telling technique, according to Rush, account for
his growing popularity among readers, while the ob-
scurity of Arden's language and setting may help to
explain his failure to achieve commercial success on
the stage.

Saurel, Renée. "Pinter, Arden, Weingarten." Les Temps
Modernes, 247 (1966), 1110-19.
    Saurel sees Arden as an original stylist who,
like Pinter and Weingarten, is a master of ambiguity.

Shrapnel, Susan. "John Arden and the Public State." The
Cambridge Quarterly, 4 (1969), 225-36.
    The language of Arden's play is examined closely
for its power of evoking a consciousness of community. Musgrave's Dance and Armstrong's Last Goodnight

are considered in this context, but Shrapnel admits to being uncertain about the role of theatre in community evolution.

Skloot, R. "Spreading the Word: the Meaning of Musgrave's Logic." Educational Theatre Journal, 27 (1975), 208-19.

In order to appeal to American audiences, Skloot suggests that a production of Serjeant Musgrave's Dance should focus on "the individual's problem of identity as it relates to the personal values of compassion, generosity, and love struggling to appear in a confused and divided self," instead of stressing the social themes. He further attempts to show that "the concealment and discovery of information is not only Arden's structural method but his theme as well."

Smith, Roger. "Rocking the Boat." Encore, 8, i (1961), 7-12.

Smith argues that the so-called left-wing theatre must arrive at a "coherent socialist ideology," despite the belief of Lindsay Anderson and others that such ideals arise out of the theatrical work itself. He proposes to draw for this framework from French and German social theorists, since he considers England to be an "intellectual backwater," in politics, philosophy, and literature. Smith sees Arden's Happy Haven as the most socially sophisticated play in years.

Styan, J. L. "The Published Play after 1956. II." British Book News: A Guide to Book Selection, 300 (August 1965), 601-05.

_____. The Dark Comedy. 2nd ed. London: Cambridge University Press, 1968. Pages 172-73.

Arden is associated with a bitter kind of comedy which is almost wholly dependent on irony.

Taylor, John Russell. Anger and After. London: Eyre Methuen, 1963. Pages 72-86.

Taylor applauds the Royal Court Theatre for its persistence in staging Arden's work, despite confused or unfavorable reaction from critics and public. He attributes this reaction to what he calls Arden's "amorality." His plays do not advocate one side of an issue or the other, but rather present the effects of that two-sided issue on the lives of individuals. Arden maintains this distance and objectivity, Taylor suggests, through overt theatricality; Arden's audience is aware of its presence in a theatre.

_____. "British Drama of the Fifties." World Theatre, 11, iii (1962), 241-54.

Taylor praises Arden for his striking theatrical effects, particularly his combination of casual and formal prose, his surprising use of music, and his sensitive treatment of old age and of conflicting value systems.

_____. "John Arden." In Modern British Dramatists, A Collection of Critical Essays. Ed. John Russell Brown. Englewood Cliffs: Prentice-Hall, 1968. Pages 83-97.

This is essentially a reprint of "John Arden" from Anger and After.

Thorne, Barry. "Serjeant Musgrave's Dance: Form and Meaning." Queen's Quarterly, 78 (1971), 567-71.

Thorne claims that Arden, in Serjeant Musgrave's Dance, incorporates the romantic plot structure and folk stylization of the Elizabethan dramatic tradition, "producing a modern Elizabethan hybrid, a tragicomedy." Thorne also points out that Arden's refusal to take sides in the issues he presents obscures the message of the play.

Trussler, Simon. "Arden--An Introduction." Encore, 12, v, (1965), 4-8. [This issue of Encore is devoted to Arden.]

Arden's "relative failure to win a mass audience" is here attributed to his flight from the metropolitan setting, his sophisticated and frequently obscure language, and his stylization and modification of Brechtian devices. Trussler, maintaining that Arden is not an amoral dramatist, as J. R. Taylor has suggested, but rather a dramatist who rejects dogma in favor of practical and thus malleable honesty. Trussler chronicles Arden's professional career calling him "the most consistently impressive of our contemporary dramatists."

_____. "British Neo-Naturalism." Drama Review, 13, ii (1968), 130-36.

Trussler examines New Wave drama as a resurrection of the "atrophying form" of naturalism. In one brief paragraph devoted to Arden, Trussler finds him less committed to naturalism than his contemporaries. Though his widely diverse plays have achieved little commercial success, Arden "may well eventually emerge as the best playwright of the new movement."

_____. John Arden (CEMW65). New York: Columbia University Press, 1973.

A broad overview of Arden's life, the reception of his plays, and a fairly detailed discussion of theme, tone, plot, characterization, and language in his plays. The book further reveals the impressive range of Arden's experimentation: "mannered comedy, grotesque farce, period problem play, autobiographical allegory, ballad opera, community drama, epic chronicle, mime play, melodrama."

_____. "Political Progress of a Paralyzed Liberal: The Community Dramas of John Arden." The Drama Review, 13, iv (1969), 181-91.
Arden's community drama, improvisations, and other experimental works are examined in detail, with special regard to their political content. Though several of the works are "autodestructive by intent," Trussler finds The Hero Rises Up to be a "potentially enduring work of art."

Tynan, Kenneth. Tynan Right and Left. New York: Atheneum, 1967. Page 21.

Wardle, Irving. "Arden: Intellectual Marauder." New Society, 9 December 1965, pp. 22-23.
Wardle discusses the non-resolution of conflict, the lack of causal links, and the mixture of the serious and obscene in Arden's plays which cause critical hostility and confusion. Wardle also points out that Arden, in many respects, is close to ancient Greek comedy, "a loose episodic form capable of accommodating high political debate side by side with knockabout fun and sex." However, Arden's practice at times falls short of his goals.

Wellwarth, George. The Theatre of Protest and Paradox. New York: New York University Press, 1964. Pages 267-73.
Wellwarth places Arden second only to Pinter in his assessment of the new dramatists. He likes the way Arden begins with an idea and organizes all his effects around it. His work is ambitious and dense without being pretentious.

Worth, Katherine J. "Avant Garde at the Royal Court Theatre: John Arden and N. F. Simpson." In Experimental Drama. Ed. William A. Armstrong. London: G. Bell, 1963. Pages 206-14.
Worth compares the works of Arden and Simpson. She finds both playwrights concerned with language and claims of Arden that he "evolves a rough, highly coloured, figurative language, based on a curious amalgam of northern dialects." She contrasts Arden's world of real life situations and major issues and his use of poetry and prose to Simpson's fantasy world and use of common speech.

II. DISSERTATIONS

Clayton, Philip T. "The Drama of John Arden as Communal
Ritual." Dissertation Abstracts International 34:
5162A (Cincinnati, 1974).
Clayton sees in Arden's own writings about drama
three major concerns--its ritual nature, its expression of community and its source in the Middle Ages.
The playwright's recurrent muse-goddess figures and
his clearly Apollonian and Dionysian master figure,
Clayton argues, posit classical dramatic conflicts
of death and rebirth, sacrifice, and heroic apothe-
osis. Despite Arden's frequently satiric critical
tone, he does suggest patterns for more successful
community structures.

Clinton, Craig D. "John Arden: A Playwright's Evolution."
Dissertation Abstracts International 34:2065A (Car-
negie-Mellon, 1973).
Critical confusion over Arden's work from its
earliest days is attributed to his seeming unwilling-
ness to take a stand on the issues he presents.
Clinton finds that his plays almost always center
and control a social rebel, over whom forces of order and control must triumph in the end. Arden's
recent collaborations with his wife, Margaret D'Arcy, mark a turning point in his career toward more
overt social and political didacticism.

Flaumenhaft, Mera J. "Politics and Technique in the
Plays of John Arden." Dissertation Abstracts International 31:5398A (Pennsylvania, 1970).
According to Flumenhaft, Arden views social or
political order as a temporary balance, achieved
through often violent struggle between the individual and a larger "problem." She examines his stage
techniques and draws substantive parallels between
Arden's work and that of Brecht and Shaw. Eight
Arden plays are examined in detail, as well as many
of his "community" experiments and improvisations.

Mack, Karin E. "Freedom and Order: A Stylistic and
Thematic Study of the Drama of John Arden." Dissertation Abstracts International 34:2638A (Columbia,
1973).
Arden's work is seen as a fusion of the socially
conscious realism and introspective experimentation
which emerged from the New Wave drama. Seven plays
are examined for their treatments of the conflict
between individual freedom and collective order.
Arden is found unwilling to commit himself to either
ideal. Rather, he presents objectively the ambiguity he sees and thus achieves a vibrant though ultimately inconclusive drama.

Matherne, Beverly M. "Established Authority in the Plays
    of John Arden." Dissertation Abstracts Internation-
    al 36:3734A (Saint Louis, 1974).
        The tension between the eccentric individual and
    the authority of the state in Arden's plays is seen
    to have roots in existentialism and the Angry Young
    Man movement. Matherne finds that, contrary to gen-
    eral critical appraisal, Arden's technique reveals a
    consistent viewpoint. His "comic reversals," she
    says, signify an upheaval, a triumph of anarchy, out
    of which temporary order arises in times of crises.
    His dramatic technique, unique at present, is com-
    pared to Brecht's and Shaw's.

McKernie, Grant F. "Politics in Modern British Drama:
    The Plays of Arnold Wesker and John Arden." Disser-
    tation Abstracts International 33:4580A (Ohio State,
    1973).
        The plays of Arden and Wesker are examined as
    representative of the "new Wave" period political
    drama. Wesker's overt socialism is contrasted with
    Arden's more objective portrayal of conflict within
    the system. The form of Arden's plays, suggests
    McKernie, grows in part from English ballad tradi-
    tion.

Roberts, Jeffrey L. "The Theatre of John Arden." Dis-
    sertation Abstracts International 32:5243A (Massa-
    chusetts, 1972).
        Despite similarities of form, Arden's plays are
    found to be entirely distinct from Brecht's. Rob-
    erts examines man's tendency toward disorder in
    Arden's plays in an attempt to clarify the author's
    viewpoint, which is generally thought to be ambigu-
    ous. In addition to his more commercial work, the
    dissertation also considers Arden's recent experi-
    mentation with free-form drama, "happenings," and
    community theatre as efforts toward more vital com-
    munication between author and audience.

III. REVIEWS

ARMSTRONG'S LAST GOODNIGHT

    The Times, 6 May 1964, p. 7d.

    Encore, 11, iv (1964), 47-51.

    New Statesman, 15 May 1964, 782-83.

    Prompt, 6 (1965), 37-38.

    Encore, 12, v (1965), 37-39.

New York Times, 7 July 1965, p. 26.

New Statesman, 16 July 1965, p. 94.

The Times, 13 October 1965, p. 31c.

Encounter, 25 October 1965, pp. 41-42.

HAPPY HAVEN

New Statesman, 16 April 1960, p. 554.

New Statesman, 24 September 1960, p. 430.

New York Times, 10 May 1963, p. 40.

HAROLD HUGGINS IS A MARTYR

New York Times, 14 July 1968, p. 4.

THE HERO RISES UP

The Times, 8 November 1968, p. 13a.

New York Times, 9 November 1968, p. 26.

ISLAND OF THE MIGHTY

The Times, 6 December 1972, p. 13b.

The Times, 9 December 1972, p. 15e. [Letter from
     John Arden and Margaretta D'Arcy.]

New York Times, 7 January 1973, II:1.

IRONHAND

The Times, 13 November 1963, p. 5a.

Encore, 11,i (1964), 48-51.

LEFT-HANDED LIBERTY

The Times, 16 June 1965, p. 17d.

New Statesman, 25 June 1965, pp. 1022-23.

Encore, 12, iv (1965), 39-41.

LIVE LIKE PIGS

The Times, 1 October 1958, p. 6c.

Spectator, 10 October 1958, p. 482.

New Statesman, 11 October 1958, p. 486.

New York Times, 8 June 1965, p. 48.

The Times, 9 February 1972, p. 10a.

NON-STOP CONNOLLY SHOW

Plays & Players, 22 (July 1975), 40-41.

Plays & Players, 23 (August 1976), 25.

SERJEANT MUSGRAVE'S DANCE

The Times, 23 October 1959, p. 18a.

Spectator, 30 October 1959, p. 594.

New Statesman, 31 October 1959, p. 574.

Illustrated London News, 7 November 1959, p. 610.

The Times, 22 February 1961, p. 13a.

New York Times, 9 March 1966, p. 44.

New York Times, 20 March 1966, II:1.

New York Times, 16 June 1968, p. 52.

SOLDIER, SOLDIER

The Times, 17 February 1960, p. 13c.

SQUIRE JONATHAN

The Times, 18 June 1968, p. 12g.

The Sunday Times, 15 July 1973, p. 37b.

New York Times, 24 December 1974, p. 10.

THE WATERS OF BABYLON

The Times, 21 October 1957, p. 3c.

WET FISH

The Times, 4 September 1961, p. 5a.

THE WORKHOUSE DONKEY

New York Times, 9 July 1963, p. 26.

New Statesman, 19 July 1963, p. 86.

Spectator, 19 July 1963, p. 83.

Illustrated London News, 20 July 1963, p. 104.

The Times, 17 February 1965, p. 16d.

ALAN AYCKBOURN

Born London, April 12, 1939

Alan Ayckbourn began his career as a writer under the pen name of Ronald Allen. His first important play under his own name was How the Other Half Loves. Though generally considered a writer of farce, Ayckbourn differs from most farceurs in two major ways. First, he seldom follows a classical formulaic plot-line. His situations are very innovative and self-consciously theatrical. Second, his dialogue contains a lot of biting satire and he seems concerned about the ethical shallowness of middle class people. Absurd Person Singular has had long runs in London and New York, and while always amusing, it explores the empty rituals of social mobility and the genuine pain of personal alienation.

PRIMARY SOURCES

I. STAGE

Absent Friends. Staged Scarborough 1974 and London 1975. London: Samuel French and Chatto & Windus, 1975.

Absurd Person Singular (also director). Staged Scarborough 1972; London 1973.

Bedroom Farce. Staged Scarborough 1975 and London 1977. London: Chatto & Windus, 1977.

Confusions. Staged Scarborough 1974 and London 1976. London: Samuel French, 1976.

Countdown, in We Who Are about to See, later called Mixed Doubles. Staged London 1969. London: Eyre Methuen, 1970.

Dad's Tale (as Ronald Allen). Staged Scarborough 1961.

Ernie's Incredible Illucinations. Staged London 1971. Published in Playbill Ore, ed. Alan Durband. London: Hutchinson, 1969.

How the Other Half Loves. Staged Scarborough 1969; ⸗
London 1970; New York 1971. London: Evans, 1972.

_____. New York: Samuel French, 1972.

Jeeves. Staged London 1975.

Just Between Ourselves. Staged Scarborough 1976.

Love after All (as Ronald Allen). Staged Scarborough
1959.

Me Times Me. Staged Scarborough 1970.

The Norman Conquests. A trilogy comprising Table Man-
ners, Living Together, and Round & Round the Garden.
Staged Greenwich 1974 and transferred to London
August 1974. London: Samuel French & Chatto and
Windus, 1975.

Pantoufle. Plaisir de France, no. 386.

_____. Trans. by Eric Kahane. L'Avant-Scene du Theatre
462 (December 1970).

Relatively Speaking. As Meet My Father, staged Scarborough 1965. As Relatively Speaking, staged
London 1967; New York 1970. London: Evans, 1968.

_____. New York: Samuel French, 1968.

The Sparrow. Staged Scarborough 1967.

The Square Cat (as Ronald Allen). Staged Scarborough
1959.

Standing Room Only (As Ronald Allen). Staged Scarborough
1962.

The Story So Far (also director). Staged Scarborough
1970.

Ten Times Table. Staged Scarborough 1977.

Time and Time Again (also director). Staged Scarborough
1971; London 1972.

Mr. Whatnot. Staged Stoke on Trent 1963; London 1964.

Xmas v Mastermind. Staged Stoke on Trent 1963.

SECONDARY SOURCES

I. CRITICISM

Joseph, Stephen. Theatre in the Round. London: Barrie
    and Rockliff, 1967. Pages 56-57, 88, 125.
         Joseph admires Ayckbourn as an actor and commends
    his use of special effects and exploitation of para-
    doxes.

Taylor, John Russell. The Second Wave. London: Eyre
    Methuen, 1971. Pages 155-62.
         Along with David Cregan and Simon Gray, Ayckbourn
    is an accomplished farceur. Taylor considers Brecht
    and the Theatre of the Absurd as influences on these
    playwrights. Ayckbourn's works are mechanically in-
    genious, but essentially shallow. He specializes in
    the "comedy of embarrassment." Taylor does not pre-
    dict great success for Ayckbourn but calls him a
    "reliable light entertainer."

II. REVIEWS

ABSURD PERSON SINGULAR

    New York Times, 3 August 1973, p. 20.

    New York Times, 9 October 1974, p. 48.

    New York Times, 20 October 1974, II:1.

HOW THE OTHER HALF LOVES

    New York Times, 7 August 1970, p. 23.

    New York Times, 11 September 1970, p. 33.

    New York Times, 30 March 1971, p. 23.

    New York Times, 4 April 1971, II:3.

NORMAN CONQUESTS

    New York Times, 17 September 1974, p. 41.

RELATIVELY SPEAKING

    New York Times, 14 July 1974, II:3.

PETER BARNES

Born London, January 10, 1931

    Peter Barnes's reputation rests primarily on his third play, The Ruling Class. Technically this play owes much to Brecht in its use of brief, highly theatrical scenes and to Pirandello in its exploration of illusion and reality. The Ruling Class is potent political satire, but it also contains the religious themes we find in Barnes's other plays. He deplores the lack of spiritual values in modern society and is appalled by the greed and exploitation he sees everywhere. His plays are both wildly amusing and outrageous. In his ability to create theatre spectacle he has few peers.

PRIMARY SOURCES

I. STAGE

The Bewitched. London: Heinemann, 1974.

The Devil Is an Ass. Adaptation of the play by Ben Jonson. Staged Nottingham 1973.

Frontiers of Farce. Staged London 1976. London: Heinemann, 1976.

Leonardo's Last Supper and Noonday Demons. [Two plays.] Staged London 1969. London: Heinemann, 1970.

Lulu. Adaptation of plays by Frank Wedekind, translated by Charlotte Beck. (Also co-director.) Staged Nottingham and London 1970. London: Heinemann, 1971.

Noonday Demons. See Leonardo's Last Supper and Noonday Demons above.

Pawns; the Plight of the Citizen-Soldier. New York: Knopf, 1971, 1972.

The Ruling Class. Staged Nottingham 1968; London 1969;
    Washington, D.C., 1971. London: Heinemann, 1969.

_____. New York: Grove Press, 1969.

Sclerosis. Staged Edinburgh and London 1965.

The Time of the Barracudas. Staged San Francisco 1963.

II. FILM

Breakout, 1959.

Not with My Wife You Don't, 1965.

Off-Beat, 1961.

The Professionals, 1960.

Ring of Spies, 1965.

The Ruling Class, 1972.

Violent Moment, 1958.

The White Trap, 1959.

III. NON-FICTION

"Ben Jonson and the Modern Stage" [a discussion].
    Gambit, 22 (1972), 5-29.

"A Past and Present High School Student's Guide to Soci-
    ety." Trace, 60 (Spring 1966), 76-79.

IV. INTERVIEW

Hennessy, Brendan. "Peter Barnes." Transatlantic Review,
    nos. 37-38 (Autumn-Winter 1970-71), 118-24.
        In this interview Barnes says the inequities of
    the class system still prevail in the home counties,
    if not in London. He looks for verbal techniques
    and expressions "like the Elizabethan's or Jaco-
    bean's." Hennessey feels in this area he is like
    the young Shaw, seeking "medieval rhythms" in the
    dialogue of his historical plays. Barnes states
    that Noonday Demons is the "purest expression up to
    now of my interest in [religious] belief," and he
    specifically refers to the alienation effect of his
    plays, although Brecht is not mentioned.

SECONDARY SOURCES

I. CRITICISM

Esslin, Martin. <u>Jenseits</u> <u>des</u> <u>Absurden</u>. Vienna: Euro-
    paverlag, 1973.

Richmond, Theo. "The Visible Worm." <u>Guardian</u>, 6 January
    1970, p. 6.

Taylor, John Russell. <u>The Second Wave: British Drama for
    the Seventies</u>. New York: Hill & Wang, 1971. Pages
    206-08.
        Taylor surveys Barnes's career as a playwright
    and screenwriter briefly but concentrates on <u>The
    Ruling Class</u>, which he calls a "glittering satirical
    charade."

II. REVIEWS

<u>BEWITCHED</u>

    <u>New</u> <u>York</u> <u>Times</u>, 29 June 1974, p. 17.

<u>LEONARDO'S</u> <u>LAST</u> <u>SUPPER</u>

    <u>The</u> <u>Times</u>, 5 December 1969, p. 7.

<u>NOONDAY</u> <u>DEMONS</u>

    <u>The</u> <u>Times</u>, 5 December 1969, p. 7.

<u>RULING</u> <u>CLASS</u>

    <u>The</u> <u>Times</u>, 9 November 1968, p. 19.

    <u>New</u> <u>York</u> <u>Times</u>, 28 February 1969, p. 31.

    <u>New</u> <u>York</u> <u>Times</u>, 25 January 1971, p. 23.

    <u>New</u> <u>York</u> <u>Times</u>, 31 January 1971, II:16.

<u>SCLEROSIS</u>

    <u>The</u> <u>Times</u>, 21 June 1965, p. 6.

ROBERT BOLT

Born Sole, Manchester, Lancashire, August 15, 1924

A graduate of Manchester University with an Exeter teaching diploma, Robert Bolt has become one of the most popular dramatists of his day. His first play, Flowering Cherry, had more in common with the New Drama than his best known play, A Man for All Seasons, since it dealt with the financial and marital problems of an English middle-class family. His marriage to Sarah Miles, his forays into movie-making, and the long runs of his historical dramas have given him a kind of celebrity status that separates him from the other playwrights listed in this volume. He is, in fact, a favorite with audiences who find his ideas clearer and more accessible than those of his possibly more distinguished contemporaries.

PRIMARY SOURCES

I. STAGE

Brother and Sister. Staged Brighton 1967; revised version Bristol 1968.

The Critic and the Heart. Staged Oxford 1957.

Doctor Zhivago: The Screenplay Based on the Novel by Boris Pasternak. London: Harvill Press, 1966; New York: Random House, 1966.

Flowering Cherry. Staged London 1957; New York 1959. London: Heinemann, 1958; New York: Samuel French, n.d.

_____. In Plays and Players, 6 (January-February 1959).

Gentle Jack. Staged London 1963. London: Samuel French, 1964; New York: Random House, 1965.

The Last of the Wine. Broadcast 1955. Staged London 1956.

A Man for All Seasons. Broadcast 1954. Staged London
_____ 1960; New York 1961. London: Heinemann, 1961; New
York: Random House, 1962 (paperback, 1966).

_____ [condensation]. In The Best Plays of 1961-62;
the Burns Mantle Yearbook, ed. by Otis L. Guernsey
Jr.; illustrated with photographs and drawings by
Hirschfeld. New York: Dodd, 1972.

_____. In Laurel British Drama: The Twentieth Century,
ed. by Robert W. Corrigan Laurel. New York: Dell,
1965.

_____. In Literary Cavalcade, ed. by Jerome Brondfield.
New York: Scholastic Magazines, n.d.

_____. In The New Theatre of Europe, ed. by Robert W.
Corrigan. Vol. I. A Delta Book. New York: Dell,
1962.

_____. In Plays of Our Time, ed. by Bennett Cerf. New
York: Random House, 1967.

_____. In Post-war Drama: Extracts from Eleven Plays,
ed. by John Hale. London: Faber & Faber, 1966.

_____. In Theatre Arts, 47 (May 1963).

_____ [record]. RCA (GB), London RB 6712/3. Notes:
Modern Play. Mono L.P. Records.

"Thomas More où l'homme seul," trans. by Pol Quentin. In
L'avant Scene, 294 (September 1963).

State of Revolution. Staged London 1977.

The Thwarting of Baron Bolligrew. Staged London 1965;
Chicago 1970. London: Heinemann, 1966; New York:
Samuel French, 1967.

_____. In Swortzell, Lowell, ed. All The World's a
Stage; Modern Plays for Young People; decorations
by Howard Simon. New York: Delacorte Press, 1972.

The Tiger and the Horse. Staged London 1960. London:
Heinemann, 1961; New York: Samuel French, n.d.

Vivat! Vivat Regina! Staged Chichester and London 1970;
New York 1972. London: Heinemann, 1971; New York:
Random House, 1972.

_____ [French's Acting edition). London: Samuel French,
1971.

36

_____. In The Best Plays of 1971-72; The Burns Mantle
        Yearbook, ed. by Otis L. Guernsey, Jr.; illustrated
        with photographs and drawings by Hirschfeld. New
        York: Dodd, Mead, 1972.

_____. Introduced by author with commentary and notes by
        E. R. Wood (Hereford Plays). London: Heinemann
        Educational Books, 1974.

II. COLLECTIONS

Three Plays. (Includes Flowering Cherry, A Man for All
        Seasons, The Tiger and the Horse.) London: Heine-
        mann, 1967.

III. SCREENPLAYS

Lawrence of Arabia, 1962.

Doctor Zhivago, 1965.

A Man for All Seasons, 1966.

Ryan's Daughter, 1970.

Lady Caroline Lamb, 1972.

_____ (director), 1972.

IV. RADIO PLAYS

The Master, 1953.

Fifty Pigs, 1953.

Ladies and Gentlemen, 1954.

A Man for All Seasons, 1954.

Mr. Sampson's Sundays, 1955.

The Last of the Wine, 1955.

The Window, 1958.

The Drunken Sailor, 1958.

The Banana Tree, 1961

V. INTERVIEW

An Interview with Tom Milne and Clive Goodwin, published
     in _Encore_ in 1961, followed by replies to further
     questions put by Simon Trussler in 1966. In Maro-
     witz, Charles and Trussler, Simon, eds. _Theatre at_
     Work. London: Eyre Methuen, 1967. Pages 62, 66-
     68, 70, 73.
         This interview covers such subjects as Bolt's
     career as a writer, his techniques, his views on
     Brecht, problems in writing non-naturalistic plays
     like _A Man for All Seasons_, personal feelings about
     Sir Thomas More, and stylization in _Gentle Jack_.

SECONDARY SOURCES

I. CRITICISM

Anderegg, Michael A. "A Myth for All Seasons: Thomas
     More." _Colorado Quarterly_, 23 (Winter 1975), 293-
     306.
         In his comparison of the play and film, _A Man for_
     All Seasons, Anderegg complains that Bolt and Zinne-
     man oversimplify the character of More, including
     little of More's wit and his life as a lawyer, dip-
     lomat, and orator. The article briefly discusses
     the mythologizing of More from his death to the
     present day and Bolt's sources for his play.

Atkins, Anselm. "Robert Bolt: Self, Shadow, and the
     Theater of Recognition." _Modern Drama_, 10 (Septem-
     ber 1967), 182-88.
         The Common Man and Thomas More in _A Man for All_
     Seasons are "two sides of an equation." Both are
     interested in the preservation of the self. More's
     self, however, is his soul, whereas the Common Man
     seeks to preserve his earthly life. Bolt prompts
     the audience to recognize and accept elements of
     both characters in themselves.

Barnett, Gene A. "The Theatre of Robert Bolt." _Dal-_
     housie Review, 48 (Spring 1968), 13-23.
         This article compares Bolt's treatment of the
     problems of self-hood and commitment in _A Man for_
     All Seasons, _The Flowering Cherry_, _The Tiger and the_
     Horse, and _Gentle Jack_.

Duprey, Richard A. "Interview with Robert Bolt."
     Catholic World, 195 (September 1962), 364-69.
         Bolt reveals his belief that two alternatives
     face modern man: a return to the old Christian val-
     ues or an espousal of a valueless world. Most men,

he feels, remain halfway between these two alterna-
tives, attempting to sustain their position and resolve the inner conflict. The playwright also dis-
dusses his choice of Thomas More as protagonist in
a play about selfhood.

Fehse, Klaus-Dieter. "Robert Bolt: A Man for All Seasons (1960)," 124-46, in Das zeitgenossische
englische Drama: Einfuhrung, Interpretation, Doku-
mentation. Frankfurt: Athenaum, 1975. Edited by
Fehse, Klaus-Dieter and Norbert Platz.
In this difficult to obtain festschrift on the
English drama Fehse draws particular attention to
More as existential hero and considers him to be
more ethical and intellectual than an impassioned
man of God.

Fosberry, M. W. "A Man for All Seasons." English Studies
in Africa, 6 (September 1963), 164-72.
Fosberry harshly criticizes Bolt for unrealistic
characters who serve as "intellectual symbols," for
ineffective imagery and symbolism, and for uncon-
vincing, although neatly phrased dialogue.

Hollis, Christopher. "Lettre de Londres: M. Robert Bolt
et St. Thomas More." La Table Ronde, Nos. 186-87
(1963), 151-57. [Tr. Philippe Leonardon.]
In a general discussion of the London theatre
season Hollis comments on the popularity of A Man
for All Seasons.

McElrath, Joseph R. "Bolt's A Man for All Seasons.
Explicator, 28, item 10, September 1969.
McElrath briefly discusses the "mud metaphor" in
A Man for All Seasons as expressive of "the total
disintegration of society."

_____. "The Metaphoric Structure of A Man for All Sea-
sons." Modern Drama, 14 (1972), 84-92.
Explores Bolt's use of water and land imagery to
"reinforce the theme of conflict between More's selfhood and the demands of Henry's England." Water
imagery suggests "cosmic background," More's selfhood, and the flow, or current, of situations and
character actions. Land imagery represents society's demands. These resonating metaphors emphasize
the presence of the individual conscience and pre-
vent a simple naturalistic interpretation of the
historical events presented in the play.

Marc'hadour, Germain. "St. Thomas More: Patron des
libres-penseurs? Reflexions sur la pièce de Bolt."
Moreana, No. 8 (November 1965), pp. 28-42.
Marc'hadour notes that playwrights have the power

to shape history with their interpretations and suggests that A Man for All Seasons will have a wider
influence than all the scholarly biographies of
More. He compares Bolt's play with Shaw's Saint
Joan. In both cases atheistic playwrights who deny
the church's concept of sainthood have "secularized"
the heroes of their plays. Bolt's More is too
cerebral, not enough of a passionate Christian.

Marowitz, Charles. "Some Conventional Words: An Interview with Robert Bolt." Tulane Drama Review, 11
(Winter 1966), 138-40.
Bolt praises convention in drama because it ful-
fills certain audience expectations and provides a
structure which conveys "delicate but immediate insights" and within which the playwright "can be
subtle, powerful."

"Notes on Robert Bolt's 'A Man for All Seasons.'" London:
Eyre Methuen (Study-aid series).

Peebles, Bernard M. "Easell vs. Eisell: A Lexicographi-
cal Lapse." Moreana, 39 (1973), 37-38.
Brief comment on the use of the word "easel" in
one of More's final remarks in A Man for All Seasons.

Pujals, Esteban. "The Globe Theatre, Londres." Filo-
logía Moderna (Madrid), I (1960), 59-63. On Graham
Greene's The Complaisant Lover and Robert Bolt's A
Man for All Seasons.
Pujals notes that Greene's play is superficially
secular but at heart a Catholic statement, whereas
Bolt's saint is depicted as a worldly man.

Purcell, Mark. "Robert Bolt: man for all media."
Cresset, 35, iv (1972), 19-21.
Purcell comments on the adaptability of A Man for
All Seasons to several media.

Reynolds, E. E. "The Significance of A Man for All
Seasons." Moreana, 23 (1969), 34-39.
Reynolds posits the universal appeal of A Man for
all Seasons as an enduring interest in Thomas More
and Bolt's accurate interpretation of More's character as a warm, witty, courageous, and honorable man.

Storari, Gilbert. "From Elizabeth I to Elizabeth II:
Two Popular Views of Thomas More." Moreana, 30
(1971), 25-28. On The Booke of Thomas More and
A Man for All Seasons.
Storari compares the Elizabethan play, The Booke
of Sir Thomas More and Bolt's A Man for All Seasons.
He finds the latter emphasizes More's intellect and
slights the hero's humor, penchant for politics, and

religious zeal. Storari also criticizes Bolt's
representation of More's stance as an isolated one.

Tees, Arthur Thomas. "The Place of the Common Man:
    Robert Bolt: A Man for All Seasons." University
    Review, 36 (October 1969), 67-71.
        Tees explores the multiple roles of the Common
    Man: "a counterbalance to More's philosophy, a
    tragic non-hero in contrast with the heroic saint,
    . . . the lecturer-commentator of a history play,
    the highly individualized allegorical figure of a
    modern medieval morality play, and the ubiquitous
    Brechtian narrator and unintended alienator."

Trewin, J. C. "Two Morality Playwrights: Robert Bolt and
    John Whiting." Experimental Drama [14] (1964),
    103-27.
        Trewin provides personal impressions of Whiting's
    Saint's Day, Marching Song, The Devils, A Penny for
    a Song, and Bolt's Flowering Cherry, A Man for All
    Seasons, The Tiger and the Horse. He attributes the
    continuing appeal of these two playwrights to their
    compelling dramatic force, their immediate involve-
    ment of the audience, and their treatment of moral
    issues.

Tucker, M. J. "The More-Norfolk Connection." Moreana,
    33 (1972), 5-13.
        Bolt distorts the historical Thomas Howard, Duke
    of Norfolk, in his portrayal of the character in A
    Man for All Seasons, representing Norfolk as an
    "over-exercised, under-educated nobleman." Tucker
    sets the record straight in his discussion of the
    historical association between More and Norfolk.

Veidemanis, Gladys. "A Play for All Seasons." English
    Journal, 55 (November 1966), 1006-14.
        A thorough teaching outline for A Man for All
    Seasons, including the necessary historical back-
    ground and analysis of the play. Veidemanis praises
    Bolt's play because it reveals man's heroic potential
    in contrast to other current works which deal in
    despair.

Wiszniowska, Marta. "Characters in Robert Bolt's Dramas
    (A Study in Internal Relations)." Kwartalnik Neo-
    filologiczny (Warsaw), 17 (1970), 147-57.
        Discusses general poetic elements in Flowering
    Cherry, The Tiger and the Horse, A Man for All
    Seasons, and Gentle Jack, and attempts to establish
    a definition of "poetic drama" in the process. The
    elements discussed include: "(1) the twofold world
    in the plays; (2) the creation of poetic characters;
    (3) a tendency to introduce some general and

abstract problems; (4) the importance of an idea to
which other elements are subject; (5) the presence
of nature and folklore components; (6) the use of
symbolism; (7) poetry as a thematic element; (8) the
use of the literary tradition of the earlier poetic
drama."

II. REVIEWS

THE CRITIC AND THE HEART

   The Times, 2 April 1957, p. 3.

FLOWERING CHERRY

   The Times, 22 November 1957, p. 8.

   New York Times, 22 October 1959, p. 46.

GENTLE JACK

   New York Times, 29 November 1963, p. 50.

   The Times, 29 November 1963, p. 18.

   Spectator, 6 December 1963, p. 754.

A MAN FOR ALL SEASONS

   The Times, 2 July 1960, p. 12.

   New York Times, 23 November 1961, p. 51.

   New York Times, 3 December 1961, II:1.

   New York Times, 23 September 1962, II:1.

   New York Times, 11 May 1963, p. 15.

THE TIGER AND THE HORSE

   New York Times, 25 August 1960, p. 26.

VIVAT! VIVAT REGINA!

   The Times, 21 May 1970, p. 11.

   New York Times, 24 May 1970, p. 80.

   New York Times, 20 July 1970, p. 21.

   New York Times, 21 January 1972, p. 27.

   New York Times, 30 January 1972, II:1.

42

EDWARD BOND

Born London, July 18, 1934

Attending state schools until he was fourteen and later serving in the army, Edward Bond has a distinctly working class background and a kind of anger and vitality that makes the young John Osborne seem genteel by comparison. Bond's plays are almost always shocking. Early Morning posits a lesbian relationship between Queen Victoria and Florence Nightingale, and Saved contains a scene in which a baby in a pram is stoned to death. Bond's plays have not been popular but the Royal Court Theatre has continued to sponsor his works because of his originality and daring. Many theatre critics believe Bond will ultimately be recognized as the outstanding dramatist of his time. At this point he appears to be a brilliant iconoclast whose vision has not yet moved beyond the private to the universal. In contrast to Stoppard's metaphysical theorizing or Pinter's somewhat stoic acceptance of human foibles, Bond appears to be searching for a workable moral code, independent of religion, which will clarify and give purpose to man's existence.

PRIMARY SOURCES

I. STAGE

A-A-America! comprising Grandma Faust and The Swing.
    Staged London 1976. London: Eyre Methuen, 1976.

Bingo: Scenes of Money and Death. London: Eyre Methuen,
    1974.

Black Mass. Staged for the Anti-Apartheid Movement, London
    1970. Included in The Pope's Wedding and Other
    Plays. London: Eyre Methuen, 1971.

_____. Best Short Plays (1972). Ed. Margaret Mayorga.
    New York: Dodd, Mead, 1972.

43

Early Morning. Staged London 1968; New York 1971. London: Calder and Boyars, 1968.

_____. New York: Hill and Wang, 1969.

The Fool. Staged London 1975. London: Eyre Methuen, 1975.

Lear. Staged London 1971. London: Eyre Methuen, 1972.

_____. New York: Hill and Wang, 1972.

Narrow Road to the Deep North. Staged Coventry 1968; London and New York 1969. London: Eyre Methuen, 1968.

_____. New York: Hill and Wang, 1968.

_____. Plays and Players, 15 (September 1968), 27-42.

Passion. Staged for the Campaign for Nuclear Disarmament, London 1971. Plays and Players (London), June 1971 and in New York Times, 1971.

The Pope's Wedding. Plays and Players, 16 (April 1969), 35-50, 79-80.

_____. Staged London 1962. The Pope's Wedding and Other Plays. London: Eyre Methuen, 1971.

Saved. Staged London 1965; New Haven, Conn. 1968; New York 1970. London: Eyre Methuen, 1966.

_____. New York: Hill and Wang, 1966.

_____. Plays and Players, 13 (January 1966), 29-44.

_____. The New Theatre of Europe, 4. Ed. Martin Esslin. New York: Dell, 1970. Pages 47-149.

The Sea. Staged London 1973. London: Eyre Methuen, 1973.

_____. New York: Hill and Wang, 1973.

Stone. Staged London 1976. London: Eyre Methuen, 1976.

Trauer zu Früh. Theatre Heute, 10 (May 1969).

III. ADAPTATIONS

The Roundheads and the Peakheads, 1970. Based on the play by Bertolt Brecht; adapted for the Royal Court Theatre.

Spring Awakening, 1974. Based on the play by Wedekind; adapted for the National Theater.

The Three Sisters, 1969. Based on the play by Anton Chekhov; adapted for The Royal Court Theatre.

The White Devil, 1976. Based on the play by John Webster; adapted for the Old Vic Theatre.

III. FILM

Blow-up, 1967. Based on a short story by Julio Cortazar.

Laughter in the Dark, 1969. Based on a novel by Vladimir Nabokov.

Michael Kohlhaas, 1969. Based on a novella by Heinrich von Kleist.

Nicholas and Alexandra, 1971.

Walkabout, 1971. Based on a novel by Vance Marshall.

IV. POETRY

"Bird." *Gambit*, 5, (1970), 55-56.

"Christ Wanders and Waits." *Gambit*, 5 (1970), 56-58.

"I Cannot Mourn." *Gambit*, 5 (1970), 47-48.

"The King with Golden Eyes." *The Pope's Wedding*. London: Eyre Methuen, 1971.

"Mr. Dog." *Gambit*, 5 (1970), 45-47.

"Mr. Dog." *The Pope's Wedding*. London: Eyre Methuen, 1971.

"Rest." *Gambit*, 5 (1970), 58-59.

"Sharpeville Sequence." *The Pope's Wedding*. London: Eyre Methuen, 1971.

V. NON-FICTION

"Beating Barbarism." *The Sunday Times*, 25 November 1973, p. 37.

"Censor in Mind." *Censorship*, 4 (Autumn 1965), 9-12.

"Drama and the Dialectics of Violence." _Theatre Quarterly_, 2 (January-March 1972), 4-14.

"The Duke in _Measure for Measure_." _Gambit_, 5 (1970), 43-45.

"The Greatest Hack: Thomas Middleton." _The Guardian_, 13 January 1966, p. 6.

"The Theatre Outside London." _Gambit_, 5 (1970), 69-74.

VI. LIBRETTO

We Come to the River, for an opera composed by Hans Werner Henze. London: Eyre Methuen, 1976.

VII. INTERVIEW

"Thoughts on Contemporary Theatre." _New Theatre Magazine_, 7 (Spring 1967), 6-12.
    Bond's rather occasional remarks mention his use of violence in _Saved_, the socially-committed aspect of the theatre, the need for experimental theatre, and its paucity because of critics.

VIII. LETTER

Theatre Quarterly, 2 (April-June 1972), 105.
    Bond castigates Arnold's review (_TQ_ 2 [January-March 1972], 15-19) for its "factual misstatements," suggesting that Marowitz' article in the _New York Times_ (Sunday, January 2, 1972) is better.

SECONDARY SOURCES

I. CRITICISM

Arnold, Arthur. "Lines of Development in Bond's Plays." _Theatre Quarterly_, 2 (January-March 1972), 15-19.
    Arnold discusses Bond's dramatic career, seeing _Saved_ as flawed by "too much realism," _Early Morning_ by "too much surrealism," while _Narrow Road to the Deep North_ "is a very successful play." Thematically, _Saved_ argues "society is the villain," _Early Morning_ that "people make their own society," whereas _Narrow Road to the Deep North_ "solves a lot of dramatic problems."

Babula, William. "Scene Thirteen of Bond's <u>Saved</u>."
<u>Modern Drama</u>, 15 (1972), 147-49.
Babula's analysis of scene thirteen argues that
the ritual actions of Pam, Harry, and especially
Len, in their performance of various household
chores, suggest a qualified optimism as the play's
theme.

Baiwir, Albert. "Le Théatre d'Edward Bond." <u>Revue de</u>
<u>l'Université Libre de Bruxelles</u> (2-3), (1973),192-
211.
Baiwir discusses Bond's censorship problem, the
shocking and controversial aspects of his works and
brief plot summaries in this overview of the playwright's canon.

Barth, Adolf. "The Aggressive 'Theatrum Mundi' of Edward
Bond: <u>Narrow Road to the Deep North</u>." <u>Modern Drama</u>
18 (June 1975), 189-200.
Barth argues that <u>Narrow Road</u> . . . is a "secularized theatrum mundi [that] in one way or another
still maintains the archetypal hope for a 'heavenly
Jerusalem' which should supplant Shogo's type of
city as well as Georgiana's. . . ." The solution,
however, is neither personal nor spiritual, but is
rather to be sought in the social realm. The play
is inconclusive as to whether Basho will realize
this hope.

Calder, John. "Le jeune littérature anglaise." <u>Quinzaine</u>
<u>Litteraire</u>, 126 (October 1-15, 1971), 5-7.
Calder briefly includes Bond in his list of promising young English writers.

Dark, Gregory. "Production Casebook No. 5: Edward Bond's
'Lear' At the Royal Court." <u>Theatre Quarterly</u>, 2
(January-March 1972), 20-31.
A synopsis of the play with its first performance
cast and a history of production.

Editors of <u>TQ</u>. "Drama and the Dialectics of Violence."
<u>Theatre Quarterly</u>, 2 (January-March 1972), 4-14.
Bond briefly relates his childhood, his first
memorable theatre experience (<u>Macbeth</u>, whom he sees
as a "Hitler"), and discusses his art, arguing his
plays are related by a similar character finally
"exorcized" in <u>Lear</u>. He discusses his "anti-natu-
ralism" and his "awareness of audience."

Elsom, John. "Spring--With a Corpse or Two." <u>The London</u>
<u>Magazine</u>, 9 (May 1969), 85-88.
Elsom discusses the theatre season and singles
out Bond for praise. He defines Bond's style:
"short narrative scenes from which comment has been

excluded but which leave symbolic impressions on the mind."

Esslin, Martin. "Bond Unbound." Plays and Players, 16 (April 1969), 32-34.
Esslin sees Saved and Narrow Road to the Deep North as both sharing "the disastrous influence of a morality based on an intellectually bankrupt religion" and "the horror of violence which expresses itself in images of violence." He reviews the current performances, finding fault with the "superficially effective clichés" of Saved.

_____. Brief Chronicles: Essays on Modern Theatre. London: Temple Smith, 1970.
This is a reprint of the preceding Esslin article.

Gordon, Giles. "Edward Bond." Transatlantic Review, 22 (Autumn 1966), 7-15. Reprinted in Behind the Scenes, ed. Joseph F. McCrindle. New York: Holt, Rinehart and Winston, 1971.
Gordon discussed with Bond the function of violence in Saved as well as its language--"basically poetic but it is also, I hope, very true to life." Bond criticizes critics for being outdated and for preferring "intellectual games" to real drama.

Gross, Konrad. "Darstellungensprinzipien im Drama Edward Bonds." Die Neuren Sprachen, 22 (1973), 313-24.
Gross studies Bond's major works and systematically analyzes them in terms of dialogue, scene structure, symbolism, time, space, and moral meaning.

Hayman, Ronald. "Bond Is Out to Make Them Laugh." The Times, 22 May 1973, p. 11.

Hobson, Harold and others. "A Discussion with Edward Bond." Gambit, 5 (1971), 5-38.
The discussion focuses on Saved, Early Morning, and Narrow Road to the Deep North. Bond makes several remarks of critical interest: "The villain of this piece is Basho," "I had this central character who runs all the way through my plays: he turns up as Scobie in the first one (Pope's Wedding) . . . he's Len in Saved . . . Arthur in Early Morning." Several comments seem designed to arouse: "I mean we would be much saner if we were cannibals." He talks about Lear, in progress, while Jane Howell, actress in and producer of several Bond plays, offers her criticism of Bond's art. Bond mentions Chekhov and Wood as dramatists he admires.

Hunt, Albert. "A Writer's Theatre." New Society, 11
    December 1975, pp. 606-07.
        Hunt begins his essay by wondering why Bond is so
    unpopular in England. He quotes Bond, who says the
    artist's role is "to analyze and explain our soci-
    ety," whose central issue is violence. Hunt feels
    Bond's failure "springs, not from the unacceptabil-
    ity of his ideas [as Bond argues], but from his in-
    creasing self-indulgence as a writer in what he him-
    self calls 'a writer's theatre.'" Bond is "a play-
    wright who has been trapped by his own literary as-
    pirations, who has lost touch with the society he is
    trying to explain."

Iden, Peter. Edward Bond. Velber: Friedrich, 1973.

Jones, D. A. N. "British Playwrights." The Listener, 80
    (August 8, 1968), 161-63.
        Jones has difficulty classifying Bond, three of
    whose plays are being done by the Royal Court. A
    serious non-comic playwright--tragic, perhaps.
    Grave, he settles on. In fact, Bond is not popular
    with many, and none of the three plays being per-
    formed have been presented publicly in London before
    due to censorship problems.

_____. Nova (June-July 1969), p. 39.

Klotz, Günther. "Erbezitat und zeitlose Gewalt, Zu Ed-
    ward Bonds LEAR." Weimarer Meiträge, 19:10 (1973),
    54-65.
        Although he mentions The Pope's Wedding, Klotz
    focuses on Bond's Lear and its many parallels with
    and departures from Shakespeare's King Lear. The
    issues of power and authority which are apparent in
    the Shakespearean classic have been adapted, rather
    drastically, to comment on the contemporary world
    scene.

Marowitz, Charles. New York Times, 2 January 1972, II:1-
    2.
        Marowitz gives a brief sketch of Bond's career
    and analyzes his interests. Terming Bond a "meta-
    physical Marxist," Marowitz sees "a sense of shock,
    or rather controlled outrage" informing all Bond's
    work. Hence, Bond is a "moralist" who smells of
    being a "revolutionary," which explains England's
    rejection of him.

Mehlin, Urs. "Die Behandlung von Liebe und Aggression
    in Shakespeares Romeo and Juliet und in Edward Bonds
    Saved." Shakespeare-Jahrbuch (Heidelberg), (1970),
    132-59.
        Mehlin finds fascinating and convincing similari-

ties between Shakespeare's <u>Romeo</u> <u>and</u> <u>Juliet</u> and
Bond's <u>Saved</u>. In particular, they are both set in
an oppressive society, which thwarts expressions of
love and tenderness, and are marked by the unexpected eruption of violence and the death of inno-
cents.

Mori, Yasuaki. "Edward Bond Tojo." <u>Eigo Seinen</u> (The
Rising Generation) (Tokyo), 115 (1969), 614.

Pasquier, Marie-Claire. "Edward Bond: Cohérence nais-
sante d'une oeuvre." <u>Cahiers de la Compagnie</u> Made-
leine Renaud-Jean Louis Barrault, 74 (1970), 36-57.
    Pasquier believes that, considered together,
Bond's plays make a powerful moral and philosophical
statement. The shocking events in the dramas are
intended to outrage his audiences so that they will
confront directly the covert brutality of contemporary "civilization."

_____. "La place d'Edward Bond dans le nouveau théâtre
anglais." <u>Cahiers de la Compagnie Madeleine</u> Renaud-
Jean Louis Barrault, 74 (1970), 21-35.
    Pasquier provides a history of Bond's censorship
problems in England.

Peter, John. "Violence and Poetry." <u>Drama</u>, 117 (Autumn
1975), 28-32.
    Peter argues that <u>Bingo</u> and <u>Narrow Road</u> share the
same object: "the utter inadequacy, indeed the harm-
fulness, of the artist as a social animal. . . ."
"Like most of Bond's plays, <u>Bingo</u> is a play of conscience." ". . . But a moral view of life means
seeing it in terms of this and their consequences.
Morality demands the responsibility of logic," something Bond fails to provide in <u>Saved</u>, <u>Early Morning</u>,
and <u>Lear</u>. Peter likes <u>The Sea</u> because it "presents
not unmotivated puppets but people." <u>Bingo</u> fails
because it is improbable and overwritten.

"P.H.S." "The Times' Diary: Overwhelmed by Hypocrisy."
<u>The Times</u>, 9 April 1968, p. 10.

Simons, Piet. "Lear van Edward Bond." <u>Ons Erfdeel</u>
(Reddem), 15 (1972), 114.
    Bond's <u>Lear</u> is the subject of brief mention here
as the work of a controversial new English playwright.

Taylor, John Russell. "British Dramatists--The New Arrivals: No. 5, Edward Bond." <u>Plays and Players</u>,
17 (August 1970), 16-18.
    Taylor traces the common theme of a "martyr fig-
ure who . . . opens himself to the worst that life

has to offer" through Pope's Wedding, Saved, and
Early Morning. He objects to Esslin's (P&P, 16
[April 1969], 32-34) "sentimental" reading of Saved.
He applauds Narrow Road . . . because it "achieves
precisely the right degree of abstraction from
everyday reality for his play to work as a parable
without raising a lot of essentially irrelevant ob-
jections in its audience's mind."

_____. The Second Wave: New British Drama for the Seven-
ties. New York: Hill and Wang, 1971. Pages 77-93.
This chapter is essentially the same article as
above with some additional plot summary.

Wardle, Irving. "The Edward Bond View of Life." The
Times, 15 March 1969, p. 21.

II. DISSERTATIONS

Jennings, Ann. "The Reactions of London's Drama Critics
to Certain Plays by Henrik Ibsen, Harold Pinter, and
Edward Bond." Dissertation Abstracts International
34:2067A (Florida State, 1973).
Jennings' dissertation is "the tracing of the
process by which plays that are initially rejected
by drama critics become standard dramas." It treats
Saved, Early Morning, Narrow Road to the Deep North,
and Lear, tracing their acceptance via new productions, articles, assimilation by other playwrights,
and use in schools.

Scharine, Richard. "The Plays of Edward Bond." Dissertation Abstracts International 34:3608A (Kansas,
1973).
Scharine presents a chronological survey of
Bond's life and major works, treating Pope's Wedding, Saved, Early Morning, Narrow Road to the Deep
North, and Lear in individual chapters, while treating lesser works as a group. He discovers that
Bond's works dwell on man's brutalization by social
abstractions such as Nationalism and Christianity,
while using Christian imagery and Oedipal symbolism
to convey their message.

III. REVIEWS

BINGO

The Sunday Times, 2 December 1973, p. 37.

New York Times, 19 August 1974, p. 32.

New York Times, 25 August 1974, II:3.

Newsweek, 23 February 1976, p. 89.

BLACK MASS

The *Times*, 1 January 1971, p. 14

EARLY MORNING

The *Times*, 8 April 1968, p. 6.

New York Times, 9 April 1968, p. 58.

Plays and Players, 15 (June 1968), 26.

Plays and Players, 16 (May 1969), 24-27.

Atlantic, August 1969, p. 100.

New York Times, 26 November 1970, p. 57.

LEAR

The *Times*, 30 September 1971, p. 11.

New York Times, 24 October 1971, p. 5.

Encounter, 37 (December 1971), 30-31.

New York Times, 29 April 1973, p. 57.

New York Times, 13 May 1973, II:1.

America, 128 (9 June 1973), 538.

Encounter, 43 (November 1974), 46-48.

NARROW ROAD TO THE DEEP NORTH

The *Times*, 25 June 1968, p. 13.

New York Times, 27 June 1968, p. 49.

The *Times*, 20 February 1969, p. 15.

Atlantic, August 1969, p. 100.

Newsweek, 24 November 1969, p. 135.

Time, 28 November 1969, p. 71.

New York Times, 2 December 1969, p. 64.

52

Saturday Review, 13 December 1969, pp. 14-15.

New York Times, 11 February 1970, p. 39.

The Times, 13 February 1970, p. 15.

Educational Theatre Journal, 22 (March 1970), 97-98.

New York Times, 7 January 1972, p. 27.

New Yorker, 15 January 1972, p. 70.

Newsweek, 17 January 1972, p. 70.

Time, 17 January 1972, p. 47.

Nation, 24 January 1972, p. 126.

America, 5 February 1972, p. 124.

New Republic, 5 February 1972, p. 32.

Educational Theatre Journal, 24 (May 1972), 195-96.

SAVED

The Times, 4 November 1965, p. 17.

The Times, 15 November 1965, p. 14.

New Society, 25 November 1965, pp. 26-27.

New Yorker, 11 December 1965, p. 228.

Contemporary Theatre: A Selection of Reviews 1966/
67, ed. Geoffrey Morgan. London Magazine Editions, 1968. Pages 41-44.

New York Times, 1 March 1970, II:10.

New York Times, 29 October 1970, p. 57.

New York Times, 1 November 1970, II:10.

New Yorker, 7 November 1970, pp. 133-35.

Newsweek, 9 November 1970, p. 88.

Time, 9 November 1970, p. 48.

Nation, 16 November 1970, p. 508.

America, 16 January 1971, pp. 47-48.

Commonweal, 22 January 1971, p. 397.

Educational Theatre Journal, 23 (March 1971), 85-86.

THE SEA

The Sunday Times, 27 May 1973, p. 35.

New York Times, 19 June 1973, p. 32.

New York Times, 19 March 1975, p. 53.

SPRING AWAKENING [original author Frank Wedekind]

New York Times, 9 September 1974, p. 42.

SIMON GRAY

Born Hayling Island, Hampshire, October 21, 1936

    Simon Gray, an erudite professor-novelist, began his play-writing career as a farceur. His improbable plots and bizarre caricatures at first reminded his audiences of Joe Orton. His first major success, Butley, proved he was a writer of greater substance and range than Orton, however, and Otherwise Engaged, another great popular success, indicates Gray's growing power as a dramatist. A graduate of Dalhousie University and Trinity College, Cambridge, Gray first demonstrated his literary skills in satiric novels. His plays, replete with literary allusions and subtle intellectual wit, examine various states of alienation and anger among educated, well-bred people and stress the difficulties of sustaining personal relationships and expressing feelings. Sophisticated London and New York audiences clearly identify with the characters and situations in Gray's recent plays.

PRIMARY SOURCES

I. STAGE

Butley. Staged Oxford and London 1971; New York 1972.
    London: Eyre Methuen, 1971.

      . Plays and Players, 19 (August 1972).

Dog Days. Staged Oxford 1976. London: Eyre Methuen,
    1976.

Dutch Uncle. Staged London 1969. London: Faber & Faber,
    1969.

The Idiot. Adapted from the novel by Dostoevsky. Staged
    London 1970. London: Eyre Methuen, 1971.

Molly. Staged Charleston, S. C., 1977.

Otherwise Engaged. Staged London 1975; New York 1976.
    In Otherwise Engaged and Other Plays. New York:

Penguin, 1975.

Plaintiffs and Defendants. In Otherwise Engaged and
    Other Plays. New York: Penguin, 1975.

Spoiled. Televised 1968; staged Glasgow 1970 and London
    1971. London: Eyre Methuen, 1971.

Sleeping Dog. Televised 1967. London: Faber & Faber,
    1968.

Two Sundays. In Otherwise Engaged and Other Plays.
    New York: Penguin, 1975.

Wise Child. Staged London 1967; New York 1972.

_____. In Plays and Players, 15 (December 1967).

_____. London: Faber & Faber, 1968.

II. TELEVISION

The Caramel Crisis, 1966.

Death of a Teddy Bear, 1967.

The Dirt on Lucy Lane, 1969.

The Man in the Sidecar, 1971.

Pig in a Poke, 1969.

Plaintiffs and Defendants, 1975.

The Princess, 1970.

Sleeping Dog, 1967.

Spoiled, 1968.

Style of the Countess, 1970.

Two Sundays, 1975.

A Way with the Ladies, 1967.

III. FICTION

Colmain. London: Faber & Faber, 1963.

A Comeback for Stark [under pen name Hamish Reade].
    London: Faber & Faber, 1969.

Little Portia. London: Faber & Faber, 1968.

Simple People. London: Faber & Faber, 1965.

IV. INTERVIEWS

Hamilton, Ian. "Simon Gray," *The New Review*, 3 (January/
   February 1977), 39-46.
   This interview provides the most thorough biography of Simon Gray available. It discusses his
childhood in France and Canada, his education at
Westminster and Cambridge and various graduate fel-
lowships he pursued after Cambridge. Gray admires
Henry James, Dickens, and George Eliot, but believes
no great novels are presently being written. The
adaptation of a short story on television brought
him in contact with Ken Trodd and other television
writers and eventually his work found its way to the
legitimate stage. Gray and Hamilton discuss the
relative merits of the protagonists in *Otherwise Engaged* and *Two Sundays* and the playwright stresses
his present commitment to theatre and quality television.

SECONDARY SOURCES

I. CRITICISM

Taylor, John Russell. "Three Farceurs." In *The Second
   Wave*. New York: Hill & Wang, 1971. Pages 156-71.
   Taylor sees Gray as primarily a farceur without a
wide-ranging appeal. The article was written prior
to *Butley* and *Otherwise Engaged* and hence describes
only the early plays and their resemblance to Joe
Orton's work.

II. REVIEWS

BUTLEY

   Saturday Review, 11 September 1971, pp. 20, 54.

   Wall Street Journal, 2 November 1972.

   Time, 13 November 1973.

OTHERWISE ENGAGED

   Observer, 7 September 1975, p. 6.

New Yorker, 6 September 1976.

PLAINTIFFS AND DEFENDANTS

The New Review, 1 (February 1975), 14-24.

TWO SUNDAYS

The New Review, 1 (November 1974), 27-38.

CHRISTOPHER HAMPTON

Born in Fayal, The Azores, January 26, 1946

Christopher Hampton is the prodigy of the London
stage since his first play, When Did You Last See My
Mother?, was successfully produced when he was only eighteen years old. Since then Hampton has continued to
write poetry, short stories, and plays of considerable
distinction. Total Eclipse took a documentary approach
to the lives of Rimbaud and Verlaine. Undoubtedly his
greatest achievement to date has been The Philanthropist.
In this play, based on Moliere's The Misanthrope, we see
the influence of Hampton's Oxford training in French and
German literature. Hampton writes wittily and generally
realistically in the Shavian tradition. He seems particularly concerned with England's changing political and
social roles in the modern world as well as with the decline of humanism everywhere.

PRIMARY SOURCES

I. STAGE

"Der Menschen-Freund." Theater Heute, no. 12 (February
        1971), 45-50.
            A truncated version of The Philanthropist in
        German.

A Doll's House. Adaptation of a play by Ibsen. Staged
        New York 1971; London 1973. New York: Samuel
        French, 1972.

Don Juan. Adaptation of a play by Moliere. Staged New
        York 1971; London 1973. New York: Samuel French,
        1973.

Hedda Gabler. Adaptation of a play by Ibsen. Staged
            Stratford, Ontario, 1970; New York 1971. New York:
        Samuel French, 1972.

Marya. Adaptation of a play by Isaac Babel, trans. by
    Michael Glenry and Harold Shuhrman. Staged London
    1967. Published in Plays of the Year. London:
    Elek, 1969.

The Philanthropist: A Bourgeois Comedy. Staged London
    1970; New York 1971; Washington, D.C. 1976. London:
    Faber and Faber, 1970.

_____. New York: Samuel French, 1971.

Savages. Staged London 1973. London: Faber and Faber,
    1973.

Tales from the Vienna Woods. Staged London 1977. [A
    translation of Odon von Horvath's play.]

Total Eclipse. Staged London 1968. London: Faber and
    Faber, 1969.

_____. New York: Samuel French, 1972.

Treats. Staged London 1976. London: Faber and Faber,
    1976.

Uncle Vanya. Adaptation of a play by Checkhov, trans. by
    Nina Froud. Staged London 1970. Published in Plays
    of the Year 39. London: Elek, 1971.

When Did You Last See My Mother? Staged Oxford, London
    1966; New York 1967. London: Faber and Faber, 1967.

_____. New York: Grove, 1967.

III. POEMS

"Absences in Rome." Delta, 34 (Autumn 1964), 22-23.

"Apostrophe." Delta, 25 (Winter 1961), 14.

"Confession." Outpost, 64 (Spring 1965), 18-19.

"Dead End." Delta, 35 (Spring 1965), 17.

"Deadlock." Pick, 2:9 (Spring 1975), 15.

"Death of a Crippled Child." Poe Ireland, 3 (Spring
    1964), 99.

"Happiness." Workshop, 15:13.

"Home for Incurables." Delta, 24 (June 1961), 13.

"Mission Doctor." Outpost, 72 (Spring 1967), 22.

"Morning News." Delta, 25 (Winter 1961), 15.

"Old Maid's Logic." Delta, 23 (February 1961), 12.

"Pimlico Garden." Delta, 27 (Autumn 1962), 6.

"Small-Talk." Delta, 24 (June 1961), 13.

"Words on an August Afternoon." Delta, 34 (Autumn 1964), 23-24.

IV. INTERVIEWS

"A Discussion." Gambit, 21:100-06.
    This is not so much an interview as a panel dis-
cussion. Wesker, Martin Esslin, Marion Boyars and
Hampton debate the problems of translating English
plays into other languages and vice versa. Hampton
says Bond's plays have been well received in Germany,
but his own Philanthropist was a failure there.

Hennessy, Brendan. "Christopher Hampton." Transatlantic
    Review, 31 (Winter 1968-69), 90-95.
    Hennessy asks Hampton about his childhood,
schooling, and early successes in the theatre.
Hampton explains his role as a script reader for the
Royal Court Theatre. He discusses his response to
success and his dislikes--advertising and television.

SECONDARY SOURCES

I. CRITICISM

"Christopher Hampton's Savages at the Royal Court Thea-
    tre." Theatre Quarterly, 3 (October-December 1973),
    79-83.
    This is a highly detailed account of the staging
of Savages. It includes a biography of Hampton, and
careful analyses of his earlier plays, especially
Total Eclipse. Robert Kidd speaks about directing
Hampton's plays and Paul Scofield describes acting
in them.

Deneulin, Alain. "The Philanthropist." Kunst en Cultuur
    (Brussels), 15 (November 1973), 14.

Esslin, Martin. "In Search of Savages." Theatre Quar-
    terly, 3:12 (October-December 1973), 79-83.
    The head of BBC Radio Drama summarizes and

elucidates criticism of Savages, a new play "of controversial content and innovative form." Esslin discusses the limitations of "instant reviewing" of a current play and includes an invaluable supply of critical notices, published in their entirety. Esslin strikes out against political and structural biases, against America's inability to understand English interactions, while stating his own belief that Hampton's play is as much about the decline of England as the plight of the Brazilian Indian. In conclusion, he writes that Savages' "tragic twentieth century dilemma" is that of a "civilized way of life which still finds insight and pleasure in poetic myth."

Pasquier, Marie-Claire and Nicole Rougier and Bernard Brugiere. "Christopher Hampton." In Le Nouveau Theatre Anglais. Paris: Librairie Armand Colin, 1969. Pages 91-92.

The authors seem to categorize Hampton primarily as an Englishman who, along with Charles Dyer and Frank Marcus, writes rather naively about homosexuals.

Salem, Daniel. La révolution théâtrale actuelle en Angleterre. Paris: Denoël, 1969. Pages 198, 221.

Salem discusses When Did You Last See My Mother?, which, though immature, gives an accurate portrait of adolescent sexual feeling, and Total Eclipse, in which the homosexual theme is treated more realistically.

Taylor, John Russell. "The Legacy of Realism." In The Second Wave. New York: Hill & Wang, 1971. Pages 191-204.

Taylor discusses Hampton as a kind of child prodigy and briefly comments on the playwright's first three works, calling him a very cerebral artist, who may possibly become "the Shaw of the seventies."

II. DISSERTATION

Schneider, Ruth. "The Interpolated Narrative of Modern Drama." Dissertation Abstracts International, 34: 6605A-06A (S.U.N.Y., Albany, 1974).

Concerned with the modern use of the interpolated narrative in Hampton's The Philanthropist, among other modern plays, Schneider says Hampton "connects the world of political chaos with the secluded world of academia, one of the last strongholds of the comedy of manners." She concludes that the uniqueness of the modern interpolated tale depends on the interdependency and intermixing of genres.

III. REVIEWS

THE PHILANTHROPIST

Wall Street Journal, 24 March 1971.

Telegraph Magazine, 9 August 1974, pp. 22-23, 25-26.

TOTAL ECLIPSE

Guardian, 7 September 1970, p. 8.

Gambit IV, 13, 110-11.

ANN JELLICOE

Born Middlesbrough, Yorkshire, July 15, 1927

        Ann Jellicoe is a product of England's Central
School of Speech and Drama and her interest in writing
plays comes second to her desire to direct them. She may
be better known as the founder of the Cockpit Theatre,
which she began in 1952, than as the author of The Knack,
her best-known work. Jellicoe is not a literary playwright; her plays are theatrical events. There are few
memorable lines, little philosophical insight or social
analysis. Early critics felt that Jellicoe played too
directly to theatre professionals, that ordinary audiences could not appreciate her consuming interest in
stage "effect." Jellicoe has directed Ibsen, Chekhov,
and Shakespeare. Since the nineteen-fifties she has been
one of the best-known women in the theatre world.

PRIMARY SOURCES

I. STAGE

Der Freischütz. Translation of the libretto by Friedrich
        Kind, music by Weber. Staged London 1964.

The Giveaway. Staged Edinburgh 1968; London 1969. Lon-
        don: Faber and Faber, 1970.

The Knack. Staged Cambridge 1961; London 1962; Boston
        1963; New York 1964.

_____. London: Encore, 1962.

_____. New York: Samuel French, 1962.

_____. In Two Plays. New York: Dell, 1964.

The Lady from the Sea. Adaptation of Ibsen's play.
        Staged London 1961.

The Rising Generation. Staged London 1967. Published
        Playbill 2, edited by Alan Durband. London, 1969.

Rosmersholm. Adaptation of Ibsen's play. Staged London
    1952; revised, staged London 1959. San Francisco:
    Chandler, 1960.

The Seagull, with Adriadne Nicolaeff. Adaptation of the
    Chekhov play. Staged London 1964.

Shelley; or, The Idealist. Staged London 1965. London:
    Faber and Faber, 1966; New York: Grove Press, 1966.

The Sport of My Mad Mother. Staged London 1958. In The
    Observer Plays. London: Faber and Faber, 1958;
    revised version, London: Faber and Faber, 1964. In
    Two Plays. New York: Dell, 1964.

Two Jelliplays (two short plays for children). Staged
    London 1974. London: Faber and Faber, 1974.

You'll Never Guess. Staged London 1973.

II. NON-FICTION

Some Unconscious Influences in the Theatre. London and
    New York: Cambridge University Press, 1967.

III. INTERVIEWS

Jellicoe, Ann. In "Theatre People Reply to Our Inquiry."
    World Theatre, 14 (January-February 1965), 44-53.
        Jellicoe provides some past and present bio-
    graphical material and discusses her association
    with the Cockpit Theatre. She speaks of directing
    her own plays and the works of the masters. A kind
    of feminism underlies her awareness of "sexual"
    politics. Many people, especially men, use sex for
    purposes of manipulation and domination. This de-
    sire to manipulate, in the extreme, leads to wars,
    fascism, etc.

Rubens, Robert. "Ann Jellicoe, Interviewed by Robert
    Rubens." Transatlantic Review, no. 12 (Spring 1963),
    27-34.
        Jellicoe discusses her failed desire to be an
    actress and her training as a director. Although
    she feels any imaginative director could stage her
    plays, she has enjoyed directing her own work and
    believes that the playwright-director combination is
    very productive. She favors improvisation. She
    would like to direct Chekhov (she did the following
    year) and feels Stanislavsky and others failed to
    recognize the humor, balance, and modernity of the
    Russian dramatist.

SECONDARY SOURCES

I. CRITICISM

Abirached, Robert. "Le Jeune Théâtre Anglais." Nouvelle
Revue Française, 29:170 (February 1967), 314-321.
   Abirached makes only brief references to Jellicoe
as one of many new talented English dramatists.

Alaiz, F. M. Lorda. Teatro Ingles de Osborne Hasta Hoy.
Madrid: Taurus, 1964.
   Alaiz discusses Jellicoe's work with the Cockpit
Theatre Club and prints an excerpt from The Sport of
My Mad Mother to illustrate her zany, theatrical
style.

Gottfried, Martin. A Theatre Divided; The Postwar American Stage. Boston: Little, Brown, 1967. Pages
218-25.
   Gottfried discusses the successful off-Broadway
run of The Knack. He refers to it as a left-wing
play, i.e., theatrically innovative, and points out
that it may contain a political allegory in which
the virginal Nancy represents neutral countries
while the suitors competing for her favors are the
United States and Russia.

Kuna, F. M. "Current Literature 1970-II, New Writing.
Drama." English Studies, 52:6 (December 1971),
565-73.
   Kuna calls The Giveaway "an uneasy mixture of
realism and fantasy." He admires Jellicoe's satire
and her ingenious plot but feels that the play is
ultimately just a tour de force because she tries
too consciously to create her "spontaneous" effects.

Kustow, Michael. "The Knack at the Royal Theatre, Bath."
In Marowitz, Charles, ed. Encore Reader. Pages 220-
23.
   Kustow compares The Knack to Godard's film Breath-
less because they both have a carefree style and
seem to mock the seriousness and self-absorption of
modern man.

Pasquier, Marie-Claire and Nicole Rougier and Bernard
Brugiere. "Artaud et le rituel." In Le Nouveau
Théâtre Anglais. Paris: Librairie Armand Colin,
1969. Pages 229-33.
   Jellicoe, along with David Rudkin, Pinter, and
Bond, is discussed as a follower of certain of
Artaud's dramatic principles. Objects, lights,
movements, attitudes, and other non-verbal elements
are more important than language in her works. She

understands the ritualistic nature of the theatre
experience. The Sport of My Mad Mother is both anti-
intellectual and rooted in universal experience.

Prickett, Stephen. "Three Modern English Plays." Philo-
    logica Pragnesia, 10 (1967), 12-21. See Arden,
    above.

Salem, Daniel. La révolution théâtrale actuelle en
    Angleterre. Paris: Denoël, 1969. Pages 57-60, 181.
        Salem offers a summary of Jellicoe's career from
    The Sport of My Mad Mother to The Giveaway. Except
    for The Knack, which he finds "insouciante," he con-
    siders Jellicoe's work somewhat immature and flawed,
    though always original.

Taylor, John Russell. Anger and After. London: Eyre
    Methuen, 1963. Pages 65-71.
        Taylor speaks of Jellicoe's unique beginnings in
    the theatre as a contest winner and director of her
    own play. He comments on her complete professional-
    ism, her relationship with the Cockpit Theatre and
    her tremendously energetic productions where she ex-
    ploits every possible theatrical device.

II. REVIEWS

THE GIVEAWAY

    The Times, 9 April 1969, p. 6.

THE KNACK

    The Times, 28 March 1962, p. 15.

    Spectator, 6 April 1962, p. 445.

    The Illustrated London News, 7 April 1962, p. 554.

    New Statesman, 13 April 1962, p. 537.

    New York Times, 28 May 1964, p. 42.

SPORT OF MY MAD MOTHER

    The Times, 26 February 1958, p. 3.

RISING GENERATION

    The Times, 24 July 1967, p. 6.

SHELLEY

    The Times, 19 October 1965, p. 16.

PETER NICHOLS

Born Bristol, July 31, 1927

A graduate of the Bristol Old Vic Theatre School, Peter Nichols also served in the Royal Air Force. He has the kind of median background which so many contemporary Englishmen and Americans have. He is neither working class nor a graduate of a prestigious university. His own background is plain but not deprived; and like the characters in his plays he has recently settled into a comfortable prosperity. So many of his plays and characters belong to a suburban milieu--distinctly late twentieth century. His basic concerns are the disintegration of the family, the loss of traditional values, the pain that accompanies self-knowledge. Humor and pathos are intermingled, as in his drama about the spastic Joe Egg and her anguished parents or in The National Health's odd mixture of morbidity and hospital jokes. Nichols always involves his audiences in his plays. His characters harangue the audience, or confide in them, and he uses many sophisticated theatrical devices. There is, perhaps, a kind of shallowness in these endeavors. The contemporary malaise is accepted too passively. There is little attempt to relate cause and effect, to protest or to change. Because Nichols' obsessions are so widely shared and because his colloquial dialogue suits the mood of the times, his works are extremely popular.

PRIMARY SOURCES

I. STAGE

"Beasts of England." Anthology selected from works of
     George Orwell; staged London 1973.

Chez Nous. London: Faber and Faber, 1974.

A Day in the Death of Joe Egg. Staged Glasgow and Lon-
     don 1967; New York 1968. London: Faber and Faber,
     1967; as Joe Egg. New York: Grove Press, 1967.

_____. The Best Plays of 1967-68. Ed. Otis L. Guernsey, Jr. New York: Dodd, Mead, 1968.

Un Jour dans la Mort de Joe Egg. Trans. by Claude Roy. L'Avant-Scene du Theatre, 442 (1 February 1970).

_____. Trans. by Claude Roy. Plaisir de France, 376 (March 1970).

Forget-Me-Not Lane. Staged London 1971. London: Faber and Faber, 1971.

_____. New York: Samuel French, 1972.

The Freeway. Staged London 1974. London: Faber and Faber, 1974.

Harding's Luck. Staged Greenwich, London 1974.

Ne m'Oubliez Pas. Adapted by Claude Roy from the English play. L'Avant-Scene du Theatre, 497 (15 June 1972).

The Hooded Terror. Televised 1963; staged Bristol 1974.

The National Health; or, Nurse Norton's Affair. Staged London 1969; Chicago 1971. London: Faber and Faber, 1970.

The National Health; A Play in Two Acts. London: Samuel French, 1973.

The National Health; or, Nurse Norton's Affair. New York: Grove Press, 1975.

Neither Up nor Down. Staged London 1972.

Privates on Parade. Staged London 1977. London: Samuel French, 1977.

II. TELEVISION

"After All." With Bernie Cooper, 1959.

"Ben Again," 1962.

Ben Spray, 1961. Published in New Granada Plays. London: Faber and Faber, 1961.

"The Big Boys." BBC, 1961.

"The Brick Umbrella." ATV, 31 May 1964.

"The Common." BBC, 1973.

"The Continuity Man." BBC, 10 March 1963.

"Daddy Kiss It Better." Yorkshire TV, 29 July 1968.

The Gorge. BBC, 4 September 1968. Published in The
    Television Dramatist, ed. Robert Muller. London:
    Elek, 1973.

"The Heart of the Country," 1962.

"Hearts and Flowers." BBC, 3 December 1970.

"The Hooded Terror." ABC-TV, 25 August 1963; staged
    Bristol 1964.

"Majesty," 1968.

Promenade, 1959. Published in Six Granada Plays.
    London: Faber and Faber, 1960.

"The Reception," 1961.

"Walk on the Grass." BBC, 1959.

"When the Wind Blows." ITV, 2 August 1965.

"Winner Takes All," 1968.

III. FILM

"Catch Us if You Can," 1965. Released in U.S. as "Having
    a Wild Weekend."

"A Day in the Death of Joe Egg," 1972.

"Georgy Girl," 1966.

"The National Health," 1973.

IV. FICTION

Patchwork of Death. New York: Holt, Rinehart & Winston,
    1965.

Piedmont and The English. London: Hugh Evelyn, 1967.

V. INTERVIEWS

Canby, Vincent. "Peter Nichols, 'Joe Egg' Author, Found
    Humor in Desperation." New York Times, 3 February
    1968, p. 22.

71

Nichols describes how he was able to turn an unpleasant personal experience into a comedy and compares Joe Egg to Orton's Entertaining Mr. Sloane. Canby also provides a very brief biography.

Hayman, Ronald. Playback 2. London: Davis-Poynter, 1973. ["essay-interviews"]
    Hayman questions Nichols on his background, discusses the author's vast television experience. He comments on Nichols' startling theatrical devices; and the playwright discusses his views on marriage, family, the welfare state.

Stott, Catherine. "Plays in the Life of Joe Egg's Dad." Guardian, 26 January 1970, p. 8.
    Penetrating, if brief, interview. Nichols discusses his writing of Joe Egg and The National Health, and talks about his future goals and his past concerns as a playwright.

SECONDARY SOURCES

I. CRITICISM

Billington, Michael. "Joe Egg's Dad." Guardian, 2 December 1971, pp. 10-11.
    Nichols discusses the production and censorship of Joe Egg, his use of music-hall techniques and his political concerns as embodied in The National Health and Forget-Me-Not Lane.

Doust, Dudley. "Making Comedy Out of a Family Tragedy." Life, 24 November 1967, pp. 106-09.
    This is a biography of Nichols' experiences with his daughter, the inspiration for Joe Egg.

Hayman, Ronald. "The Mimic Man." The Times, 31 March 1971, p. 11.
    Hayman includes biography, professional history, brief critical commentary, and lengthy quotes of Nichols' discussion of his writing. Primarily he is concerned with Joe Egg, The National Health, and Forget-Me-Not Lane.

Hewes, Henry. "The British Bundle." Saturday Review, 11 September 1971, pp. 20, 54.
    Included here is a plot summary of Butley and Old Times and a review and superficial analysis of Nichols' Forget-Me-Not Lane and Osborne's West of Suez.

The National Health Program. London: The National The-
     atre, 1968.

Stiles, G. W. "Some Thoughts on Two Modern English Come-
     dies." Unisa English Studies, 9 (September 1971),
     10-16.
          Stiles compares Orton's What the Butler Saw and
     Nichols' The National Health. In both he finds a
     topsy-turvy world in which traditional values are
     perverted. The welfare state has created a complex
     bureaucracy and man is helpless to act; he can only
     laugh at his own absurdity.

Taylor, John Russell. "British Dramatists--The New Ar-
     rivals: No. 1, Peter Nichols." Plays and Players,
     17 (April 1970), 48-51.
          Taylor analyzes Nichols' development as a drama-
     tist from his television plays up to Forget-Me-Not
     Lane. He sees a "running theme in Nichols' work,
     the mutually destructive relations between children
     and adults." Taylor forecasts a "new direction" in
     Nichols' later plays.

_____. The Second Wave. London: Eyre Methuen, 1971.
          Reprint with slight changes of the article in
     Plays and Players.

Weightman, John. "Metaphysical Voids." Encounter, 43
     (December 1974), 64-66.
          Weightman considers Ayckbourn's The Norman Con-
     quests and Nichols' The Freeway. In Ayckbourn's
     trilogy "a technical gimmick takes precedence over
     content." Weightman criticizes the lack of finesse.
     The jokes are not "fitted to the personalities of
     the characters," and it is simply "the nondescript
     muddle in a lower-middle-class household." He
     criticizes Nichols' The Freeway on two points: the
     characters are "traditional theatrical types" with-
     out enough variety to successfully represent English
     society; Nichols has not thought out his political
     theme fully, creatively, or carefully enough.

II. REVIEWS

"THE BRICK UMBRELLA"

     The Times, 1 June 1964, p. 14.

"THE CONTINUITY MAN"

     The Times, 11 March 1963.

"DADDY KISS IT BETTER"

The Times, 30 July 1968, p. 11.

FORGET-ME-NOT LANE

The Times, 2 April 1971, p. 10.

New York Times, 17 August 1971, p. 27.

New York Times, 8 April 1973, p. 79.

New York Times, 22 April 1973, II:1.

Newsweek, 30 April 1973, p. 87.

"THE GORGE"

The Times, 5 September 1968, p. 7.

"HEARTS AND FLOWERS"

The Times, 4 December 1970, p. 10.

"THE HOODED TERROR"

The Times, 26 August 1963, p. 12.

A DAY IN THE DEATH OF JOE EGG

The Times, 21 July 1967, p. 6.

New York Times, 2 February 1968, p. 26.

Nation, 19 February 1968, pp. 247-49.

Reporter, 7 March 1968, p. 44.

America, 9 March 1968, pp. 330-31.

The Times, 3 December 1971, p. 13.

THE NATIONAL HEALTH

The Times, 17 October 1969, p. 15.

New York Times, 19 October 1969, p. 75.

Plays and Players, 17 (December 1969), 22-25.

The Times, 20 January 1971, p. 12.

Catholic World, 212 (March 1971), 314-15.

The Times, 9 March 1973, p. 15.

Nation, 2 November 1974, pp. 444-45.

New Republic, 2 November 1974, p. 32.

"WHEN THE WIND BLOWS"

The Times, 3 August 1965, p. 11.

JOE ORTON

Born Leicester, 1933 (date unknown); died London, August 9, 1967

Joe Orton is the only playwright in this bibliography who is no longer living. In a few short years Orton wrote prodigiously and created several classic English comedies. His intense involvement with the theatre, his controversial personal life, and his shocking murder have led critics of the new Renaissance to compare Orton's life to Christopher Marlowe's brief but meteoric career. Of course, there are no similarities in the works of the two writers. Orton seems to have inherited the wit and a dedication to aesthetic ideals associated with Oscar Wilde. Sometimes he pictures an enigmatic Pinteresque environment with unexpected violence and odd, silent characters. Nearly always the more shocking events in Orton's plays contrast with the genteel, even pretentious dialogue of his characters. Freud, the Roman Catholic Church, the welfare state, and sexual stereotypes are all treated satirically. As in farce, the playwright frequently confounds our expectations: honest people are wrongly accused of crimes while thieves, murderers, or degenerates live happily ever after. The lack of major social or moral commitments--except, perhaps, a subtle endorsement of bisexuality and a plea for human compassion in all areas of life--make Orton's plays seem superficial to many. Yet theatre sophisticates and intellectuals value Orton all the more for his lack of didacticism and his commitment to pure art.

PRIMARY SOURCES

I. STAGE

Entertaining Mr. Sloane. London: Hamish Hamilton, 1964.

_____. Plays and Players, 11 (July 1964) (Act I); 11 (August 1964), 17-24 (Act II); 12 (September 1964), 17-24 (Act III).

_____. New York: Grove Press, 1965.

_____. _Forms of Drama_. Ed. James L. Calderwood and H. C. Tolliver. Englewood Cliffs: Prentice Hall, 1969.

Loot. London: Eyre Methuen, 1967.

_____. New York: Grove Press, 1968.

_____. _New English Dramatists 13_. Harmondsworth: Penguin Books, 1968.

"Until She Screams." _Oh, Calcutta_. Ed. Kenneth Tynan. New York: Grove Press, 1969.

_____. _Evergreen Review_, 13 (August 1969), 49-54.

_____. _Evergreen Review_, 14 (May 1970), 51-53.

What the Butler Saw. London: Eyre Methuen, 1969.

_____. New York: Samuel French, 1969.

_____. _The Best Plays of 1969-1970_. Ed. Otis L. Guernsey, Jr. New York: Dodd, Mead, 1971.

II. TELEVISION

Crimes of Passion. (Consists of two television plays: "The Ruffian on the Stair" and "The Erpingham Camp.") London: Eyre Methuen, 1967.

_____. New York: Samuel French, 1968.

"The Erpingham Camp." See _Crimes of Passion_ above.

Funeral Games; and The Good and Faithful Servant. London: Eyre Methuen, 1970.

The Good and Faithful Servant. See _Funeral Games_ above.

"The Ruffian on the Stair." See _Crimes of Passion_ above.

_____. _Best Short Plays, 1968-1972_. Ed. Margaret Mayorga. New York: Dodd, Mead, 1972.

III. RADIO

"The Ruffian on the Stair." _New Radio Drama_. London: BBC, 1966.

IV. FICTION

Head to Toe. London: Anthony Blond, 1971.

_____. London: Panther Books, 1971.

V. NON-FICTION

"The Bitter Bit." Plays and Players, 11 (August 1964),
16.

"Joe Orton to Frank Marcus" (a letter). The London Magazine, 9 (July-August 1969), 56.

VI. INTERVIEW

Gordon, Giles. "Joe Orton." Transatlantic Review, 24
(Spring 1967), 93-100. Reprinted in Behind the
Scenes. Ed. Joseph F. McCrindle. New York: Holt,
Rinehart and Winston, 1971.
    Orton discusses Entertaining Mr. Sloane and Loot,
his views of himself as a playwright, his term in
prison, his morality and taste, and his writing history.

SECONDARY SOURCES

I. CRITICISM

Clurman, Harold. Nation, 16 August 1976, pp. 123-24.
[On Pinter, Stoppard, Orton.]
    Clurman calls Orton's work satires but believes
Orton enjoys rather than deplores "the sadism and
foulness of the environment he depicts" in Entertaining Mr. Sloane and Loot.
    He feels Stoppard has a desire to "communicate
matters of philosophical import," but his plays remain "hollow." Critical analysis of Travesties as
"debonair frivolity."
    Clurman briefly mentions Pinter's Old Times as
preface to a longer discussion of No Man's Land.
He finds the latter "glacial," reflecting "a society
at a dead end."

"Death of a Playwright" [short obituary]. Time, 15 September 1967, p. 40.

Elsom, John. "The Man Who Said 'No' and the Man Who Said
'Well' . . ." The London Magazine, N.S. 9 (April
1969), 91-95.

Orton is a writer of farce, particularly What the
Butler Saw. Orton is distinguished by the quality
of his insight: "He would state innocently the
thoughts we try to suppress and . . . reveal how
rigid and unlikely our fantasies are."

Fox, James. "The Life and Death of Joe Orton." Sunday
Times Magazine, 22 November 1970, p. 44.

Fraser, Keath. "Joe Orton: His Brief Career." Modern
Drama, 14 (1971), 413-19.
This is a critical discussion of Orton's major
works. Fraser concludes that Entertaining Mr.
Sloane and Loot will be "among comedies still per-
formed in fifty years."

Fridshtein, F. "Ochen' nepriyatnye p'esy Dzho Ortona."
["The Very Unpleasant Plays of Joe Orton"]. Teatr
(Moscow), 5 (1971), 129-31.
Fridshtein deplores the immorality and decadence
of Orton's work. He believes Orton's vision is
selfish and eccentric and that the civilization he
portrays is beyond hope.

Gosling, Ray. "Creatures of the Body." The Times
(London), 25 January 1971, p. 7.

Hunt, Albert. "What Joe Orton Saw." New Society, 17
April 1975, pp. 148-50.
Hunt compares Orton to "early Shaw" in that both
presented their personal view of our society. Orton,
in Loot and What the Butler Saw, uses comedy to
"demolish a whole way of looking at 'recognisable
reality.'"

Kerr, Walter. Tragedy and Comedy. [On Entertaining Mr.
Sloane.] New York: Simon and Schuster, 1967.
Pages 317-19.
Kerr cites "Joe Ordway's" [sic] Entertaining Mr.
Sloane as an example of comedy that "acknowledges
the disappearance of affirmation," and asserts that
the play can be comedy only if the audience brings
a normative view of life for it to work against.

Lahr, John. "Artist of the Outrageous." Evergreen Review, 14 (February 1970), 30-34, 83-84.
Lahr combines selections from Giles Gordon's interview with critical comment on Orton's work. Lahr
feels that Orton reveals "social insanity" and his
use of farce extends "to an audience the possibility
of humility and care."

Marcus, Frank. "Comedy or Farce?" The London Magazine,
    N.S., 6 (February 1967), 73-77.
        Marcus interestingly provides his own definitions
    of comedy and farce, and then discusses Loot as a
    farce.

Marowitz, Charles. "Farewell, Joe Orton." New York
    Times, 7 April 1968, II:1.

"Mr. Joe Orton: New Wave Dramatist" [obituary]. The
    Times, 10 August 1967, p. 8.

Nicoll, Allardyce. English Drama: A Modern Viewpoint.
    London: Harrap, 1968.
        Nicoll offers brief plot summaries of Entertain-
    ing Mr. Sloane and Loot with a later mention of the
    former, implying that it is not "serious" drama.

Schneider, Alan. "'Mr. Sloane's' Director Talks Back."
    New York Times, 31 October 1965, II:5.

Spurling, Hilary. "Early Death." Spectator, 18 August
    1967, p. 193.

Stiles, G. W. See Nichols above.

Taylor, John Russell. "British Dramatists--The New Ar-
    rivals--No. 7, The Late and Lamented Joe Orton."
    Plays and Players, 18 (October 1970), 14-17.
        This is an overview of Orton's works. Those
    plays produced during his lifetime, Taylor feels,
    are evidence of his "genuine and extraordinary"
    talent. Those produced posthumously seem, "at best,
    rough drafts."

_____. The Second Wave: New British Drama for the Seven-
    ties. New York: Hill and Wang, 1971. Pages 125-40.
        This is a reprint with slight revision of the
    article appearing in Plays and Players cited above.

Thompson, Christian. "Joe Orton und das englische Thea-
    ter der sechziger Jahre." Muk, 19 (1973), 321-41.

Trussler, Simon. "Theatre Reviews: Second Generation
    London." The Drama Review, 12 (Winter 1968), 171-76.
        Orton "chose mannered comedy as the vehicle which
    could best combine [his] sense of private pain and
    of the farcical incongruity of things."

II. DISSERTATION

Galassi, Frank. "The Absurd Theatre of Joe Orton and N.
    F. Simpson." Dissertation Abstracts International

(1972) 32:5930A (New York University).
Galassi shows that, although Orton and Simpson
use many comic techniques of the French absurdists,
the two playwrights present a "message of social and
political satire . . . within a dramatic farcical
medium."

III. REVIEWS

CRIMES OF PASSION

New Yorker, 8 November 1969, p. 156.

Nation, 17 November 1969, pp. 546-47.

CRIMES OF PASSION; THE RUFFIAN ON THE STAIR

New York Times, 27 October 1969, p. 54.

CRIMES OF PASSION; ERPINGHAM CAMP; RUFFIAN ON THE STAIR

New York Times, 9 November 1969, II:3.

ENTERTAINING MR. SLOANE

The Times, 7 May 1964, p. 20.

The Times, 30 June 1964, p. 13.

Time, 22 October 1965, p. 103.

Saturday Review, 30 October 1965, p. 74.

Educational Theatre Journal, 18 (March 1966), 66-67.

Drama: The Quarterly Theatre Review (Autumn 1975),
   49.

FUNERAL GAMES [TV]

The Times, 27 August 1968, p. 9.

Plays and Players, 16 (October 1968), 56.

The Times, 1 December 1970, p. 13.

LOOT

The London Magazine, 6 (February 1967), 73-77.

New York Times, 19 March 1968, p. 40.

New Yorker, 30 March 1968, p. 103.

New York Times, 31 March 1968, II:1.

Drama: The Quarterly Theatre Review (Autumn 1975),
49.

WHAT THE BUTLER SAW

The Times, 17 December 1968, p. 14.

Plays and Players, 16 (April 1969), 24-27.

New York Times, 5 May 1970, p. 56.

New Yorker, 16 May 1970, p. 106.

Educational Theatre Journal, 12 (October 1970), 314-
15.

New York Times, 27 June 1971, II:7.

Drama: The Quarterly Theatre Review (Autumn 1975),
49-51.

JOHN OSBORNE

Born London, December 12, 1929

Although Pinter may be the most important playwright in the new British Renaissance, John Osborne is undoubtedly the founder of the movement. Osborne's first stage plays were collaborations with Stella Linden and, later, Anthony Creighton. But his fame rests on Look Back in Anger, which was presented to a dazzled audience at the Royal Court Theatre on May 8, 1956. Osborne has written many other fine plays, and either Luther or Inadmissible Evidence may be his most challenging and mature work. But Look Back in Anger retains a mythological significance for the English and the new British theatre. Jimmy Porter, Anger's legendary "angry young man," was identified with Osborne biographically and spiritually. Primarily, however, he stood for all the bright, disillusioned young men who found themselves disoriented and in pain a decade after World War II. Peter Barnes, Simon Gray, Peter Nichol, and, in fact, virtually all the major English playwrights writing today were stirred into action by Osborne. He has moved from scathing political indictments of England and capitalism toward more psychologically and philosophically oriented drama. He is a gifted playwright, of course, but a revered patron saint of the movement as well.

PRIMARY SOURCES

I. STAGE

A Bond Honoured. London: Faber and Faber, 1966.

The Devil Inside. Staged London 1949.

The End of the Old Cigar. Faber and Faber, 1975.

The Entertainer. London: Faber and Faber, 1957; New
     York: Criterion Books, 1958.

_____. The Best Plays of 1957-1958. Ed. Louis Kronen-
     berger. New York: Dodd, Mead, 1958.

_____. Postwar Drama: Extracts from Eleven Plays. Ed.
John Hale. London: Faber and Faber, 1966.

Epitaph for George Dillon. London: Faber and Faber,
1958; New York: Criterion Books, 1958. (Coauthored
with Anthony Creighton.)

_____. The Best Plays of 1958-1959. Ed. Louis Kronen-
berger. New York: Dodd, Mead, 1959.

_____. Theatre Arts, 46 (March 1962).

_____. A Treasury of the Theatre. Vol. 2. 4th ed. Ed.
John Gassner and Bernard Dukore. New York: Simon
& Schuster, 1970.

Four Plays: West of Suez, A Patriot for Me, Time Present,
The Hotel in Amsterdam. New York: Dodd, Mead, 1972.

Hedda Gabler. Faber and Faber, 1972.

Inadmissible Evidence. London: Evans Brothers, 1965;
London: Faber and Faber, 1965; New York: Grove
Press, 1965.

_____. The Best Plays of 1965-66. Ed. Otis L. Guernsey,
Jr. New York: Dodd, Mead, 1966.

_____. The New Theatre of Europe 3. Ed. R. W. Corrigan.
New York: Dell, 1968.

Look Back in Anger. London: Faber and Faber, 1957; New
York: Criterion Books, 1957; Chicago: Dramatic,
1959.

"Anger." New York Times, 13 October 1957, VI:32-34.
[Selections.]

Look Back in Anger. The Best Plays of 1957-1958. Ed.
Louis Kronenberger. New York: Dodd, Mead, 1958.

_____. Broadway's Best, 1958: The Complete Record of the
Theatrical Year. Ed. John Chapman. New York:
Doubleday, 1958.

_____. Twentieth Century Drama England, Ireland and the
United States. Ed. Ruby Cohn. New York: Random
House, 1960.

_____. Masters of Modern Drama. Ed. H. M. Block and
R. G. Shedd. New York: Random House, 1962.

_____. Plays of Our Time. Ed. Bennett Cerf. New York:
Random House, 1967.

Luther. London: Faber and Faber, 1961; New York: Criterion Books, 1962; Chicago: Dramatic, 1961.

————. *America's Lost Plays.* New York: Dodd, Mead, 1964.

A Patriot for Me. London: Faber and Faber, 1966; New York: Random House, 1970.

Personal Enemy (Coauthored with Anthony Creighton). Staged Harrogate 1953.

The Picture of Dorian Gray: A Moral Entertainment. London: Faber and Faber, 1973.

A Place Calling Itself Rome. Faber and Faber, 1973.

Plays for England: Under Plain Cover and the Blood of the Bambergs. London: Faber and Faber, 1963; New York: Criterion Books, 1964.

Plays for England (Under Plain Cover and the Blood of the Bambergs) and The World of Paul Slickey. New York: Grove Press, 1966.

A Sense of Detachment. London: Faber and Faber, 1973.

Three Plays. New York: Criterion Books, 1959.

Time Present and The Hotel in Amsterdam. London: Faber and Faber, 1968.

Very Like a Whale. London: Faber and Faber, 1971.

Watch It Come Down. London: Faber and Faber, 1975.

West of Suez. London: Faber and Faber, 1971.

West of Suez; A Patriot for Me; Time Present; The Hotel in Amsterdam; Four Plays. New York: Dodd, Mead, 1973.

West of Suez. Chicago: Dramatic, 1974.

The World of Paul Slickey. London: Faber and Faber, 1958; New York: Criterion Books, 1961.

II. FILM

The Charge of the Light Brigade. A Woodfall production in 1968; directed by Tony Richardson; screenplay by John Osborne and Charles Wood.

The Entertainer. A Woodfall Production in 1960; directed
    by Tony Richardson; screenplay by John Osborne and
    Nigel Kneale.

Inadmissible Evidence. A Woodfall production in 1968;
    directed by Anthony Page; screenplay by John Osborne.

Look Back in Anger. A Woodfall production in 1959;
    directed by Tony Richardson; screenplay by Nigel
    Kneale with additional dialogue by John Osborne.

Tom Jones. A Woodfall production in 1962; directed by
    Tony Richardson; screenplay by John Osborne. Pub-
    lished version New York: Grove Press, 1964. Rev.
    ed. 1965.

_____. London: Faber and Faber, 1964.

III. TELEVISION

The Gift of Friendship: A Play for Television. London:
    Faber and Faber, 1972.

Jill and Jack: A Play for Television. London: Faber and
    Faber, 1975.

The Right Prospectus: A Play for Television. London:
    Faber and Faber, 1970.

A Subject of Scandal and Concern. Best Short Plays of
    the World Theatre 1958-1967. Ed. Stanley Richards.
    New York: Crown, 1968.

A Subject of Scandal and Concern: A Play for Television.
    London: Faber and Faber, 1961.

A Subject of Scandal and Concern. Chicago: Dramatic,
    1971.

Very Like a Whale. London: Faber and Faber, 1971.

IV. NON-FICTION

"That Awful Museum." Twentieth Century, 169 (February
    1961), 212-16.

"Berliner Ensemble." London Times, 5 September 1963,
    p. 13d.

"Dr. Agostinho Neto." London Times, 2 October 1961,
    p. 13d. [Letter to editor.]

"The Epistle to the Philistines." London Tribune, 13
     May 1960, p. 9.

"Intellectuals and Just Causes: A Symposium." Encounter,
     29 (September 1967), 3-4.

"Introduction" in International Theatre Annual, Number
     Two. Ed. Harold Hobson. London: Calder, 1957.

"A Letter to My Fellow Countrymen." London Tribune, 18
     August 1961, p. 11.

"Letter to the Editor." Spectator, 12 April 1957, p. 486.

"On Critics and Criticism." London Telegraph, 28 August
     1966, p. 6.

"On the Thesis Business and the Seekers After Bare Ap-
     proximate: On the Rights of the Audience and the
     Wink and the Promise of the Well-Made Play." London
     Times, 14 October 1967, p. 20c.

"Playwrights and South Africa." London Times, 16 May
     1968, p. 13e.

"Revolt in Cuba." London Times, 19 April 1961, p. 13e.
     [Letter to editor.]

"Sex and Failure." In The Beat Generation. Eds. Gene
     Feldman and Max Greenberg. New York: Citadel, 1958.

"They Call It Cricket." In Declaration. Ed. Tom
     Maschler. New York: McGibbon and Kee, 1958.

"Threat to a Theatre for Nottingham." London Times, 4
     June 1960, p. 7d. [Letter to editor.]

"Transatlantic Air Race." London Times, 12 May 1969,
     p. 11.

"Trial of Two Rolling Stones: Informing the Police."
     London Times, 4 July 1957, p. 11c.

"A Working Man." London Times, 2 September 1968, p. 7d.

"The Writer and His Age." London Magazine, 4 (May 1957),
     47-49.

V. INTERVIEWS

Alvarez, A. "John Osborne and the Boys at the Ball."
New York Times, 28 September 1969, II:1,6.
    Alvarez explores some of the ironies of Osborne's
new-found prosperity. The playwright defends his
treatment of homosexuality in A Patriot For Me,
affirming his seriousness of purpose, denying
charges of sensationalism.

Booth, John. "Rebel Playwright." New York Times, 2
November 1958, II:3:1

Cagerne, Walter, ed. The Playwrights Speak. New York:
Walter Wager, 1967. Pages 127-28.
    A BBC "Face to Face" interview--the general
achievements, themes, goals of Osborne's career are
discussed. Osborne appears to be a thorough-going
theatre professional. He is defensive about charges
that his later plays lack the social bite of Look
Back in Anger. As an artist he wants the freedom
to explore many ideas and techniques in the theatre.

Devlin, Polly. "John Osborne." Vogue, June 1964, pp.
98-99, 152, 168.
    Osborne attempts to explain his views on social
injustice, class struggle and human needs to the
Vogue reader.

"Good-Natured Man." New Yorker, 26 October 1957, pp. 36-
37.
    This is a typical New Yorker sketch contrasting
Osborne's personal geniality with Jimmy Porter's
celebrated rudeness and hostility.

"Talk with a Playwright." Newsweek, 24 February 1958,
p. 62.

Tynan, Kenneth. "John Osborne Talks to Kenneth Tynan."
London Observer, 7 July 1968, p. 21.

_____. "John Osborne Talks to Kenneth Tynan." London
Observer, 30 June 1968, p. 21.

_____. "John Osborne Talks to Kenneth Tynan--Candidly."
Atlas, 16 (September 1968), 53-57.
    This interview combines the conversations of the
two interviews above. The playwright discusses his
own career and contributions in the context of the
modern theatre. He discusses his theme of anger,
the new school of drama that has grown up around
him, his new play Time Present, and his explorations
of other media, such as TV and film. Osborne gives

an overview of the major social issues facing England in 1968--problems of drug abuse, student rebellion, changing values and traditions.

Watts, Stephen. "Playwright John Osborne Looks Back-- And Not in Anger." New York Times, 22 September 1963, p. 1:2.

SECONDARY SOURCES

I. CRITICISM

Abirached, Robert. "Le Jeune Théâtre Anglais." Nouvelle Revue Française, 29 (February 1967), 314-21.
     This is an early recognition of Osborne's primacy in the New English theatre movement, emphasizing the effect of the Welfare State and other social changes on the drama.

Adania, Alf. "Osborne azi, la Amsterdam." România Literara 30 (January 1969), 22.

Adell, Alberto. "Lope, Osborne y los críticos." Insula (Madrid) 22 (June 1967), 7.

Adelman, Irving and Rita Dworkin. Modern Drama: A Checklist of Critical Literature on Twentieth Century Plays. Metuchen, N.J.: Scarecrow Press, 1967. Pages 236-38.
     This is a now outdated bibliography of Osborne's works; yet it covers the first ten years of Osborne's theatre career effectively.

Allsop, Kenneth. The Angry Decade. London: Peter Owen, 1958. Pages 96-132, 135-40.
     Allsop provides a very early recognition of the impact Look Back in Anger would have on British drama. He analyzes Anger and the Entertainer. Biographical data and some contemporary reactions to the plays are also included.

Alvarez, A. "Anti-Establishment Drama." Partisan Review, 26 (Fall 1959), 606-11.
     Alvarez discusses the realistic and naturalistic techniques of young English dramatists, such as Osborne, who want to alert audiences to anti-humanistic forces in the modern world and to make them acknowledge their pain, frustration, and anger.

Anikist, A. "Ot Osborna k Mersu." Teatăr, 6 (1969), 147-57.
     Anikist gives a Yugoslavian view of recent

British drama, concentrating on Osborne's emphasis
on class conflict.

Ansorge, Peter. "No People Like Show People." _Plays and
Players_, 14, v (1967), 60-63.
This is a brief discussion of some of the new
playwrights who have brought life to the British
stage, including Osborne.

Bailey, Shirley Jean. "John Osborne: A Bibliography."
Twentieth Century Literature, 7 (1961), 118-20.
The contents of this brief bibliography are
presently available in more recent publications.

Balakian, Nona. "The Flight from Innocence." _Books
Abroad_, 33 (Summer 1959), 260-70.
Archie Rice, George Dillon, and Jimmy Porter are
all defeated spirits, yet they are not "tragic" personalities. Balakian compares Allison Porter to
Ibsen's Nora. This is a general article on British
writers who are social realists eschewing the old
myths of the empire. Mostly novelists are discussed.

Banham, Martin. _Osborne_. Edinburgh: Oliver and Boyd,
1969.
Banham's emphasis is on Osborne's impact as a
leader in a new theatre movement rather than on the
playwright's social or political appraisals of English life. The individual plays are studied in
terms of their expert craftsmanship and the new life
they bring to the English stage.

Barbour, Thomas. "Theatre Chronicle." _Hudson Review_, 11
(Spring 1958), 118-20.
Barbour has a basically unfavorable response to
Look Back in Anger. Barbour links Osborne's ap-
proach to modern American realists and concludes
he is more of a journalist than artist.

Barker, Clive. "_Look Back in Anger_--The Turning Point."
Zeitschrift für Anglistik und Amerikanistik, 14
(1966), 367-71.
Barker considers _Look Back in Anger_ primarily a
transitional play which freed serious British dramatists from a slavish devotion to T. S. Eliot's
techniques. He appears to value Behan's work more
highly than Osborne's.

Bäumgart, Wolfgang. "Die Gegenwart des Barocktheaters."
_Archiv für das Studium der Neueren Sprachen und
Literaturen_, 113/198 (1961), 65-76.
This contains scant references to Osborne, as
well as Arthur Miller and other modern dramatists

who were currently popular in Germany.

Baxter, Kay M. Contemporary Theatre and the Christian
Faith. New York: Abington, 1967. Pages 79-88.
    Baxter views Osborne's angry, doubting protago-
nists as proof of a worldwide decline in Christian
commitment. Her interpretations of Look Back in
Anger, The Entertainer, and Luther may possibly shed
some light on modern spiritual attitudes but clearly
do not provide much insight into Osborne's plays.

_____. Speak What We Feel: A Christian Looks at the Con-
temporary Theatre. London: SCM Press, 1964.
    This is virtually an earlier version of the above.

Beaven, John. "Unlucky Jim." Twentieth Century, 160
(July 1956), 72-74.
    Beaven discusses Osborne's debt to Tennessee
Williams and relates Look Back in Anger to Streetcar
Named Desire. He also compares Jimmy Porter to the
protagonist of Kingsley Amis's Lucky Jim.

Bentley, Eric. The Life of the Drama. New York:
Atheneum, 1964. Pages 287-88.
    The "angry" theatre movement is accused of being
self-pitying and undisciplined.

Blau, Herbert. The Impossible Theatre. New York: Macmillan, 1964. Pages 213-20.
    Blau provides some biographical information about
Osborne and his social protest and describes specific events which influenced The Entertainer and Look
Back in Anger.

Bode, Carl. "Redbrick Cinderellas." College English, 20
(April 1959), 331-37.
    A useful article for Americans unaware of the
caste system in British education. Bode properly
identifies Jimmy Porter as the prototype of a new
postwar Englishman--educated at an "unfashionable"
university, impatient with social injustice, unwilling
to be absorbed into the complacent middle class.

Bonnerot, Louis. "John Osborne." Études Anglaises, 10
(1958), 378-91.
    A Frenchman serves an early appraisal of the
Royal Court Theatre, Osborne, and the growing power
of "angry theatre."

Bradbrook, M. C. English Dramatic Form: A History of Its
Development. New York: Barnes and Noble, 1965.
Pages 178, 186-88.
    This work contains a very brief discussion of Os-
borne's ability to capture contemporary attitudes

and frustrations in workable dramatic situations.

Brahams, Caryl. "The World of John Osborne." John O'London's, 26 November 1959, p. 292.

Brown, Ivor. "The High Froth." Drama, 87 (Winter 1967), 32-34.
  Brown comments on the voluble protagonists of Osborne's plays and wishes they would spill those words on someone or something good.

Brown, John Russell. "Introduction." Modern British Dramatists. Ed. John Russell Brown. Pages 9-10.

_____, ed. Modern British Dramatists: A Collection of Critical Essays. Englewood Cliffs: Prentice Hall, 1968. Pages 9-10, 47-57, 117-21.
  This is one of the 20th Century views series and provides an excellent collection of essays on the New Drama. Brustein and Marowitz are among the contributing authors. Strongest emphasis is on Osborne though other authors are discussed.

_____. Theatre Language: A Study of Arden, Osborne, Pinter, and Wesker. London: Allen Lane, The Penguin Press, 1972. Pages 118-57.

Browne, E. Martin. "A Look Round the English Theatre: Summer and Fall, 1966." Drama Survey, 5 (Winter 1966-67), 297.

Brustein, Robert. Seasons of Discontent. New York: Simon and Schuster, 1965. Pages 196-200.
  This essay on Osborne's Luther generally deplores the playwright's lack of control over his materials.

_____. "Theatre Chronicle." Hudson Review, 12 (Spring 1959), 98-101.
  Brustein describes Osborne's role in revising Epitaph for George Dillon for production. He notes Osborne's growing strength as a dramatist and compares Osborne's philosophical approach to George Orwell's.

_____. The Theatre of Revolt. Boston: Little, Brown, 1964. Pages 27, 316.
  Osborne gains his strength from his rebellion against society and the conventions of British theatre.

_____. The Third Theatre. New York: Knopf, 1969. Pages 146-48.
  Brustein's chapter on Inadmissible Evidence criticizes the play for its one-dimensional character-

ization and sermonizing but admits the power of the
protagonist's explosive self-hatred.

Buskens, John. "De Humorist: John Osborne--K.N.S.
Antwerpen." Vlaamse Gids, 52 (1968), vi:13.

Calisher, Hortense. "Will We Get There by Candlelight?"
Reporter, 4 November 1965, pp. 38-40, 42, 44.
Calisher gives an analytical summary of the first
decade of Osborne's career in the theatre in a witty,
perceptive, thorough study.

Carnall, Geoffrey. "Saints and Human Beings: Orwell,
Osborne, & Gandhi." In Essays Presented to Amy G.
Stock, Professor of English, Rajasthan University,
1961-65. Jaipur: Rajasthan University Press, 1965.
Carnall links Osborne to Orwell, which has been
done by other critics but he also compares them with
Gandhi. In the manner of Sartre he points out the
shared existential strength and idealism of the
three men.

Carter, A. V. "John Osborne: A Re-Appraisal." Revue
Belge de Philologie et d'Histoire, 44 (1966), 971-76.
Carter values Osborne's ability to portray contemporary man's sense of alienation. The playwright
is less a social reformer than a social realist,
less a healer than a diagnostician.

Carter, Alan. John Osborne. Edinburgh: Oliver and
Boyd, 1969.
A full length study of Osborne as a social protest playwright. All of the author's plays through
Hotel in Amsterdam are discussed. Carter's knowledge of English, social issues and Osborne's response to these is valuable, especially to an American reader a decade later.

Chiari, J. Landmarks of Contemporary Drama. London:
Jenkins, 1965. Pages 109-15.
Chiari provides brief critical discussions of
several early Osborne plays and Chiari's evolution
of

Churchill, Randolph. "Portrait of the Artist as an Angry
Young Gentleman." Encounter, 10 (January 1958), 66-
68.
Churchill offers a somewhat reactionary defense
of English social institutions and expresses hostility toward social critics (such as Osborne) whom he
feels should be grateful for their own advantages.

Clurman, Harold. *Lies Like Truth*. New York: Macmillan, 1958. Pages 167, 190-92.

_____. *The Naked Image*. New York: Macmillan, 1966. Pages 101-04.
Clurman's books are primarily collections of reviews. His initial comments on *Look Back in Anger* are included.

Cohn, Ruby. *Currents in Contemporary Drama*. Bloomington: Indiana University Press, 1969. Pages 5-6, 12-15, 123-24, 209.
Cohn provides discussion of the obvious Brechtian influence on *Luther*.

_____ and Bernard Dukore, eds. *Twentieth Century Drama: England, Ireland, the United States*. New York: Random House, 1966. Pages 542-44.
Osborne's role as the new young leader of British drama is discussed.

Coleman, Arthur and Gary R. Tyler. *Drama Criticism*. Denver: Swallow Press, 1966. Pages 169-71.
This is a brief, unannotated bibliography now out of date.

Colquitt, Betsy. "Editorial: The Limited View of *Look Back in Anger*." *Descant*, 4 (Fall 1959), 2, 48.
Colquitt gives a generally negative appraisal of *Look Back in Anger* with feminist overtones.

Corina, Leslie. "Still Looking Back." *New Republic*, 10 February 1958, p. 22.

Darricarrère, Jacqueline. "Nuevo Brote de Arte Dramático en Inglaterra." *Revista de Occidente*, 35 (February 1966), 217-25. In Spanish.
This is a general study of English drama, particularly those playwrights who have been sponsored by the Royal Court. Many plays are mentioned, but the greatest praise is reserved for *Look Back in Anger*.

Deming, Barbara. "John Osborne's War Against the Philistines." *Hudson Review*, 11 (Autumn 1958), 410-19.
Deming gives detailed analyses of *The Entertainer* and *Look Back in Anger*, but these plays fail to convince Deming of Osborne's success as a social reformer. Rather she sees him and his protagonists as victims of their own snobbery and hypersensitivity.

Dempsey, D. "Most Angry Fella." *New York Times Magazine*, 20 October 1957, pp. 22, 25-27.
This is an early profile of Osborne in which the playwright resists the Angry Young Man label and

proclaims himself more artist than reformer.

Denty, Vera D. "The Psychology of Martin Luther." Catholic World, 194 (November 1961), 99-105.
Denty gives a lay Catholic's view of Osborne's success in Luther, a play which she generally praises. This is not surprising since Osborne's Luther is more of an existential hero than a religious reformer, a man of ambiguous and often secular motives.

Dobree, Bonamy. "No Man's Land." Sewanee Review, 65 (1957), 309-16.
Dobree surveys the "angry" school of letters and offers particular praise for Osborne's contributions.

Downer, Alan S. "Total Theatre and Partial Drama: Notes on the New York Theatre, 1965-66." Quarterly Journal of Speech, 12 (October 1966), 225-36.
Downer compares "Inadmissible Evidence" to "Death of a Salesman" since both Osborne and Miller have managed successfully to portray inner states of mind in a stage setting. He emphasizes the destructive impact of contemporary society on the psychological well-being of the two heroes.

Driver, Tom F. Romantic Quest and Modern Query. New York: Delacorte, 1970. Pp. 455-56.
Driver notes the power of Osborne's rhetoric in the longer stage monologues but he feels that Osborne is more important as a sociological phenomenon than as a dramatist.

Droll, Morton. "The Politics of Britain's Angry Young Men." Western Political Quarterly, 12 (June 1959), 555-57.
A general survey of the educated postwar Englishman's view of the old order, the welfare state, and the continuing class struggle.

Dukore, Bernard. "Portrait of a Would-Be Artist." Western Speech, 30 (Spring 1966), 68-81.
In this character analysis of the character George Dillon, Dukore examines the way Dillon is corrupted by bourgeois values and surrenders his identity as an artist.

Duncan, Ronald. "A Preface to the Sixties." London Magazine, 7 (July 1960), 15-19.
Duncan questions Osborne's reputation as a revolutionary dramatist, illustrating the point that his vision never goes beyond Shaw's or Ibsen's.

Dupee, F. W. "Isn't Life a Terrible Thing, Thank God."
Partisan Review, 25 (Winter 1958), 122-26. Reprinted in Dupee's "The King of the Cats" and Other
Remarks on Writers and Writing under the title
"England Now--Ariel or Caliban."
     Dupee discusses England's social dilemma, calling
the popularity of Look Back in Anger an index of
public discontent.

_____. "The King of the Cats" and Other Remarks on
Writers and Writing. New York: Farrar, Strauss and
Giroux, 1965. Pages 196-200.

Dyson, A. E. "Look Back in Anger." Critical Quarterly,
1 (Winter 1959), 318-26. Reprinted in Modern British Dramatists. Ed. John Russell Brown. Pages 47-
57.
     Dyson defines "the Angry Young Man" myth and
closely analyzes Jimmy Porter as supreme representa-
tive of the type. He believes Osborne neither sen-
timentalizes nor maligns Jimmy.

Elsom, John. "A Bond with Nahum Tate." London Magazine,
6, (November 1966), 73-76.
     Elson considers A Bond Honored to be an inferior
adaptation of La fianza satisfecha.

Esslin, Martin. "Brecht and the English Stage." Tulane
Drama Review, 11 (Winter 1966), 63-70.
     This is an analysis of Brecht's influence on Os-
borne and other English dramatists.

_____. Reflections: Essays on Modern Theatre. Garden
City: Doubleday, 1969. Pages 78, 81, 84-85, 167.
     Esslin objects to Osborne's misrepresentation of
historical fact and milieu in Luther and A Patrol
for Ore. He fails to see the metaphysical significance of these works, however, or to account for
their power and effectiveness as drama.

_____. The Theatre of the Absurd. Garden City: Double-
day, 1969. Pages 101-02, 379.
     Esslin briefly discusses the ways in which Os-
borne is similar to and different from the absurdists.

_____. "Where Angry Young Men Led." New York Times,
8 May 1966, II:4-5.

Faber, M. D. "The Character of Jimmy Porter: An Approach
to Look Back in Anger." Modern Drama, 13 (May
1970), 67-77.
     Faber suggests a psychoanalytic alternative to
the more usual sociological approach to Jimmy

Porter. Jimmy is motivated by oral fixations and neuroticism, not his reactions to the class system.

Farrar, Harold. John Osborne. (CEMW67) New York and London: Columbia University Press, 1973.
All of Osborne's plays are flawed and at least five are "bad." He is not a playwright of ideas, yet he is an exciting dramatist because "he has articulated as fully as any writer the central experience of his age."

Findlater, Richard. "The Angry Young Man." New York Times, 29 September 1957, II:1:6.

_____. The Future of the Theater. London: The Fabian Society, 1959.
Findlater explores the relationship between England's economic and social problems and the kind of theatre that developed after World War II. Osborne's and other playwrights' responses to conditions are alluded to.

Flint, Martha and Charlotte Garrard. "Le Diable et le Bon Dieu and an Angry Young Luther." Journal of European Studies, 2 (1972), 247-55.
This is a perceptive analysis of Luther. The authors point out the relevance of the historical Luther's problems to those of contemporary English society.

Fraser, G. S. The Modern Writer and His World. Harmondsworth: Penguin, 1964. Pages 223-33.
Fraser relates Osborne to Tennessee Williams and to Brecht. He applies Adlerian criteria to his analysis of Jimmy Porter's personality. Osborne blends traditional characterizations and language with unconventional attitudes toward English institutions. (Esslin and other critics have been more perceptive in their recognition of the originality and unique impact of Osborne's dialogue.)

Freedman, Morris. The Moral Impulse. Carbondale: University of Southern Illinois Press, 1967. Pages 116-17.
Freedman compares Jimmy Porter with Tennessee Williams' Kowalski (Streetcar Named Desire), showing how one rejects, the other accepts, the shallow dictums of a profit-oriented society.

Gascoigne, Bamber. Twentieth Century Drama. New York: Hutchinson, 1962. Pages 196-98.
Gascoigne praises Osborne and Luther.

Gassner, John. Dramatic Soundings. New York: Crown, 1968. Pages 612-14.
Gassner generally offers unfavorable comments on Osborne's plays. He seems to object to the complaining nature of his protagonists.

_____. Theatre at the Crossroads. New York: Holt, Rinehart and Winston, 1960. Pages 173-77.
This is a superficial survey of Osborne's early work. Gassner is noncommittal.

Gersh, Gabriel. "The Theatre of John Osborne." Modern Drama, 10 (September 1967), 137-43.
This article offers a biographical interpretation of the first decade of Osborne's career as playwright. The ups and downs of Osborne's fame and prosperity are related to his plays and the characters are seen to manifest the playwright's own slightly paranoid vision of life. Gersch offers some good insights but his conclusions are highly speculative.

Graef, Hilda. "Why All This Anger?" Catholic World, 188 (November 1958), 122-28.
Graef maintains that beneath its surface of modern sociological topics, Look Back in Anger is essentially a reworking of the Cain and Abel story.

Granger, D. "Themes for New Voices." London Magazine, 3 December 1956), 41-47.
This is a very early statement of Osborne's potential importance as a playwright for the English stage and a timely discussion of economical and political realities which have prepared audiences to receive his message.

Grindin, James. Postwar British Fiction. Berkeley: University of California Press, 1963. Pages 51-64. Reprinted in John Osborne: Look Back in Anger, A Casebook.
Grindin urges critics to note more carefully the personal relationships in Look Back in Anger and to consider the play an investigation of love and human communication rather than a social document.

Hahnloser-Ingold, Margrit. Das Englische Theater und Bert Brecht: Die Dramen von W. H. Auden, John Osborne, John Arden in Ihrer Beziehung zum Epischen Theater von Bert Brecht und den Gemeinsamen Elisabethanischen Quellen. Bern: Francke, 1970.
The Brechtian influence on Osborne is given its fullest treatment here. The author's study of Arden is equally thorough. Brecht's techniques are de-

fined and compared to copious selections from the
English writers.

Hall, Stuart. "Beyond Naturalism Pure." Encore (November-December 1961), 12-19. Reprinted in The Encore
Reader.
    The treatment by Wesker, Arden, and Osborne of
the anti-hero of contemporary culture is seen to be
an extension of the naturalist mode of presentation.
Osborne is particularly successful in combining
naturalism with a subtle symbolism, thereby making
protagonists like Jimmy or Archie part of a metaphoric design.

Haltresht, Michael. "Sadomasochism in John Osborne's 'A
Letter to My Fellow Countrymen.'" Notes on Contemporary Literature, 4, Fall 1975, 10-12.
    Osborne's attitude toward his audiences and
toward his fellow countrymen is that of a reforming
moralist who knows people enjoy being berated.

Hancock, Robert. "Anger." Spectator, 5 April 1957,
pp. 438-39. (Reply by Osborne in the Spectator, 13,
April 1957, B.)
    This is a partial portrait of the newly discov-
ered playwrights and the latter's somewhat testy
corrections.

Hare, Carl. "Creativity and Commitment in the Contemporary British Theatre." Humanities Association
Bulletin, 16 (Spring 1965), 21-28.
    Almost a decade after Osborne's opening at the
Royal Court, Hare assesses the vitality of the new
theatre movement he spawned.

Hartley, Anthony. "Angry Romantic." Spectator, 18 May
1957, p. 688.

Hartley, Walter. "Useful Criticism." London Times, 15
June 1966, p. 13d.

Hayman, Ronald. John Osborne. New York: Ungar, 1968.
2d ed. Melbourne: Heinemann Educ. Australia, 1970.

_____. John Osborne. (World Dramatists). New York:
Ungar, 1972.
    Hayman suggests that Osborne is preoccupied with
his heroes' quest for a kind of existential self-
definition and suggests that his plays therefore
lack thematic and stylistic variety. Though it is
debatable whether Osborne's dominating protagonists
are the weakness or the strength of his plays, Hayman's insightful analysis in separate chapters of
Osborne's works from Look Back in Anger to West of
Suez is well-organized and informative.

Heilman, Robert B. Tragedy and Melodrama: Versions of Experience. Seattle: University of Washington Press, 1966. Pages 138, 145-48, 297-98.
Heilman discusses Look Back in Anger and Inadmissible Evidence as polemical theatre pieces.

Hilton, Frank. "Britain's New Class." Encounter, 10 (February 1958), 59-63.
Hilton asserts that Jimmy Porter belongs to a new social class--one embittered by a working class past but softened by present bourgeois comforts. Porter is a kind of 1930s rebel in a drastically changed Europe. His anger derives more from confusion over his own social identity than from a genuine concern with political realities.

Hollis, Christopher. "Keeping Up With the Rices." Spectator, 18 October 1957, pp. 504-05.

Holloway, John. "Tank in the Stalls: Notes on the School of Anger." Hudson Review, 10 (Autumn 1957), 424-29.
Holloway traces Porter's literary "genealogy" to H. G. Wells's Kipps. He accurately predicts that Porter will be a prototype for a new English stage hero.

Hughes, Catherine. "John Osborne's Generation Gap." America, 11 October 1969, pp. 295-97.
Hughes contrasts the rebellious heroes of Osborne's early works with the rather conformist protagonists of later plays, such as Time Present.

Hunter, G. K. "The World of John Osborne." Critical Quarterly, 111 (Spring 1961), 76-81.
Investigating Osborne's early plays, Hunter cites conflicts between individual needs and the demands of society as a source of dramatic energy.

Huss, Roy. "John Osborne's Backward Halfway Look." Modern Drama, 6 (May 1963), 20-25.
Huss subjects Look Back in Anger to Freudian analysis and describes Porter's oedipal conflicts and sado-masochistic behavior.

Hussey, Charles. "Osborne Looks Forward in Anger." New York Times, 25 October 1964, VI:71.

I[hlenfeld], K[urt]. "Osborne's Luther." Eckart Jahrbuch (1961-1962), pp. 312-15.
The author finds Luther intelligent and highly dramatic but questions its historical accuracy.

<u>John</u> <u>Osborne</u>: <u>A</u> <u>Symposium</u>. London: Royal Court Theatre, 1966.
 Ten years after <u>Look</u> <u>Back</u> <u>in</u> <u>Anger</u> opened at the Royal Court, dramatists connected with the theatre, such as John Auden and other literary personalities, evaluate Osborne's achievement.

Karrfalt, David H. "The Social Theme in Osborne's Plays." <u>Modern</u> <u>Drama</u>, 13 (May 1970), 78-82.
 Modern man's sense of isolation from his community and its institutions is seen to be a source of despair in Osborne's plays. The playwright's sympathy lies with protagonists who confront a meaningless world with an existential awareness.

Kato, Kyohei. "An Essay on John Osborne." In <u>Collected</u> <u>Essays</u> <u>by</u> <u>Members</u> <u>of</u> <u>the</u> <u>Faculty</u>, No. 13. <u>Kyoritsu,</u> Japan: Kyoritsu Women's Junior College, 1969. In Japanese.

Kennedy, Andrew K. "Old and New in London Now." <u>Modern</u> <u>Drama</u>, 11 (February 1969), 437-46.
 Kennedy's appraisal of the theatre season in London includes rather deprecating comments on <u>Time</u> <u>Present</u> and <u>The</u> <u>Hotel</u> <u>in</u> <u>Amsterdam</u>, which he sees as failed Chekhovian naturalism.

Kerr, Walter. <u>The</u> <u>Theater</u> <u>in</u> <u>Spite</u> <u>of</u> <u>Itself</u>. New York: Simon & Schuster, 1963. Pages <u>129-31</u>.
 This is basically a reprint of an early <u>Look</u> <u>Back</u> <u>in</u> <u>Anger</u> review, citing the power and freshness of Osborne's talent.

_____. <u>Tragedy</u> <u>and</u> <u>Comedy</u>. New York: Simon & Schuster, 1967. Pages 325-27.

Kershaw, John. <u>The</u> <u>Present</u> <u>Stage</u>. London: Fontana, 1966. Pages 21-41.
 Kershaw praises Osborne's deft handling of colloquial speech and finds in <u>Look</u> <u>Back</u> <u>in</u> <u>Anger</u> a work which thematically and stylistically challenges stereotyped views of British life and theatrical conventions. Audience empathy with the character's emotional crises is a major factor in the play's success.

King, Seth S. "Britain Damned by John Osborne." <u>New</u> <u>York</u> <u>Times</u>, 19 August 1961, p. 4:1.

Kitchin, Laurence. <u>Drama</u> <u>in</u> <u>the</u> <u>Sixties</u>. London: Faber and Faber, 1966. Pages <u>185-91</u>.
 Kitchin compares Osborne's emergence as a dramatist of international significance and his leadership of a theatrical movement with the rise of

Luther and Protestantism.

_____. _Mid-Century Drama_. London: Faber and Faber, 1960. Pages 99-101, 104-06. Comments on Osborne reprinted _John Osborne_, _Look Back in Anger_, _A Casebook_.
A brief article valuable in that it discusses the Royal Court Theatre's original decision to accept _Look Back in Anger_ for production.

_____. "Realism in the English Mid-Century Drama." _World Theatre_, 14 (January-February 1965), 17-26.
This is a brief survey of English drama since the advent of Osborne. The new interest in working class life, everyday speech, and social conflicts is discussed.

_____. "Theatre--Nothing But Theatre." _Encounter_, 10 (April 1958), 39.

Knight, G. Wilson. "The Kitchen Sink: On Recent Developments in Drama." _Encounter_, 11 (December 1963), 48-54.
Knight contrasts the realistic drama of Osborne and its concern with problems of the proletarian with the sophisticated and more philosophical absurdist dramas of N. F. Simpson and the French playwrights.

Kuin, J. "Religieuze Problematiek bij schrijvers zonder geloof." _Roeping_, 38 (1962), 34-50.
Kuin wonders if Osborne's _Luther_ behaves like a theologian as modern social reformer.

Lahr, John. "Poor Johnny One-Note." _Evergreen Review_, 12 (December 1968), 61-63, 93-95.
Lahr gives a very negative appraisal of Osborne's work, arguing a steady decline of his powers since _Look Back in Anger_, a weakening of his social message and artistic self-discipline.

Landstone, Charles. "From John Osborne to Shelagh Delaney." _World Theatre_, 8 (Autumn 1959), 203-16.
Landstone associates Osborne's meteoric rise with critic Kenneth Tynan's powerful support. He discusses the "angry" circle and comments on Shelagh Delaney's _Taste of Honey_.

Langmann, F. H. "The Generation That Got Lost Staying Home: A Letter to Jimmy Porter." _Theoria_, 11 (1958), 29-30.
One of many contemporary repudiations of Jimmy Porter, this article is a "letter" to Porter, the man, deploring his self-pity and gutlessness.

Leech, Clifford. The Dramatist's Experience. New York:
    Barnes and Noble, 1970. Page 140.

Leslie, P. "The Angry Young Man Revisited." Kenyon Re-
    view, 27 (Spring 1965), 344-352.
        A conventional appraisal of Look Back in Anger's
    seminal position in the new drama and Osborne's more
    moderate social analyses.

Lewis, Allan. The Contemporary Theater. New York:
    Crown, 1971. Pages 315-35.
        Surveying the Osborne canon from Look Back in
    Anger to The Hotel in Amsterdam, Lewis praises Look
    Back in Anger and faults nearly all the subsequent
    plays, especially Luther.

Leyburn, Ellen D. "Comedy and Tragedy Transposed."
    Yale Review, 53 (Summer 1964), 553-62.
        Leyburn prefers Arthur Miller and Tennessee
    Williams to Osborne whose characters seem "disagree-
    able" to her.

"Look Back in Anger in Sweden." London Times, 13 May
    1957, p. 14b.

Lumley, F. New Trends in Twentieth Century Drama. Lon-
    don: Barrie and Rockliff, 1967. Pages 221-32, 255.
        This article covers Osborne's work up through
    the time of A Bond Honoured. Lumley considers Os-
    borne a dramatist of great stature, one who has
    matured without ceasing to experiment.

McCarthy, Mary. "A New Word." Harper's Bazaar, April
    1958, pp. 176-78.
        Briefly, McCarthy compares Osborne to Shaw as a
    social realist and praises his insights into the op-
    pressive nature of contemporary society. Jimmy
    Porter is seen as the "conscience" of his circle.

_____. "Odd Man In." Partisan Review, 26 (Winter 1959),
    100-06.
        This time McCarthy compares Epitaph for George
    Dillon to plays by Genet and O'Neill which explore
    the artist's world.

_____. Sights and Spectacles. London: Heinemann, 1959.
    Pages 184-96.
        McCarthy finds an integrity in Porter's arrogance
    and his refusal to explain his position fully or to
    attract the sympathy of moderates through rational
    argument.

Magee, Bryan. The New Radicalism. London: Secker and
    Warburg, 1962. Page 180.

Mander, John. *The Writer and Commitment*. London: Secker
   and Warburg, 1961. Pages 179-211.
   Mander considers *Look Back in Anger* an ineffective play because he feels the minor characters are
carelessly drawn and the audience is left without
any unbiased perspective for forming social judg-
ments.

Mannes, Marya. "A Question of Timing." *Reporter*, 14
   November 1957, p. 38.

Marowitz, Charles. "The Ascension of John Osborne."
   Tulane Drama Review, 7 (Winter 1962), 175-79. Reprinted in *Modern British Dramatists* and *John Os-*
   borne: Look Back in Anger, A Casebook.
   Marowitz has studied Osborne's religious skepti-
cism, particularly as it is manifest in characters
like Porter, Dillon, Rice, and Luther. He correctly
assesses the existentialist attitudes of Osborne's
Luther.

Martin, Graham. "A Look Back at Osborne." *Universities*
   and Left Review, 7 (Autumn 1959), 37-40.
   In retrospect Osborne's disgust with modern institutions seems almost mild. He alerted audiences
to conditions which are now widely recognized.

Millgate, Michael. " A Communication: A Good Word for
   England." *Partisan Review*, 24 (Summer 1957), 428-31.
   Millgate applauds *Look Back in Anger* as a sign of
healthy protest in the theatre. Millgate compares
Jimmy Porter to Kingsley Amis's Lucky Jim and other
new works.

_____. "An Uncertain Feeling in England." *New Republic*,
   9 September 1957, pp. 16-17.

Milne, Tom. "The Hidden Face of Violence." *Encore*, 7
   (1960), 14-20. Reprinted in *Modern British Drama-*
   tists and *The Encore Reader*.
   Milne posits that Osborne's plays lie midway between the affirmative vision of Eliot's and Fry's
Christian dramas and Harold Pinter's atheistically
existential dramatic statements. In particular Osborne's treatment of sex and violence seems more
credible to avenge audiences than the random abstract
menace of Pinter's world.

_____. "*Luther* and *The Devils*." *New Left Review*, 12
   (November-December 1961), 55-57.
   Milne explores the use of history in contemporary
theatre and takes exception to widespread acceptance
of the Brechtian historical modes of drama. In particular he finds the use of history in Whiting's

The Devils and Osborne's Luther misleading and lim-
iting.

"Mr. Osborne Looks On In Anger." London Times, 9 June
1966, p. 14d.

Morgan, Edwin. "That Uncertain Feeling." In The Encore
Reader: A Chronicle of the New Dramas. Ed. by
Charles Marowitz, Tom Milne, and Owen Hale. London:
Eyre Methuen, 1965. Pages 52-55.
    Morgan believes that Osborne, Arthur Miller, and
Tennessee Williams have all revitalized the stage
with more naturalistic speech patterns. Further-
more, Osborne has done much to emphasize feeling
rather than intellect in the theatre.

"Moscow Looks Back in Anger." London Times, 19 December
1969, p. 7e.

Nathan, David. "John Osborne--Is His Anger Simmering."
The Curtain Rises. Comp. Dick Richards. London:
Frewin, 1966. Pages 244-47.

Nicoll, Allardyce. "Somewhat in a New Dimension." In
Contemporary Theatre. Eds. John Russell Brown and
Bernard Harris. London: Arnold, 1962. Pages 77-95.
Reprinted in John Osborne: Look Back in Anger, A
Casebook.
    Nicoll emphasizes the newness of Osborne's tech-
nique. He avoids needless exposition in Look Back
in Anger and omits the conclusion. This sharpens
the play's naturalism as well as the tensions between Porter and Allison. Nicoll considers Osborne's
subjectivism and obvious identification with his
characters a strength.

Nightingale, Benedict. "Osborne's Old Times." New
Statesman, 27 August 1971, p. 277.

Northouse, C. and T. P. Walsh. John Osborne. Boston:
G. K. Hall, 1974.
    One of the most recent and most thorough bibliog-
raphies of Osborne's works. The annotations are
perceptive and detailed. Foreign citations, however, are somewhat scanty. The secondary bibliography is arranged alphabetically under the year it
was published. Critics of popular culture will appreciate this approach since one can see the impact
of each Osborne play on audiences and watch the
growing popularity of the playwright. But it is
time-consuming to survey the writings of a single
critic since his articles may be listed in many different sections.

Novick, Julius. _Beyond Broadway_. New York: Hill and Wang, 1968. Page 150.

O'Brien, Charles H. "Osborne's _Luther_ and the Humanistic Tradition." _Renascence_, 21 (Winter 1969), 59-63
O'Brien notes similarities between Osborne's portrayal of Luther and early accounts of the theologian's life by Erasmus. O'Brien notes certain existential elements in Osborne's protagonist, which are clearly anachronistic, but mainly believes the characterization is dramatically effective.

O'Connor, John J. "The Three Faces of John Osborne." _Audience_, 6 (Spring 1969), 108-13.
O'Connor believes that the protagonists of _George Dillon_, _Look Back in Anger_, and _The Entertainer_ appear to have diverse, even contradictory, personalities but sees they have all been shaped by environmental forces to some degree and capture audience sympathy in similar ways.

Odajima, Yuji. _J. Osborne_. Tokyo: Kenkyusha, 1970.

Oppel, Horst. "John Osborne: _Look Back in Anger_." In _Das Moderne Englische Drama: Interpretationen_. Berlin: Erich Schmidt, 1963. Pages 316-30.
Oppel begins by citing the enormous impact _Look Back in Anger_ has had on English theatre. He explores the social issues in the play and analyzes the imagery from a psychoanalytic viewpoint--for example, the sexual imagery of the bears and squirrels game. He concludes that, although the play is excellent, Osborne, like most modern dramatists, has not found a dramatic form that fully suits his talents. He is caught instead between naturalistic and psychological drama.

"Osborne's Random Sortie." _London Times_, 23 January 1968, p. 81.

Osztovits, Levente. "John Osborns." In _Az angel irodalom a husz adik száz udban_. Eds. Laszlo Bát and István Kristó-Nagy. Budapest: Gundolat, 1970. Pages 231-58. In Hungarian.
Osborne's beginnings at the Royal Court Theatre, the tremendous success of _Look Back in Anger_, and his social realism are all noted, though there is a general feeling that his early work was stronger than the plays that followed.

Palmer, Helen H. and Anne Jane Dyson. _European Drama Criticism_. Hamden, Conn.: Shoestring Press, 1968. Pages 305-10.

This Shoestring press bibliography of Osborne's
works from 1957 to 1965 is not annotated.

Peinert, Dietrich. "'Bear' and 'Squirrel' in John Osborne's Look Back in Anger." Literatur in Wissenschaft und Unterricht (Kiel) 1 (1968), 117-22.
Peinert does an extensive imagery study of Look
Back in Anger, which he uses as the clue to understanding of the play's psychological undercurrents.

Peel, Marie. "Power and Pattern v. Morality 1. Poetry
and Drama." Books and Bookmen, 18, i (1972), 38-42.
This contains several brief references to Osborne's anti-establishment views.

_____. "Violence in Literature." Books and Bookmen, 17,
v (1972), 20-24.
Jimmy Porter is a good example of the modern
anti-hero who mistreats people yet who captures
the audience's sympathy.

Playfair, Giles. "Phoney War." Spectator, 17 June 1966,
p. 754.

Popkin, Henry. "Brechtian Europe." Drama Review, 12
(Fall 1967), 156-57.
This is a brief discussion of Brechtian technique
in Luther.

_____. "Theatre II." Kenyon Review, 20 (Spring 1958),
309-10.
Popkin describes the underlying pessimism in Look
Back in Anger where neither political change nor
personal redemption through love offer solutions to
suffering and alienation.

_____. "Williams, Osborne, or Beckett?" New York Times
Book Review, 13 November 1960, pp. 32-33-119-21.
This is an evaluation of the relative merits and
popularity of three contemporary playwrights writing
for three distinctly different cultures.

Post, Robert M. "The Outsider in the Plays of John Os-
borne." Southern Speech Communication Journal, 39
(Fall 1973), 63-75.
All of Osborne's characters are outside society.
His dramas are primarily studies of human aberra-
tion.

Price, Martin. "The London Season." Modern Drama, 1
(May 1958), 53-59.
Price complains that Osborne's characters are
often too self-involved to be interesting. Only
Olivier's acting makes Archie Rice truly complex.

"Putting Drama in Touch with Contemporary Life: Two Years of the English Stage Company." London Times, 19 March 1958, p. 3b.

Robson, W. W. Modern English Literature. London: Oxford University Press, 1970. Pages 116, 157-58.
Robson uses Osborne as an example of a writer whose original interests were political but whose later works have focused more on personal and philosophical issues.

Rogers, Daniel. "Look Back in Anger--to George Orwell." Notes and Queries, 9 (1962), 310-11.
In a brief Notes and Queries comment, Rogers feels that Jimmy Porter quotes Orwellian philosophy in Look Back in Anger and that Orwell's ideas are less biased and more interesting than those of Osborne's spokesman.

_____. "'Not for Insolence, But Seriously': John Osborne's Adaptation of La fianza satisfecha." Durham University Journal, 29 (1968), 146-70.
This is a detailed comparison of A Bond Honoured and its source, Lope de Vega's La fianza satisfecha. Generally laudatory, the article notes Osborne's forcefulness as a translator and his instinct for good theatre which leads to some fairly substantive alterations. Contemporary themes of alienation and the concept of selfhood depart strongly but interestingly from Lope's model.

Rogoff, Gordon. "Richard's Himself Again: Journey to an Actor's Theatre." Tulane Drama Review, 11 (Winter 1966), 29-40.
Rogoff maintains that while Osborne created the illusion of starting a new kind of drama, his later works have marked him not as a revolutionary but as a traditionalist.

Rollins, Ronald G. "Carroll and Osborne: Alice and Alison in Wild Wonderland." Forum (Houston), 7 (Summer 1969), 16-20.
Look Back in Anger is compared to Alice in Wonderland which is seen as a source of imagery, theme, and characterization for Osborne. It is wise to remember that the late 1960s saw a great revival of interest in Lewis Carroll, especially on the scholarly level.

Roy, Emil. British Drama Since Shaw. Carbondale: University of Southern Illinois, 1972. Pages 100, 106, 115, 123-24, 128.
Roy alludes to Osborne's works many times in his overall assessment of British drama. He particu-

larly admires Inadmissible Evidence and compares
Osborne to Pinter in his ability to describe the
modern sense of alienation theatrically.

Rupp, Gordon E. "John Osborne and the Historical Luther."
     The Expository Times, 73 (February 1962), 147-51.
     Erik Erikson's Young Man Luther is discussed as
the primary source of Osborne's Luther and Rupp
meticulously points out discrepancies between the
stage hero and the historical Luther.

_____. "Luther and Mr. Osborne." Cambridge Quarterly, 1
     (Winter 1965-66), 28-42.
     This article is similar to the one above, with
more emphasis on Osborne's distortion of Luther to
make him an angry young man.

Sahl, Hans. "John Osborne." Welt und Wort, 14 (1959),
     36-37. In German.
     This is a brief evaluation of Osborne's career to
date and his impact on British theatre.

Scott-Kilvert, Ian. "The Hero in Search of a Dramatist:
     The Plays of John Osborne." Encounter, 9 (December
     1957), 26-30.
     Scott-Kilvert appreciates Osborne's success in
challenging the over-emphasis on upper class life
in English drama and the playwright's personal
grievances with English society. But he suggests
that Osborne is "essentially stagey" and questions
his ability to continue captivating large audiences.

Selz, Jean. "John Osborne et Jimmy Porter." Les Lettres
     Nouvelles, 61 (June 1958), 908-11
     The French critic briefly explores parallels be-
tween Osborne's own life and views and Jimmy
Porter's.

Servadio, Gaia. "Il Dandy con il metra spara salve." La
     Fiera Litteraria, 1 August 1968, p. 14.

Seymour, Alan. "Maturing Vision." London Magazine, 5
     (October 1965), 75-79.
     Here Seymour attempts to correct the overstate-
ment of his May article by pointing out that his
characters progress in terms of philosophical awareness and that A Patriot for Me is more intellectually complex and skillful than any of Osborne's previous efforts.

_____. "Osborne V.C." London Magazine, 5 (May 1965),
     69-74.
     This is a generally negative account of Osborne's
achievement to date, with special scorn for George

Dillon and an overall criticism of the author's
mastery of stage techniques, writing ability, and
conformed ideas.

Shayon, Robert Lewis. "Luther, Whose Identity Crisis?"
Saturday Review, 17 February 1968, p. 42.

Sherry, Ruth Forbes. "Angry Young Men." Trace (May-June
1960), pp. 33-37.
Jimmy Porter is briefly noted as an example of a
prevalent psychological phenomenon in English life
and literature.

Shostakov, D. "Monologi Dzhona Osborne." Ihostranaya
literatura, 7 (1967), 112-16.

Sigal, Clancy. "Looking Back Without Anger." Commonweal,
8 May 1970, pp. 186-88.
Sigal discusses briefly the social background of
the angry movement and gives some biographical notes
on Osborne and his contemporaries.

Spacks, Patricia Meyer. "Confrontation and Escape in Two
Social Dramas." Modern Drama, 11 (May 1968), 61-72.
Look Back in Anger is compared negatively in
terms of characterization and impact to Ibsen's A
Doll's House.

Spanos, William V. The Christian Tradition in Modern
British Verse Drama. New Brunswick, N.J.: Rutgers
University Press, 1967. Pages 336-37.
Osborne is included briefly as an example of a
popular modern dramatist who, unlike Eliot and Fry,
is not primarily a "Christian" writer.

Spender, Stephen. "London Letter: Anglo-Saxon Attitudes."
Partisan Review, 25 (Winter 1958), 110-16.
Spender compares Osborne to Dylan Thomas. Osborne is an effective social critic who perceives
the negative influence of a powerful state on traditional human relationships.

_____. "Notes from a Diary." Encounter, 7 (August 1956),
71.

_____. "Notes from a Diary." Encounter, 11 (December
1958), 75-77.
Spender, writing in Poland, complains that Osborne's attack on English social problems seems
naive in Poland where human rights are virtually
ignored.

Stefanov, Vasil. "Spoluki na mladostta. Piesata 'Osborne ses gnjai nazad' vav Varnenskija dramat
teatar." Teatar, 21, 3 (1968), 43-44. In Yugoslavian.
This is a Yugoslavian reaction to a performance
of Look Back in Anger, emphasizing Porter's resent-
ment of the English class system.

Stoppard, Tom. "'A Very Satirical Thing Happened to Me
on the Way to the Theatre Tonight." Encore, 10
(March-April 1963), 33-36.
Stoppard notes that there are three satirical
comedies playing in London simultaneously. One is
Osborne's Under Plain Cover which he finds too close
to the truth to be genuine satire and foolish besides. The famous Stoppard wit and word-play is
apparent even in this very slight article.

Stroman, B. "Maarten Luther en John Osborne." Vlaamse
Gids, 45 (September 1961), 633-35.

_____. "Tweërlei Afstotendheid." Vlaamse Gids, 49
(November 1965), 746-47.

Sundrann, Jean. "The Necessary Illusion." Antioch Review, 18 (Summer 1958), 236-44.
Sundrann believes The Entertainer illustrates the
conflicts of old and new values in an era of great
transition. England's angry men are really mourning
a loss of meaning and purpose.

"Sweete Alisoun." London Times Literary Supplement, 25
January 1957, p. 49.

Takada, Mineo. "A Non-U-Intelligentsia Dramatist." In
Annual Reports of Studies, Vol. 23. Kyoto: Doshi-
sha Women's College of Liberal Arts, 1972. Pages
146-88.
Osborne is described as a brilliant, successful
dramatist who has avoided the label of an "establishment" playwright. "U" values are Oxford and
Cambridge values, tradition-bound and upper middle
class.

Taylor, John Russell. Anger and After: A Guide to the
New British Drama. London: Eyre Methuen, 1962.
Pages 29-66. Reprinted in John Osborne: Look Back
in Anger, A Casebook.
Although Taylor properly credits Osborne as the
inspirational force behind the new English drama, he
feels the playwright himself is highly overrated and
that his talents have steadily deteriorated over the
years.

_____. The Angry Theater. New York: Hill and Wang,
1962. Pages 39-57.
    Taylor praises Dillon where Osborne maintained
some distance from his protagonist but feels that
his later plays lack imagination, spirit, objective.
He does, however, acknowledge Osborne's excellent
craftsmanship.

_____. "British Drama of the Sixties." In On Contempo-
rary Literature. Ed. Richard Kostelanetz. New
York: Avon, 1964. Pages 90-96.
    Taylor again acknowledges Osborne's historical
role in the new drama but the angry movement is seen
as a short-lived aberration.

_____. "Inadmissible Evidence." Encore, 9 (November-
December 1964), 43-46. Reprinted in John Osborne:
Look Back in Anger, A Casebook.
    At last, Taylor feels, Osborne has written a
strong play on the subject that he handles best--
alienation. He goes on to compare Inadmissible Evidence to Fellini's movie, 8-1/2.

_____, ed. John Osborne: Look Back in Anger, A Casebook.
London: Macmillan, 1968.
    This casebook is a testament to the legendary im-
pact of Look Back in Anger. Many English and foreign reviews of performances are given. Essays by
Osborne which elucidate his social ideas are included. Evaluations of the play are provided by
George Wellwarth, Katherine Worth, Lindsay Anderson,
and other distinguished theatre critics. Taylor's
introduction provides a balanced overview.

_____. "Ten Years of the English Stage Company." Tulane
Drama Review, 11 (Winter 1966), 120-31.
    Taylor offers a general discussion of the English
Stage Company's first ten years and Osborne's role
in its success. Specific Osborne plays, performed
by the company, are evaluated.

Thomas, Michael. "Translator's Dilemma." Plays and
Players, 13, vi (1966), 53.

Trilling, Ossia. "The New English Realism." Tulane Drama
Review, 7 (Winter 1962), 184-93.
    Osborne and others have shattered stereotypes
about British behavior and have attempted to portray
the life-styles of the average postwar Englishman.

_____. "The Young British Drama." Modern Drama, 111
(September 1960), 168-77.
    A general essay on British playwrights which
places Osborne at the center of the group.

114

Trussler, Simon. "British Neo-Naturalism." The Drama
    Review, 13 (Winter 1968), 130-36.
        Osborne's influence on Wesker and others is dis-
    cussed and he is credited with introducing the
    themes which will dominate the stage for years to
    come.

_____. "His Very Own Golden City: Interview." Tulane
    Drama Review, 11 (Winter 1966), 192-202. (Interview
    with Wesker.)
        Wesker acknowledges his debt to Osborne in this
    interview.

_____. John Osborne. London: Longmans, Green, 1969.
        This Longman's pamphlet is an encapsulated ver-
    sion of the study below.

_____. The Plays of John Osborne: An Assessment. Lon-
    don: Victor Gollancz, 1969.
        Trussler's full-length study of Osborne contains
    plot-summaries and critical interpretations of all
    the author's plays to date. The study is rather im-
    pressionistic. Trussler does not impose a set the-
    matic structure or overemphasize biographical de-
    tails, but his admiration for the playwright is con-
    sistent.

Tynan, Kenneth. "Men of Anger." Holiday, 23 (April
    1958), 92-93, 177, 179, 181-82, 184. Reprinted in
    Tynan's Tynan on Theatre as "The Angry Young Move-
    ment."
        Although this is a general study of the angry
    movement, Osborne's work is always center stage.
    Tynan is sympathetic with the social grievances of
    the group.

_____. "A Phony or a Genius?" London Observer, 16 Feb-
    ruary 1958, p. 12.

_____. Tynan on Theatre. Harmondsworth: Penguin, 1964.
    Pages 130-32, 173-76, 205-07.
        Early Tynan reviews of Look Back in Anger, The
    Entertainer, and Epitaph for George Dillon are in-
    cluded here as well as the essay "Men of Anger,"
    cited above.

_____. Tynan Right and Left. New York: Atheneum, 1967.
    Pages 5-6, 77-79, 109-10.

Valette, Jacques. "Lettres Anglo-Saxonnes: La Souete
    Anglaise et le Théâtre de John Osborne." Mercure de
    France, 333 (June 1958), 342-46.
        This is an early French essay on the English

social malaise as it is revealed in the plays of John Osborne.

Van de Perre, H. _John Osborne, boze jonge man_. The Hague: Tielt, 1962.
A Dutch investigation of Osborne's early works, discusses his fostering of the "angry" movement.

Van der Veen, Adriaan. "Boze Jongelieden in een Zich Vernieuwend Engeland." _Vlaamse Gids_, 43 (April 1959), 232-36.

Van Lokhorst, Emmy. "Toneelkroniek: _Wrok tegen het verleden_." _De Gids_, 120 (1957), xii, 404-07.
Van Lokhorst gives what is essentially a plot summary of _Look Back in Anger_, but she notes that Osborne and the English Stage Company have introduced the angry youth, already familiar in fiction in England (Kingsley Amis) and in France (Françoise Sagan), to the stage and that this joint enterprise is causing considerable excitement.

Ward, A. C. _Twentieth Century English Literature_. London: Eyre Methuen, 1964. Pages 11, 138, 140.
Ward is rather skeptical of _Look Back in Anger_'s success which he attributes in part to enthusiasm for the Royal Court Theatre itself.

Wardle, Irving. "The World of John Osborne." _London Times_, 6 July 1968, p. 18e.

_____. "Revolt Against the West End." _Horizon_, 5 (January 1963), 26-33.
Wardle sees Osborne and his followers as the hope of the British theatre. An antidote to the commercialism of Piccadilly and to the dramatic packaging of stereotyped British characters and situation.

Watt, David. "Class Report." _Encore_ (September 1957). Reprinted in _The Encore Reader_. Eds. Charles Marowitz, Tom Milne, and Owen Hale. London: Eyre Methuen, 1965. Pages 56-61.
Look Back in Anger introduced the educated lower middle class protagonist to the English stage. Unlike the working class men and women he sympathizes with, this protagonist can articulate his woes and attack the society which perpetrates them.

Weiss, Samuel. "Osborne's Angry Young Play." _Educational Theatre Journal_, 12 (December 1960), 285-88.
Weiss considers _Look Back in Anger_ the signal play of the new movement. Osborne understands the relationship between the psychological tensions of the Porters' marriage and modern English society.

Wellwarth, George E. The Theatre of Protest and Paradox.
    New York: New York University Press, 1964. Pages
    52, 197, 221, 222-34, 258, 274, 293. Reprinted in
    John Osborne: Look Back in Anger, A Casebook.
        Wellwarth questions whether Osborne's plays are
    truly social protests. Look Back in Anger appears
    to him to be a Strindbergian battle of the sexes.
    Only Paul Slickey offers genuine social criticism
    and he believes Osborne's career is degenerating.

Wesker, Arnold. "Center 42: The Secret Reins." En-
    counter, 25 (March 1962), 3-6.
        Wesker defends Osborne's picture of English so-
    ciety in Look Back in Anger and calls for the estab-
    lishment of an art center which will help create a
    better English society.

West, Atlick. "John Osborne." Filologiai Kozlony, 9
    (January-June 1963), 129-34.

Whiting, John. "Luther." London Magazine, 1 (October
    1961), 57-59. Reprinted in Whiting's On Theatre.
        Whiting summarizes Osborne's career to date and
    notes that the playwright's personality has increas-
    ingly intruded itself onto the stage so that the
    protagonist, Luther, and the playwright John Osborne
    are the same man.

Williams, Raymond. Drama from Ibsen to Brecht. New
    York: Oxford University Press, 1969. Pages 318-22.
        Look Back in Anger is a striking depiction of a
    modern, alienated subculture.

_____. "The New English Drama." Twentieth Century, 170
    (1961), 169-80. Reprinted in Modern British Drama-
    tists.
        This is an overview of the new drama with Os-
    borne's place clearly defined.

_____. "Recent English Drama." In The Modern Age. Ed.
    Boris Ford. Harmondsworth: Penguin, 1964. Pages
    487-88, 501-07.
        Williams repeats much of the material in the
    article above.

Wilson, A. "New Playwrights." Partisan Review, 25
    (Fall 1959), 631-34.
        Osborne and the Royal Court Theatre are seen to
    have revitalized the English stage.

Wohlfahrt, Paul. "'Berliner Westwochen' mit Osborne's
    'Luther.'" Begegnung, 18 (September 1963), 262.

Worsley, T. C. "Minority Culture." New Statesman, 26
January 1957, p. 97.

Worth, Katherine J. "The Angry Young Man: John Osborne."
In Experimental Drama. Ed. William A. Armstrong.
London: G. Bell, 1963. Pages 147-68. Reprinted in
John Osborne: Look Back in Anger,: A Casebook.
In this largely affirmative evaluation of Os-
borne's career, Worth asserts that the playwright
applied social criticism in the mode of Shaw and
Galsworthy to the contemporary English scene with
great success. She sees progress in his continued
craftsmanship and conceptualizing.

_____. "Shaw and John Osborne." The Shavian, 2 (October
1964), 29-35.
This is a thorough comparison of the two playwrights which explores their shared idealism and
their similar approaches to stage realism.

"Wrath at the Helm?" London Times, 26 May 1969, p. 7c.

Wyatt, Woodrow. Distinguished for Talent. London:
Hutchinson, 1958. Pages 116-22.
This is an early appraisal of Osborne with emphasis on Look Back in Anger, his great popular success and influence.

Young, Wayland. "London Letter." Kenyon Review, 17
(Autumn 1956), 642-47.
Young recognizes the revolutionary aspects of
this new play.

II. DISSERTATIONS

Athanason, Arthur Nicholas. "John Osborne: From Appren-
ticeship to Artistic Maturity." Dissertation Ab-
Stracts International 33:6898A-12A (Pennsylvania
State, 1972).
"John Osborne's journey from apprenticeship (The
Devil Inside Him, Personal Enemy, and Epitaph for
George Dillon) to artistic maturity (Inadmissible
Evidence) has been marked by the influence of many
established playwrights and novelists both in form
and style," including Brecht, Lawrence, Miller,
Priestley, Strindberg, Waugh, Williams, and the
music hall.

Brohaugh, Clair Bernhardt. "John Osborne and the Theme
of Authority." Dissertation Abstracts International
36:8068A-12A (Nebraska, 1975).
"This thematic study of ten plays by John Osborne [Look Back in Anger, A Bond Honoured, Time

Present, A Place Calling Itself Rome, Epitaph for
George Dillon, The Entertainer, Inadmissible Evidence, A Portrait for Me. The Hotel in Amsterdam]
emphasizes his continuing interest in man's relationship to various kinds of authority. In his
early plays, he focuses on the conflict between the
individual and the repressive institutions and conventions of society. In subsequent plays he explores the internal--as opposed to the external--
conflicts of protagonists who try to cope with problems of identity and responsibility. In more recent
plays he presents characters at peace with themselves and their world, or characters whose relationship to authority has a symbolic or allegorical
significance."

Brookbank, Charles D. "The Theme of Boredom in Selected
    Modern Dramas." Dissertation Abstracts Internation-
    al 32:5929A-10A (Minnesota, 1971).
        "Osborne's realistic plays offer a variety of
    bored characters. Boredom in Epitaph for George
    Dillon is born of disillusionment, while the boredom
    of Jimmy Porter, in Look Back in Anger, is militant
    and, insofar as Jimmy 'acts' to become bored, maso-
    chistic. Redl, in A Portrait for Me, overcomes
    boredom when his repressed instinctual aim, homo-
    sexuality, surfaces."

Budd, Dirk Ronald. "The Vicissitudes of the Osborne Pro-
    test from 1956 to 1964." Dissertation Abstracts In-
    ternational 30:1163A-03A (Pennsylvania, 1968).
        Budd examines the roots of Osborne's anger, its
    changing expression from Look Back in Anger through
    The Entertainer and Luther, to Plays for England,
    and its influence on "other playwrights from the
    lower strata of society."

Conlon, Patrick Owen. "Social Commentary in Contemporary
    Great Britain, as Reflected in the Plays of John
    Osborne, Harold Pinter, and Arnold Wesker." Disser-
    tation Abstracts International 29:3713A-10A (North-
    western, 1968).
        Conlon studies these three as members of "a wave
    of new dramatists, largely from the working class,
    who have specialized in outspoken social commentary."
    "Chapter II traces Osborne's work from his realistic
    first plays in which would-be artists on the fringes
    of British life comment bitterly on the pervasive
    grayness of the Welfare State and the persisting in-
    equities of the class system, through plays such as
    Luther when the author adopts Brechtian devices . . .
    to . . . A Bond Honoured [which] . . . suggests the
    nihilist. . . ."

Gilliard, Bari Lynn. "Men in Crisis: Vision and Form in John Osborne's Major Plays. _Dissertation Abstracts International_ 36:1526A-3A (Utah, 1975).
    "John Osborne's avowed purpose as a dramatist is "to make people feel, to give them lessons in feeling." ". . . An analysis of Osborne's six major plays, _Look Back in Anger_, _The Entertainer_, _Luther_, _Inadmissible Evidence_, _A Portrait for Me_, and _West of Suez_, reveals both the conception and execution of the playwright's dramatic vision of feeling."

Hinchey, James Francis. "John Osborne as Social Critic and Dramatic Artist: The Theme of Isolation and Estrangement in His Works." _Dissertation Abstracts International_ 32:6977A-12A (Wisconsin, 1972).
    "Each of the playwright's major works is examined separately, so that the theme of isolation and the consistent questioning of the ethos of twentieth-century Western civilization can be seen to be woven as a common thread throughout Osborne's drama. By tracing the pattern of his social concerns and by indicating the manner in which John Osborne's dramaturgy departs from that of British playwrights who preceded him, one can see that he has been a catalyst whose work precipitated a new wave of non-establishment theatre in Great Britain."

Lee, Sandra Marie. "John Osborne and the Ironic Comedy of Failure: A Study of Comic Subject and Techniques." _Dissertation Abstracts International_ 36:320A-1A (Loyola, 1975).
    "This study applies the concept of ironic comedy (developed from the comic theories of Bergson, Merideth, Frye, Langer) to the subject matter, dramatic forms, and audience response of Osborne's plays from 1957 to 1973. The most open comic contest in all the plays is between a member of society and the values of that society. There is also a more essential confrontation between the Osborne hero's idealized self-image of elevated vitality and will _and_ the private personal reality of failures to transcend natural human limitations."

Moore, Robert Barry. "The Published Stage Plays of John Osborne, 1956-1968: A Critical Exploration." _Dissertation Abstracts International_ 32:7123A-12A (Denver, 1971).
    "This dissertation, although concerned with Osborne's social and political comments, investigates the playwright's protagonists as manifestations of the existential crisis common to much contemporary literature and explores and [sic] the playwright's relation to the theatre of the Absurd."

Strane, Robert Erskine. "Gasconade for the End of
the World: The Plays of John Osborne." American
Doctoral Dissertations, 1966, p. 118 (Yale, 1966).
Strane emphasizes the despair and alienation of
Osborne's world and the existential responses of his
protagonists. He provides an excellent survey of
the first decade of theatrical activity and critical
response following the opening of Look Back in Anger.

Van Niel, Pieter Jan. "The Plays of John Osborne--The
Experiments and the Results." Dissertation Abstracts International 33:4576A-08A (Stanford, 1972).
Van Niel stresses the psychological profundity of
Osborne's play. He has praise for A Patriot for Me,
which he sees as a key to Osborne's complex characterization. This is an imaginative, original study.

III. REVIEWS

A BOND HONOURED

   The Times, 8 June 1966, p. 13e.

   The Times, 10 June 1966, p. 12e.

   The Times, 11 June 1966, p. 11c.

   The Times, 18 June 1966, p. 11d.

   The Times, 24 June 1966, p. 13d.

   Encounter, 27 (August 1966), 45-47.

THE ENTERTAINER

   The Times, 13 March 1957, p. 3b.

   Twentieth Century, 161 (June 1957), 583-85.

   New York Times, 13 February 1958, p. 22:2.

   New York Times, 23 February 1958, II, 1:1.

   Saturday Review, 1 March 1958, p. 24.

   The Times, 20 October 1959, p. 4a.

EPITAPH FOR GEORGE DILLON

   The Times, 27 February 1957, p. 3c.

   The Times, 12 February 1958, p. 3e.

The Times, 30 May 1958, p. 16e.

New York Times, 5 November 1958, p. 44:1.

New Yorker, 15 November 1958, pp. 101-03.

New York Times, 16 November 1958, II:1:1.

New York Times, 29 December 1960, p. 17:1.

New Yorker, 14 January 1961, pp. 68, 70, 72.

The Times, 8 December 1972, p. 13.

HOTEL IN AMSTERDAM

The Times, 4 July 1968, p. 13f.

New York Times, 17 August 1968, p. 17:1.

London Magazine, 8 (September 1968), 102-06.

INADMISSIBLE EVIDENCE

The Times, 10 September 1964, p. 8d.

The Times, 18 March 1965, p. 9c.

The Times, 29 September 1965, p. 14a.

New York Times, 1 December 1965, p. 52:1.

The Times, 31 December 1965, p. 13b.

National Review, 5 April 1966, pp. 325-26.

The Times, 3 February 1971, p. 11a.

Sheed, Wilfred. The Morning After. New York:
     Farrar, Straus and Giroux, 1971. Pp. 154-56.
     Reprint from Commonweal.

LOOK BACK IN ANGER

The Times, 9 May 1956, p. 3d.

Reporter, 18 October 1956, pp. 33-35.

The Times, 12 March 1957, p. 3e.

The Times, 11 September 1957, p. 3e.

New Yorker, 28 September 1957, pp. 153-54.

New York Times, 2 October 1957, p. 28:2.

The Times, 3 October 1957, p. 7d.

New Yorker, 12 October 1957, pp. 93-94.

New York Times, 13 October 1957, II:1:1.

Christian Century, 23 October 1957, pp. 1262-63.

The Times, 25 April 1958, p. 3e.

New York Times, 1 November 1968, p. 38:1.

Sight and Sound (Autumn 1961), pp. 10-13.

LUTHER

The Times, 7 July 1961, p. 15a.

The Times, 28 July 1961, p. 13a.

Encounter, 17 (August 1961), 51-53.

Reporter, 15 October 1961, pp. 50-53

Critic, 20 (February-March 1962), 53-55.

New York Times, 11 September 1963, p. 46:3.

New York Times, 26 September 1963, p. 41:1.

The Times, 27 September 1963, p. 16e.

New York Times, 6 October 1963, II:1:1.

New Republic, 19 October 1963, pp. 28, 30-31.

Reporter, 24 October 1963, pp. 54,55-56.

National Review, 5 November 1963, pp. 446-48, 449.

A PATRIOT FOR ME

The Times, 1 July 1965, p. 17c.

New York Times, 6 October 1969, p. 58:1.

New York Times, 12 October 1969, II:1:1.

National Review, 30 December 1969, pp. 1334-35.

A SENSE OF DETACHMENT

   The Times, 5 December 1972, p. 14.

TIME PRESENT

   The Times, 24 May 1968, p. 7a.

   New York Times, 2 June 1968, II:3:6.

   New York Times, 5 July 1968, p. 20:1.

WEST OF SUEZ

   The Times, 18 August 1971, p. 8c.

   Encounter, 37 (November 1971), 56-58.

THE WORLD OF PAUL SLICKEY

   New York Times, 6 May 1959, p. 48:7.

   Twentieth Century, 167 (January 1960), 29-38.

HAROLD PINTER

Born Hackney, London, October 10, 1930

     Harold Pinter may well be the most respected writer
for the stage in the world today. Some consider Samuel
Beckett a greater artist, but Pinter is still a relatively young man and is at the peak of his powers. Beckett
reads all of Pinter's scripts and makes suggestions on
them and the latter considers Beckett his master. Yet
Pinter, more than anyone else in this century, has
changed our expectations for stage language and has made
more traditional treatments of stage space, action, and
language seem ridiculous and pretentious. He is an enigma to critics. Some consider him an absurdist (the Beckett influence), others an existentialist, and some the
ultimate naturalist. Pinter is a genuine theatre person.
He has been an actor, writer, and director and is almost
totally involved in the world of the stage. Perhaps it
is the tension between Pinter's use of the absurdist tradition, with its baffling non sequiturs and purposeless
activities, and his naturalistic use of language, dialect,
and precise, believable detail that gives Pinter his
unique hold on drama. His earliest play, The Room, was
performed in 1957, but it was The Homecoming, ten years
later, which brought Pinter worldwide recognition. The
proliferation of scholarship concerning his playwriting
in the past decade is unequalled. He may not be as brilliant as Stoppard, as entertaining as the Shaffers, or as
startling as Bond. Yet he is the "Shakespeare" of his
age, the central figure in the New Wave.

PRIMARY SOURCES

I. STAGE

"Applicant." In A Slight Ache and Other Plays. London:
    Eyre Methuen, 1961.

       . In The Dwarfs and Eight Revue Sketches. New
    York: Dramatists Play Service, 1965.

The Basement. In Tea Party and Other Plays. London:
    Eyre Methuen, 1967.

_____. In The Lover, Tea Party, The Basement. New York:
    Grove Press, 1967.

The Birthday Party. London: Encore, 1959.

The Birthday Party, and Other Plays. London: Eyre
    Methuen, 1960. Revised ed. 1965. [Includes The
    Room and The Dumb Waiter.]

The Birthday Party, and The Room. New York: Grove Press,
    1961. [Includes The Dumb Waiter.]

The Birthday Party. In Seven Plays of the Modern Theater.
    Ed. Harold Clurman. New York: Grove Press, 1962.

_____. In Post-War Drama: Extracts from Eleven Plays.
    Ed. John Hale. London: Faber and Faber, 1966.

"The Black and White." In One to Another, by John
    Mortimer, N. F. Simpson, and Harold Pinter. London:
    Samuel French, 1960.

_____. The Spectator, 1 July 1960, p. 16. [In prose.]

_____. In A Slight Ache and Other Plays. London: Eyre
    Methuen, 1961.

_____. In Theatre Today. Ed. David Thompson. Harlow,
    Essex: Longman, 1965.

_____. In The Dwarfs and Eight Revue Sketches. New
    York: Dramatists Play Service, 1965.

_____. Flourish (magazine of the Royal Shakespeare
    Theatre Club) (Summer 1965).

_____. The Transatlantic Review, 21 (Summer 1966), 52.

The Caretaker. London: Eyre Methuen, 1960.

The Caretaker, and The Dumb Waiter: Two Plays. New York:
    Grove Press, 1961.

The Caretaker. In The Best Plays, 1961/62. Ed. Henry
    Hewes. New York: Dodd, Mead, 1962.

The Caretaker and The Room. New York: Grove Press, 1962.

The Caretaker. Speculum, 8 (1965).

_____. In The New British Drama. Ed. Henry Popkin. New York: Grove Press, 1964.

_____. In Twelve Modern Dramatists. Ed. Raymond Cowell. London: Pergamon Press, 1967.

The Collection. London: Samuel French, 1962.

_____. In Three Plays: A Slight Ache, The Collection, The Dwarfs. New York: Grove Press, 1962.

_____. In America's Lost Plays. New York: Dodd, Mead, 1963.

_____. In The Best Plays of 1962-63. Ed. Henry Hewes. New York: Dodd, Mead, 1963.

The Collection and The Lover. London: Eyre Methuen, 1966. [Includes the prose piece "The Examination."]

"Dialogue for Three." Stand, 6, iii (1963), 4-5.

The Dumb Waiter. In The Birthday Party and Other Plays. London: Eyre Methuen, 1960.

_____. In Twentieth Century Drama, England, Ireland, The United States. Ed. Ruby Cohn. New York: Random HOuse, 1960.

_____. In The Birthday Party and The Room. New York: Grove Press, 1961.

_____. In The Caretaker and the Dumb Waiter: Two Plays. New York: Grove Press, 1961.

_____. In New English Dramatists 3. Ed. Tom Maschler. Harmondsworth: Penguin, 1961.

_____. In The Room and The Dumb Waiter. London: Eyre Methuen, 1966.

The Dwarfs. In A Slight Ache and Other Plays. London: Eyre Methuen, 1964.

_____. In Three Plays: A Slight Ache, The Collection, The Dwarfs. New York: Grove Press, 1962.

The Dwarfs and Eight Revue Sketches. New York: Dramatists Play Service, 1965. [Includes "Trouble in the Works," "The Black and White," "Request Stop," "Last to Go," "Applicant," "Interview," "That's All," "That's Your Trouble."]

The Homecoming. London: Eyre Methuen, 1965.

_____. New York: Grove Press, 1966.

_____. The Best Plays of 1966-1967. Ed. Otis L. Guern-
sey, Jr. New York: Dodd, Mead, 1967.

_____. Rev. ed. London: H. Karnac, 1968.

_____. Manuscript notes and a page of the typescript
reproduced. London Magazine, N.S. 100 (July-August
1969).

Henrik Ibsen's Hedda Gabler. Adaptation. Chicago:
Dramatic, 1974.

"Interview." In Dwarfs and Eight Revue Sketches. New
York: Dramatists Play Service, 1965.

Landscape. London: Pendragon Press, 1968.

_____. Evergreen Review, 68 (July 1969).

Landscape and Silence. London: Eyre Methuen, 1969.
[Includes Night.]

_____. New York: Grove Press, 1970. [Includes Night.]

"Lost to Go." In A Slight Ache and Other Plays. London:
Eyre Methuen, 1961.

_____. In Theatre Today. Ed. David Thompson. Harlow,
Essex: Longman, 1965.

_____. In The Dwarfs and Eight Revue Sketches. New
York: Dramatists Play Service, 1965.

The Lover. New York: Dramatists Play Service, 1965.

_____. In The Collection and The Lover. London: Eyre
Methuen, 1966.

The Lover, Tea Party, The Basement. New York: Grove
Press, 1967.

Monologue. London: Covent Garden Press, 1973.

Night. (In We Who Are about to . . . , later called
Mixed Doubles; staged London 1969). Included in
Landscape and Silence. London: Eyre Methuen, 1969;
New York: Grove Press, 1970.

A Night Out. London: Samuel French, 1961.

_____. In A Slight Ache and Other Plays. London: Eyre
Methuen, 1961.

_____. In Early Plays: A Night Out, Night School, Revue Sketches. New York: Grove Press, 1968.

Night School. In Tea Party and Other Plays. London: Eyre Methuen, 1967.

_____. In Early Plays: A Night Out, Night School, Revue Sketches. New York: Grove Press, 1968.

No Man's Land. London: Eyre Methuen, 1975.

_____. New York: Grove Press, 1975.

Old Times. London: Eyre Methuen, 1971.

_____. New York: Grove Press, 1971.

"Request Stop." In A Slight Ache and Other Plays. London: Eyre Methuen, 1964.

_____. In The Dwarfs and Eight Revue Sketches. New York: Dramatists Play Service, 1965.

The Room. In The Birthday Party and Other Plays. London: Eyre Methuen, 1960.

_____. In The Caretaker and The Room. New York: Grove Press, 1962.

_____. The Room and The Dumb Waiter. London: Eyre Methuen, 1967.

Silence. Lanscape and Silence. London: Eyre Methuen, 1969.

_____. Landscape and Silence. New York: Grove Press, 1970.

Sketches by Pinter. In Early Plays: A Night Out, Night School, Revue Sketches. New York: Grove Press, 1968.

A Slight Ache and Other Plays. London: Eyre Methuen, 1961. [Includes A Night Out, The Dwarfs, and the revue sketches "Trouble in the Works," "The Black and White," "Request Stop," "Last to Go," and "Applicant."]

A Slight Ache. In Three Plays: A Slight Ache, The Collection, The Dwarfs. New York: Grove Press, 1962.

"Special Offer." In Harold Pinter. Ed. Arnold Hinchliffe. New York: Twayne, 1967.

Tea Party. London: Eyre Methuen, 1965.

_____. New York: Grove Press, 1966.

Tea Party, and Other Plays. London: Eyre Methuen, 1967.
   [Includes The Basement and Night School.]

Tea Party. In The Lover, Tea Party, The Basement. New
   York: Grove Press, 1967.

_____. Rev. ed. London: H. Karnac, 1968.

_____. In Three Plays: Tea Party, The Basement, and The
   Lover. New York: Grove Press, 1968.

"That's All." In The Dwarfs and Eight Revue Sketches.
   New York: Dramatists Play Service, 1965.

"That's Your Trouble." In The Dwarfs and Eight Revue
   Sketches. New York: Dramatists Play Service, 1965.

Three Plays: A Slight Ache, The Collection, The Dwarfs.
   New York: Grove Press, 1962.

Three Plays: Tea Party, The Basement, and The Lover.
   New York: Grove Press, 1968.

"Trouble in the Works." In One to Another, by John
   Mortimer, N. F. Simpson and Harold Pinter. London:
   Samuel French, 1960.

_____. In A Slight Ache and Other Plays. London: Eyre
   Methuen, 1961.

_____. In The Dwarfs and Eight Revue Sketches. New
   York: Dramatists Play Service, 1965.

II. FILM

The Servant, 1962.

The Caretaker (The Guest), 1963.

The Pumpkin Eater, 1964.

The Quiller Memorandum, 1966.

Accident, 1967.

The Birthday Party, 1968.

Langrishe, Go Down, 1970.

The Go-Between, 1969.

The Homecoming, 1971.

A la Recherche du Temps Perdu, 1973.

The Last Tycoon, 1976.

[Published Screenplays]. Five Screen Plays. London:
    Eyre Methuen, 1971; New York: Grove Press, 1973.
    [Contents: Accident, The Go-Between, The Pumpkin
    Eater, The Quiller Memorandum, The Servant.]

III. TELEVISION

Night School, 1960.

The Collection, 1963.

The Lover, 1963.

Tea Party, 1965.

The Basement, 1967.

IV. RADIO PLAYS

A Slight Ache, 1959.

The Dwarfs, 1960.

A Night Out, 1960.

Landscape, 1968.

V. POETRY

"Afternoon." Twentieth Century, 169 (1961), 218.

_____. Poetry Northwest, 8, i (1967), 5.

"All of That." Times Literary Supplement, 69 (1970),
    1436.

"Chandeliers and Shadows." Poetry London, 19 (August
    1950).

"The Error of Alarm." Poetry Northwest, 8, i (1967), 3.

"European Revels." Poetry London, 20 (November 1950).

New Poems, 1967: A P.E.N. Anthology of Contemporary
    Poetry. Ed. Harold Pinter, et al. London: Hutch-
    inson, 1968.

131

"New Year in the Midlands." <u>Poetry London</u>, 19 (August 1950); 20 (November 1950).

"One a Story, Two a Death." <u>Poetry London</u>, 22 (Summer 1951).

<u>Poems</u>. Comp. Alan Clodd. London: Enitharmon Press, 1968.

"Rural Idyll." <u>Poetry London</u>, 20 (November 1950).

"The Table." <u>Poetry Northwest</u>, 8, i (1967), 4.

VI. NON-FICTION

"Art as Therapy, Hobby, or Experience." In <u>Essays in Honor of William Gallacher</u>. Berlin, 1966. Pages 234-36.

"Beckett." In <u>Beckett at Sixty: A Festschrift</u>. London: Calder, 1967.

"Harold Pinter Replies." <u>New Theatre Magazine</u>, 11, ii (1961), 8-10.

"The Knight Has Been Unruly: Memories of Sir Donald Wolfit." <u>The Listener</u>, 79 (1968), 501.

<u>Mac</u>. London: Pendragon Press, 1968. Reprinted in <u>Harper's Bazaar</u>, November 1968, pp. 234-35.

"Memories of Cricket." <u>Daily Telegraph Magazine</u>, May 1969.

"Pinter on Beckett." <u>New Theatre Magazine</u>, 2, iii, p. 3.

"Pinter's Reply to Open Letter by Leonard Russell." <u>Sunday Times</u>, 14 August 1960, p. 21.

"Speech: Hamburg 1970." <u>Theatre Quarterly</u>, 1 (July-September 1971), 3-4.

"Writing for Myself." <u>Twentieth Century</u>, 168 (December 1960), 172-75.

"Writing for the Theatre." <u>Evergreen Review</u>, 33 (August-September 1964), 80-82.

VII. INTERVIEWS

Bakewell, Joan. "In an Empty Bandstand--Harold Pinter in Conversation with Joan Bakewell." <u>Listener</u>, 6

November 1969, pp. 630-31.
Pinter briefly discusses his views on two famous actor-managers, Donald Wolfit and McMaster, the germ of The Room and The Birthday Party, and how the echoes of past words and phrases have influenced his writings.

Bensky, Lawrence. "Harold Pinter: An Interview." Paris Review, 10 (Fall 1966), 13-37. Also in Writers at Work: The Paris Review Interviews. 3rd series. New York: Viking, 1967. Pages 347-68.
Pinter discusses, among other topics, his career as a playwright, his writing methods, the reception and writing of The Room, The Birthday Party, The Caretaker, and The Dwarfs, the difficulties of directing his own plays, the violence and humor in his plays, the relative lack of autobiography in his works, and his traditional outlook on writing plays. Pinter also devotes time to explain how his characters develop, come alive, for him.

_____. "Pinter: Violence Is Natural." New York Times, 1 January 1967, p. 7.

Cavander, Kenneth. "Filming the Caretaker: Harold Pinter and Clive Donner, Interviewed by Kenneth Cavander." Transatlantic Review, 13 (Summer 1963), 17-26. Reprinted in McCrindle, Joseph, ed. Behind the Scenes. New York: Holt, Rinehart, 1971.
In this comic interview, Pinter and director Clive Donner talk enthusiastically of their experiences in filming The Caretaker, from its casual conception through the actual shooting. In particular they discussed the differences in balance, timing, and rhythm between the stage and film, and the financial problems which they overcame.

Dean, Michael. "Harold Pinter Talks to Michael Dean." Listener, 6 March 1969, p. 312.

"Dialogue for Three." Stand, 6, iii (1963), 4.

Gussow, Mel. "A Conversation [Pause] with Harold Pinter." New York Times Magazine, 5 December 1971, 42-43, 126-36.
In this long informative interview Gussow focuses attention on Old Times and Pinter's relationship with Beckett. In addition, Pinter discusses playwriting, screenwriting, his interest in poetry, his political views, and the reactions of critics to his plays. Also the topic of pauses and silences in his plays and their "meaning" is discussed.

"Harold Pinter." New York Times, 27 October 1968, II:3.

"Interview with Harold Pinter." Daily Mirror, 26 March 1965.

"Interview with Harold Pinter." New York Times, 10 September 1967, II:3.

"Mr. Harold Pinter--Avant-Garde Playwright and Intimate Revue." The Times, 16 November 1959, p. 4.

Packard, William. "An Interview with Harold Pinter." First Stage, 6, ii (1967), 82.

"Pinter Between the Lines." Sunday Times, 4 March 1962, p. 25.

Pugh, Marshall. "Trying to Pin Down Pinter: Interview with Marshall Pugh." Daily Mail, 7 March 1964.

Thompson, Harry. "Harold Pinter Replies: Pinter Interviewed by Harry Thompson." New Theatre Magazine, 11, ii (1961), 8-10.
    Pinter objects to critics who "impose" meaning on his plays. He defends his techniques on the basis of their effectiveness in the theatre and avoids analyzing content.

Tynan, Kathleen. "In Search of Harold Pinter: Interview with Kathleen Tynan." Evening Standard, 25 and 26 April 1968.

"Two People in a Room; Playwriting." New Yorker, 25 February 1967, pp. 34-36.
    In this friendly chat in his Fifth Avenue apartment during the Broadway run of The Homecoming, Pinter briefly discusses his earlier life, his interest in poetry and the increasing demands of writing due to his developing "concern for economy and discipline" and a consequent loss of poetic freedom.

SECONDARY SOURCES

I. BIBLIOGRAPHIES

Adelman, Irving, and Rita Dworkin. "Harold Pinter." In their Modern Drama. Metuchen, N.J.: Scarecrow Press, 1967. Pages 241-42.

Gale, Steven H. "Harold Pinter: An Annotated Bibliography 1957-1971." Bulletin of Bibliography, 29 (1972), 46-56.

Gordon, Lois G. "Pigeonholing Pinter: A Bibliography."
Theatre Documentation, 1, i (1968), 3020.

Imhof, Rüdiger. Pinter: A Bibliography. Theatre Facts
Supplement, Bibliography Series 1. London and Los
Angeles: TQ Publications, 1975.

Majstrak, Manfred, and Hans Rossman. "Harold Pinter."
Bibliographie der Interpretationen: English. Dort-
mund, 1972. Pages 117-20.

Palmer, David S. "A Harold Pinter Checklist." Twentieth
Century Literature, 16 (1970), 287-96.

Schroll, Herman T. Harold Pinter: A Study of His Reputation (1958-1969) and a Checklist. Metuchen, N.J.:
Scarecrow Press, 1971.

II. CRITICISM

Abirached, Robert. "Le Jeune Théâtre Anglais." Nouvelle
Française, 29 (February 1967), 314-21.
    Along with Arden, Jellicoe, and Saunders, Pinter
has absorbed the lessons of absurdism and the angry
movement, adding a unique psychological element of
his own.

Adler, T. P. "Pinter's Night: A Stroll Down Memory Lane."
Modern Drama, 17 (1974), 461-65.
    Night, which presents the reminiscences of a
couple in their forties, explores the effect of time
on memory. Adler finds this "compressed, intense,
and poetic short drama" atypical for Pinter as an
"unequivocal celebration" of married love.

Ahrens, Rudiger. "Das moderne englische Drama: Moglich-
keiten der Behandlung im Unterricht der gymnasialen
Oberstufe." Der fremdsprachliche Unterricht, 4,
xiii (1970), 15-28.
    This is an account similar to Allgaier's below.

Alexander, Nigel. "Past, Present, and Pinter." Essays
and Studies by Members of the English Association,
27 (1974), 1-17.
    Alexander examines the pressure of the past on
the present and future of Pinter's characters in The
Caretaker, The Birthday Party, The Homecoming, and
Old Times, and the resultant atmosphere of hopeless-
ness. The characters' "belief in their free will,
and the audience's awareness of their completely
conditioned state, creates a remarkable dramatic
tension."

Allgaier, Dieter. "Harold Pinter's 'The Caretaker' als
    Lese und Diskussionsstoff in der gymnasialen Ober-
    stufe." Die Neueren Sprachen, 19 (1970), 556-66.
        Allgaier begins by placing Pinter in the movement
    so sensationally brought to life by Osborne in 1956.
    Next he tells how a group of German students were
    given The Caretaker to read, followed by a list of
    study questions on the play. The result is a very
    interesting analysis by close-reading.

Allison, Ralph, and Charles Wellborn. "Rhapsody in an
    Anechoic Chamber: Pinter's Landscape." Educational
    Theatre Journal, 25 (1973), 215-25.
        This is an intricate exploration of rhapsodic
    elements in Landscape, focusing on the periodic
    rhythm created by the recurrent images, the transi-
    tions between the past and present, the juxtaposi-
    tion of words and silences, the occurrence of
    thoughts, unrelated to preceding dialogue, and gram-
    mar and punctuation. The audience must interpret
    subjectively what Pinter has presented objectively
    and thus become an "integral part of the theatrical
    experience."

Amend, Victor E. "Harold Pinter: Some Credits and Deb-
    its." Modern Drama, 10 (1967), 165-74.
        Amend traces Pinter's kinship with Beckett, Kaf-
    ka, and Brecht before he points out Pinter's defi-
    ciencies and limitations: (1) ambiguous symbolism;
    (2) ambiguous character motivation; (3) limitations
    inherent in demonstrating the lack of communication;
    (4) his choice of characters without nobility; and
    (5) a "negative approach to values." Amend includes
    The Room, The Birthday Party, The Caretaker, A
    Slight Ache, The Dwarfs, and The Collection in his
    discussion.

Angus, William. "Modern Theatre Reflects the Times."
    Queen's Quarterly, 70, ii (1963), 255-63.
        Angus believes modern dramatists are not fulfill-
    ing their responsibilities to audiences. Pinter and
    others reveal sick societies but in a very passive
    subjective way.

Aronson, Steven M. L. "Pinter's 'Family' and Blood
    Knowledge." In The Homecoming: Harold Pinter, A
    Casebook. Ed. John Lahr. New York, 1971.
        Pinter has "shaped" The Homecoming to intensify
    the dynamics of family life. The play is psycholog-
    ically more realistic than many people realize.

Aragones, Juan Emilio. "Dos hermeticas piezas breves de
    H. Pinter." La Estafeta Literaria, 31 (February
    1967).

Arden, John. "The Caretaker." New Theatre Magazine, 4
(July 1960), 29-30.
Arden examines the orchestration and the new
brand of Realism in The Caretaker, which explores
the "inconsequentials" of life.

Armstrong, William, ed. Experimental Drama. London:
G. Bell, 1963. Pages 128-146.

_____. "Tradition and Innovation in the London Theatre,
1960-1961." Modern Drama, 4, ii (1961), 184-95.
Armstrong provides a brief mention of Pinter as a
playwright of the "new movement," and he includes a
plot summary of The Caretaker.

Ashworth, Arthur. "New Theatre: Ionesco, Beckett, Pinter." Southerly, 22, iii (1963), 145-54.
Ashworth sees resemblances between Pinter and the
French absurdists but also perceives a vein of English realism in the playwright. Pinter borrows from
both traditions and shares elements with Kafka as
well.

Aylwin, Tony. "The Memory of All That: Pinter's Old
Times." English (London), 22 (1973), 99-102.
Aylwin discusses the old and new techniques and
themes of Old Times and examines the characters'
attempts in this play to recapture the past and to
separate truth from fantasy.

Baker, William and Stephen E. Tabachnick. Harold Pinter.
Edinburgh: Oliver and Boyd, 1973; New York: Barnes
and Noble, 1974.
In this thorough exploration of the themes, characters, atmosphere, dialogue, and use of time in
Pinter's major plays and film scripts, Baker and
Tabachnick emphasize the effects of the playwright's
past on his writings and his efforts to universalize
the particular. Baker and Tabachnick also provide
a discussion of five poems ("New Year in the Midlands," "Stranger," "The Error of Alarm," "Afternoon," and "Chandeliers and Shadows"), a list of
Pinter's school activities at Hackney Downs School,
and a selected bibliography.

_____. "Reflections on Ethnicity in Anglo-Jewish Writ-
ing." Jewish Quarterly, 21, i-ii (1973), 94-97.
Baker finds that of the three Jewish writers,
Arnold Wesker, Bernard Kops, and Harold Pinter, Pinter "proves the most successful in at once recapturing and universalizing personal memories" of his
early environment.

Barber, John. "Pinter the Incomplete." London Daily
    Telegraph, 16 November 1970, p. 6.

Báti, Lázló and István Kristó-Nagy, eds. Az Angol Iro-
    dalom a Huszadik Században (English Literature in
    the Twentieth Century). Budapest: Gondolat, 1970,
    Vol. 2, pp. 259-76.

Beckerman, Bernard. Dynamics of Drama: Theory and Method
    of Analysis. New York: Knopf, 1970. Pages 238-39.
    Beckerman shows how the audience must complete
    the meaning of a Pinter scene.

Beckmann, Heinz. "Harold Pinter." Zeitwende, 31 (1960),
    858-59.
    Beckmann notes that the early Pinter appears
    similar to the French absurdists in his methods.

Berkowitz, G. M. "Pinter's Revision of The Caretaker."
    Modern Literature, 5 (February 1976), 109-16.
    Berkowitz maintains that Pinter's revisions in
    every case tend to increase ambiguity rather than
    to clarify issues.

Bernard, F. J. "Beyond Realism: The Plays of Harold Pin-
    ter." Modern Drama, 8 (1965), 185-91.
    Bernard notes the lyrical quality of Pinter's dia-
    logue and studies the techniques with which Pinter
    transcends realism to create a kind of naturalism so
    pure it seems like poetry.

Bigsby, C. W. E. "Pinter." In Contemporary Dramatists.
    Ed. James Vinson. London: St. Martin's , 1973.
    Pages 608-13.
    This article provides a short biography and a list
    of awards, publications, and theatrical activities
    as well as a concise outline of The Room, The Birth-
    day Party, The Dumb Waiter, The Caretaker, The Home-
    coming, Landscape, Silence, Night, and Old Times.
    Bigsby sees Pinter moving from a sense of threat in
    his earlier works to a "fascination with the sub-
    stance of reality and the significancy of memory"
    in his later works. Throughout, however, Pinter's
    "fundamental theme is the struggle for survival."

Billington, Michael. "Our Theatre in the Sixties." In
    Theatre 71. Ed. Sheridan Morley. London, 1971.
    Pages 208-33.
    Pinter has moved ahead of Osborne, Wesker, et al.
    and is seen as a world leader in the drama. The
    Homecoming and other plays are discussed in detail.

138

Blau, Herbert. The Impossible Theatre. A Manifesto.
New York: Macmillan, 1964. Pages 254-56.
This is a conversational and philosophical examination of the theatre in America. Birthday Party
and A Slight Ache are used as examples in a discussion of the author's doubts about Theater of the
Absurd.

_____. "Politics and the Theatre." Wascana Review, 2,
ii (1967), 5-25.
Blau discusses the challenge to modern theatre to
"help to recultivate a sense of political man"
through the representation of action, "purposive,
cadential, complete." He examines the quest for
self and the problems of identity and dispossession
in several poems and plays, including Pinter's The
Homecoming.

Bleich, David. "Emotional Origins of Literary Meaning."
College English, 31, i (1969), 30-40.
Bleich looks at two critical and emotional responses to Pinter's The Caretaker and attempts to
"demonstrate how a literary meaning is made; how it
develops from the subject's emotional response to
the work, and moves along its projective path to the
status of (at least provisional) fact." He suggests
that the same "intrapsychic forces" control both
critical and creative processes.

Boulton, James T. "Harold Pinter: The Caretaker and
Other Plays." Modern Drama, 6 (1963), 131-40.
Boulton compares Pinter with Kafka, especially in
their shared theme of modern man's vulnerability to
random violence.

Bovie, Palmer. "Seduction: The Amphitryon Theme from
Plautus to Pinter." Minnesota Review, 7, iii-iv
(1967), 304-13.
Plautus, Molière, Dryden, and finally Pinter have
been intrigued by the theme of the husband cuckolded
in his own home.

Bowen, John. "Accepting the Illusion." Twentieth Century, 169 (1961), 153-65.
Bowen takes a look at definitions of realism and
naturalism in relation to modern British dramatists,
and links Pinter's work to Ionesco's.

_____. "Changing Fashions in the English Theatre." The
Listener, 60 (1958), 269.

Bradbrook, M. C. English Dramatic Form: A History of Its
Development. New York: Barnes and Noble, 1965. 188-90.
Bradbrook notes Pinter's concentration on the

room as a dramatic setting, on non-verbal communication and the breakdown of ordinary speech patterns.

Bray, J. J. "The Ham Funeral." Meanjin, 21 (March 1962), 32-34.
    This is a note on the influence of Patrick White's works in Pinter.

Bredella, Lothar. "Die Intention und Wirkung literarischer Texte . . . ." Der fremdsprachliche Unterricht, Jg. 7, 25 (February 1973), 34-49.
    The best approach to Pinter is to study what his characters say and do, to make no assumptions based on one's previous experience.

Brine, Adrian. "Mac Davies Is No Clochard." Drama, 61 (Summer 1961), 35-37.

Brody, Alan. "The Gift of Realism: Hitchcock and Pinter." Journal of Modern Literature, 3 (1973), 149-72.
    Brody examines Hitchcock's Shadow of a Doubt and Pinter's The Birthday Party as individual visions of their authors and as representatives of the contemporary development of film and theater. Brody compares and contrasts the plot, the dream-like milieu, and the characters of these two "suspense thrillers" in which "conflict is expressed in disjunction between language and action."

Brook, Peter, et al. "Artaud for Artaud's Sake." Encore, 11, iii (1964), 20-31.
    In this discussion of Artaud's works, Shaffer praises Pinter's "extraordinary musicianship in writing and the conjuring up of atmospheres."

Brooke, Nicholas. "The Characters of Drama." Critical Quarterly, 6 (1964), 78-82.
    This contains a one-line slur on Pinter's lack of "dramatic intelligence."

Brooks, Mary E. "The British Theatre of Metaphysical Despair." Literature and Ideology (Montreal) 12 (1972), 49-58.
    Pinter is linked once again to Beckett. His characters are permanently alienated, have no core of belief, are victims of nameless ominous forces.

Brown, John R. "Dialogue in Pinter and Others." In his (ed.) Modern British Dramatists. Englewood Cliffs, N.J.: Prentice-Hall, 1968. Pages 122-144. Reprinted from Critical Quarterly, 7 (1965), 223-43.
    Brown explores two important influences in Pinter--the plays of Chekhov and Beckett. Their impact on his method of composing, dialogue is especially crucial.

_____. "Introduction." In his (ed.) Modern British Dramatists. Englewood Cliffs, N.J.: Prentice-Hall, 1968. Pp. 1-14.
 Brown provides an overview of Pinter's career to date, his innovations in theatre language and his impact on the new drama.

_____. "Mr. Pinter's Shakespeare." Critical Quarterly, 5 (1963), 251-65.
 Like Shakespeare and Ionesco, Pinter understands that non-verbal communication, such as pauses, gestures, and unspoken feelings delineates character as much as direct address.

_____. Theatre Language: A Study of Arden, Osborne, Pinter and Wesker. London: Allen Lane, 1972. Pages 15-117.

Browne, E. Martin. "A Look Round the English Theatre, 1961." Drama Survey, 1 (1961/62), 227-31.

Brustein, Robert. "The English Stage. Tulane Drama Review, 10 (1966), 127-33.
 Brustein provides glancing mention of Pinter, who "excludes statement from his work altogether."

_____. Season of Discontent. New York: Simon and Schuster, 1965. Pages 180-83. Reprinted from New Republic, 23 October 1961, pp. 29-30.

_____. The Theatre of Revolt. Boston: Little, Brown, 1964. Pages 26-27.

_____. "Thoughts from Abroad." In his The Third Stage. New York: Alfred Knopf, 1969. Pages 117-22.
 Brustein is concerned by "Pinter's reluctance to invent in his works anything more than atmosphere." Although he finds the first act of The Homecoming promising, he concludes that the denouement is "mere exploitation of the bizarre."

Bryden, Ronald. "Pinter." London Observer, 19 February 1967, p. 11.

_____. "A Stink of Pinter." New Statesman, 69 (1965), 928.

_____. "Three Men in a Room." New Statesman, 67 (1964), 1004.

Burghardt, Lorraine Hall. "Game Playing in Three by Pinter." Modern Drama, 17 (1974), 377-88.
 Burghardt proposes game theory as a possible single frame of reference for explicating meaning in Pinter's plays as applied specifically to The Dumb Waiter, The Birthday Party, and Tea Party. She

141

sees a progression in these plays from "a concern
with the complex interactions of many towards the
complex perception of one disturbed, confused man."

Burkman, Katherine H. The Dramatic World of Harold Pinter: Its Basis in Ritual. Columbus: Ohio State
University Press, 1971.
    This excellent book reveals the archetypal pat-
terns behind Pinter's dramatic situations. She argues for the very deep humanity of his plays. For
an example of her technique, see below.

_____. "Pinter's A Slight Ache as Ritual." Modern Drama,
11 (1970), 326-35.
    Burkman sees Greek fertility ritual used as struc-
ture in A Slight Ache. Edward and the matchseller
are seen as "alazon" and "eiron," while Flora acts
as "fertility goddess." The play is a "tragicomic
vision" in which "fertility itself is mocked" and
Pinter's subject is a crisis of identity, his theme,
the alienation of modern man.

Caine, Cindy. "Structure in the One-Act Play." Modern
Drama, 12, iv (1970), 390-98.
    Caine uses The Dumb Waiter and Beckett's Krapp's
Last Tape as examples of the thesis that modern one-
act plays exhibit a polar division of classical
structure. Their concern is rather with "what is
happening? instead of what will happen next?"

Callen, A. "Comedy and Passion in the Plays of Harold
Pinter." Forum of Modern Language Studies, 4, iii
(1968), 299-305.
    Callen believes that although the situations in
Pinter's plays may seem bizarre, as in The Homecoming, his insights into human feelings and pas-
sions are extremely perceptive.

_____. "Stoppard's Godot: Some French Influences on
Post-War English Drama." New Theatre Magazine, 10
(April 1960) i, 22-30.
    Callen focuses on the influence of Ionesco and
Beckett on Stoppard, but discusses the French influence on Pinter and N. F. Simpson as well. Like
Beckett, Pinter creates tension through rhythmic
variations and his characters use banal language to
hide emotions. Pinter's plays also reveal series
of emotional states and contain minimal narrative.

Canaday, Nicholas, Jr. "Harold Pinter's 'Tea Party':
Seeing and Not-Seeing." Studies in Short Fiction
(Newberry Coll., S.C.), 6 (1969), 580-85. [Dis-
cusses short story version.]
    Canaday explores the central metaphor of sight in

"Tea Party." This work displays many of the same
concerns of other Pinter plays: usurpation, betrayal, blurred reality, "annihilation of an individual," and sexual mastery.

Capone, Giovanna. Drammi per voci: Dylan Thomas, Samuel
Beckett, Harold Pinter. Bologna: Patron, 1967.

Carat, J. "Harold Pinter et W. Gombrowicz." Preuves
(November 1965), 75-77.
Carat discusses the Parisian theatre season. He
compares Yvonne, a play written thirty years ago by
Gombrowicz, which has retained its freshness and
relevance, to Pinter's The Collection and The Lover.
He sees the two Pinter plays as absurdist dramas.

Carpenter, Charles A. "The Absurdity of Dread: Pinter's
The Dumb Waiter." Modern Drama, 16 (1973), 279-85.
This is an interesting reading of The Dumb Waiter
as strictly comedy, with no metaphysical overtones.
Carpenter sees it as farce, at times parodying Ab-
surdist theatre.

_____. "What Have I Seen, the Scum or the Essence?
Symbolic Fallout in Pinter's Birthday Party." Modern
Drama, 17 (1974), 389-402.
This is a psychological, symbolic analysis. Both
Goldberg and Meg are struggling for possession of a
child, Stanley. The birthday party is seen as a rebirth from the womb-world Meg has created for Stanley to the knowledge of the outside world, a "gener-
alized society-Hell," that Goldberg forces upon him.

Case, L. L. "'The Ticket' Or Pinter Parodied." New York
Times, 16 May 1965, II:6.

Chiari, J. Landmarks of Contemporary Drama. London: H.
Jenkins, 1965. Pages 119-26, 202-07.
Pinter's ability to create puzzling but beauti-
fully structured drama is noted. The Caretaker is
one of Chiari's favorites.

Christophery, Jules. "Artaud and Pinter." Nouvelle Revue
Luxembourgeoise Academia (1971), 197-204.
Pinter understands the first lesson of Artaud--
to alert an audience to the possibility that the sky
may come crashing down at any time. He also stresses feeling rather than intellect and the terror of
ambiguity.

Clurman, Harold. The Naked Image. New York: Macmillan,
1966. Pages 101-14.
This is a theatrical, rather than dramatic or
literary, analysis of The Caretaker, The Dumb

Waiter, The Collection, The Room, A Slight Ache, and
The Lover. Clurman offers his interpretation briefly and discusses Pinter's theatrical technique.

Cohen, Mark. "The Plays of Harold Pinter." Jewish Quarterly, 8 (Summer 1961), 21-22.
Cohen is particularly interested in Pinter's obsession with sadistic behavior, violence, pointless
cruelty. The playwright's sympathies with victims
of the Nazis may be relevant here.

Cohen, Marshall. "Theater 67." Partisan Review, 34
(1967), 436-44.
Cohen reviews production of Galileo, Mailer's The
Deer Park, Albee's A Delicate Balance, and Pinter's
The Homecoming. Cohen praises the subtlety and
"rhetorical brilliance" of this last play which focuses on the role of "the contradictory female, at
once mother, mistress and whore," but finds it
"fragmentary, evasive and often pointlessly para-
doxical."

Cohn, Ruby. "The absurdly Absurd: Avatars of Godot."
Comparative Literature Studies, 2 (1965), 233-40.
Cohn discusses the metaphysical absurdity in
Beckett's Waiting for Godot, Pinter's The Dumb
Waiter, and Bromberg's Defense of Taipei, comparing
their situations, rhythms, and characters. "Although the three dramas are built on the same pat-
tern--exploration of a relationship based on loyalty
to a transcendent power--that relationship disinte-
grates in the three successive plays."

_____. Currents in Contemporary Drama. Bloomington:
Indiana University Press, 1969. Pages 15-17, 78-81,
177-81.
This includes most of the insights which appear
in her articles listed here. She notes his works
are a fascinating blend of naturalism and absurdism.

_____. "Latter Day Pinter." Drama Survey (Minneapolis),
3 (1964), 367-77.
⟶ Pinter like most contemporary playwrights explores the themes of illusion versus reality. Plays
such as The Birthday Party are enigmatic because
they depict the very subjective nature of our experience.

_____. "The World of Harold Pinter." Tulane Drama Re-
view, 6, iii (1962), 55-68.
Cohn observes a villain-victim conflict at the
heart of Pinter's early dramas. Man seems to relate
only on a sadomasochistic level in these plays.

_____ and Bernard Dukore, eds. Twentieth Century Drama:
England, Ireland, The United States. New York:
Random House, 1966. Preface to The Dumb Waiter.
Pinter is located in the New English drama but
often resembles the French absurdists to a great
degree.

Cook, David. "Of the Strong Breed." Transition, 3
(1964), 38-40.
Pinter is seen to be an influence on Wole Suyin-
ka, a chronicler of Nigerian life.

_____ and Harold F. Brooks. "A Room with Three Views:
Harold Pinter's The Caretaker." Komos, 1 (1967),
62-69.
Brooks emphasizes the sympathetic, humanistic,
and realistic elements in The Caretaker, focusing
on character analysis. "Pinter's men are responsible, and so the corrollary of his compassion is his
indictment, or at least passionate criticism, of
their submission, to forces of fear, separation and
illusion."

Corrie, Tim. "The Homecoming." New Theatre Magazine, 6,
ii (1965), 31-32.
This is a brief, early interpretation of the
play, which Corrie believes is a deliberate enigma.

Cowell, Raymond. Twelve Modern Dramatists. Elmsford,
N.Y.: Pergamon Press, 1967. Pages 134-35.
Cowell's introduction to Pinter pictures the
playwright as an enigmatic sophisticate, philosophically akin to the French avant garde.

Craig, H. A. L. "Poetry in the Theatre." New Statesman
and Nation, 12 November 1960, pp. 734, 736.
Although there are few verse dramatists in the
modern theatre, Pinter's pure supra-realistic dialogue is a kind of poetry.

"Cues." Plays and Players, 21, i (1973), 17.

Curley, Daniel. "A Night in the Fun House." Midwest
Monographs (University of Illinois), 1, i (1967),
1-2.

Davison, Peter. "Contemporary Drama and Popular Dramatic
Forms." In Aspects of Drama and the Theatre.
Sidney: Sidney University Press; London: Eyre
Methuen, 1965. Pages 164-66, 175-79, 181-87.
Davison makes general remarks on Pinter's links
to absurdism and his deliberately enigmatic effects.

Dawick, John. "'Punctuation' and Patterning in The Homecoming." Modern Drama, 14 (1971), 37-46.
    This is an analysis of Pinter's use of non-verbal
dramatic devices in The Homecoming to emphasize significant "sub-textual implications." Dawick defines
and examines five types: hesitation, pause, silence,
blackout, and curtain.

Dennis, Nigel. "Pintermania." New York Review of Books,
17 December 1970, pp. 21-22.
    The escalating popularity of Pinter is discussed.
Analyzing his works has become an intellectual game.

Deurbergue, Jean. "Sujet, personnage, parole, dans The
Caretaker de Harold Pinter." Recherches Anglaises
et Américaines, 5 (1972), 47-62.
    The Caretaker is seen to be an extremely logical
psychological study of personal dependencies.

Dias, Earl J. "The Enigmatic World of Harold Pinter."
Drama Critique, 11, iii (1968), 119-24.
    In The Homecoming and other works we are always
presented with possible facts or explanations but
they are deliberately never confirmed.

Dick, Kay. "Mr Pinter and the Fearful Matter." Texas
Quarterly, 4, iii (1961), 257-65.
    One of many articles which explores the methods,
both verbal and non-verbal, by which Pinter's characters reveal themselves to audiences. They usually remain isolated from the other characters but
the audience sympathizes with their failed attempts
at communication.

Donoghue, Denis. "The Human Image in Modern Drama."
Lugano Review, 1, iii-iv (1965), 155-68.
    Donoghue admires the theatricality but not the
moral content of plays such as The Birthday Party
and The Caretaker.

_____. "London Letter: Moral West End." Hudson Review,
14 (1961), 93-103.
    Donoghue believes the mood of Fellini's La Dolce
Vita sets the tone for English attitudes in the
theatre. He objects to Pinter's cynicism about
human nature.

Donovan, J. "The Plays of Harold Pinter (1957-61): Victims and Victimization." Recherches Anglaises et
Américaines, 5 (1972), 35-46.
    A struggle for power is considered the central
dramatic and thematic issue in this essay. Surpris-
ingly, the most predatory characters at first appear
passive and quiet.

Douglas, Reid. "The Failure of English Realism." Tulane Drama Review, 7 (1962), 180-83.
This is a brief mention of The Caretaker: "It has no plot, no development, no comment--and no purpose. . . ."

Downer, Alan S. "The Doctor's Dilemma: Notes on the New York Theater, 1966-67." Quarterly Journal of Speech, 53, iii (1967)., 213-23.
This is a brief discussion of The Homecoming as produced on Broadway during the 1966-67 season.

_____. "Experience of Heroes: Notes on the New York Theater, 1961-1962." Quarterly Journal of Speech, 48, iii (1962), 261-70.
Self-delusion and fantasy protects the main characters in The Caretaker from despair.

_____. "Old, New, Borrowed and (a Trifle) Blue: Notes on the New York Theatre, 1967-1968." Quarterly Journal of Speech, 54, iii (1968), 199-211.
This is a brief discussion of The Birthday Party as produced on Broadway during the 1967-68 season.

Drescher, Horst. "Die englische Literatur." In Modern Weltliteratur. Eds. Gero von Wilpert and Ivar Ivask. Stuttgart, 1972. Pages 323-26.
Pinter is mentioned along with Osborne and other writers of the new wave. His plays are considered to be more ambiguous, more closely related to the absurd dramatists.

_____. "Einleitung." In Englische Literatur der Gegenwart in Einzeldarstellung. Ed. H. W. Drescher. Stuttgart, 1970. Pages 17 ff.

Duberman, Martin. "Theatre 69." Partisan Review, 36 (1969), 483-500.
Duberman reviews the 1968-69 theatre season, focusing on "black" plays and "new theater." He briefly criticizes the quick shifts in mood and scene in Pinter's Tea Party and Basement.

Dukore, Bernard F. "The Pinter Collection." Educational Theatre Journal, 7 (1974), 81-85.
Form is content in Pinter's work. The Collection concerns a group of potential adulterers. There are unsuccessful attempts to establish their innocence or guilt. Desire for power is seen as the key in sexual relationships.

_____. "The Theatre of Harold Pinter." Tulane Drama Review, 6, iii (1962), 43-54.
     This is an examination of Pinter's major plays. Pinter presents "an unreal reality or a realistic unreality," which is "a horrifying picture of contemporary life."

_____. "A Woman's Place." Quarterly Journal of Speech, 52 (1966), 237-41.
     Dukore sees four pairs of characters between the generations in The Homecoming. Each parallels the other in character and actions among "a cluster of interwoven images; battles for power among human animals, mating rites, and a dominant wife-mother in a den of sexually maladjusted males."

Eigo, James. "Pinter's Landscape." Modern Drama, 16 (1973), 179-83.
     Eigo offers an interpretive reading of the monologues in Landscape emphasizing their points of interrelation.

Eilenberg, Lawrence I. "Rehearsal as Critical Method: Pinter's Old Times." Modern Drama, 18 (1975), 385-92.
     Eilenberg views the rehearsal of a play as an expression of the "critical methods by which the interpreters (actor, director, designer) arrive at their conclusion (the production itself)." He uses as example a "rehearsal game" which he analyzes as indicative of both the type and structure of power in the play.

Ekbom, Torsten. "På jakt efter en identitet: Harold Pinter och den absurda traditionen." Bonniers Litterära Magasin, 31 (1962), 809-14. In Swedish.
     Pinter's techniques are those of the absurdists and Camus has influenced his philosophy. The Dwarfs, The Caretaker, and other plays are discussed.

Engler, Balz. "Shakespeare und das moderne Theater--Eine Konfrontation auf der Buhne." Deutsche Shakespeare-Gesellschaft West Jahrbuch (1971), 18-22.
     To demonstrate the "modernity" of Shakespeare, a theatre group performed Shakespeare's Henry V and Richard III along with Wilder's Our Town and Pinter's Birthday Party. Engler has summarized the discussion by German scholars of the event.

English, Alan C. "Feeling Pinter's World." Ball State University Forum, 14, i (1973), 70-75.
     English criticizes those who seek intellectual solutions to Pinter's riddle. One must feel the

emotions in his plays--such as fear and anger--to
understand Pinter's profound understanding of the
human psyche.

Esslin, Martin. "The Absurdity of the Absurd." Kenyon
    Review, 22 (1960), 670-73.

_____. "Brecht, the Absurd, and the Future." Tulane
    Drama Review, 7, iv (1963), 43-54.
    Brecht's epic theatre and the French theatre of
    the absurd have been the primary influences in re-
    cent theatre. Few writers seem to be ready to at-
    tempt anything new.

_____. Brief Chronicles: Essays on the Modern Theatre.
    London, 1970. Pages 190-198.

_____. "Der Commensense der Nonsense." In Sinn oder
    Unsinn: Theater unserer zeit, Bd. III. Stuttgart,
    Basel, 1962. Pages 123-146.

_____. "Godot and His Children: The Theatre of Samuel
    Beckett and Harold Pinter." In Experimental Drama.
    Ed. William A. Armstrong. London: G. Bell, 1963.
    Pages 128-46. Also in Modern British Dramatists.
    Ed. John R. Brown. Englewood Cliffs, N.J.: Pren-
    tice-Hall, 1968. Pages 58-70.
    Pinter is compared with Beckett. The Room and
    and The Birthday Party are analyzed. Neither writer
    believes in social progress or life-after-death.
    Yet Esslin sees no cause for despair since both
    authors accept mankind with love and compassion, but
    without illusions.

_____. Harold Pinter. Hannover: Friedrich Verlag,
    1967. In German.
    This is the German version of Esslin's book-
    length studies of Pinter, though it only covers the
    early plays.

_____. "Harold Pinter, un dramaturge anglais de l'ab-
    surde." Preuves, No. 151, pp. 45-54.
    Discussing The Room, The Dumb Waiter, The Birth-
    day Party, A Slight Ache, and The Caretaker, Esslin
    asserts the essentially poetic nature of Pinter's
    plays and suggests one should approach them as meta-
    phors of experience, as one does with the French ab-
    surdists.

_____. "New Form in the Theatre." In his Reflections:
    Essays on Modern Theatre. Garden City, N.Y.:
    Doubleday, 1969. Pages 3-10.

_____. The Peopled Wound: The Work of Harold Pinter.
London: Eyre Methuen; Garden City, N.Y.: Doubleday, 1970.
    Esslin links Pinter to the modern existential
tradition and cites his preoccupation with alienation and the creation of self. Certain characters
--such as Ruth in The Homecoming--define themselves and emerge as free characters; but others
are locked into fixed roles by the pressures of
society on their own lack of will. Esslin blends
Sartrean philosophy with Freudian psychology in a
curious and interesting way.

_____. Pinter: A Study of His Plays. London: Eyre
Methuen, 1973.
    Esslin includes material from his earlier writ-
ings but also does a perceptive analysis of Old
Times.

_____. "Pinter Translated." Encounter, 30, iii (1968),
45-47.
    This is a brief comic article in which Esslin
discusses hilarious mistranslations of Pinter's
plays into German.

_____. The Theatre of the Absurd. Garden City, N.Y.:
Doubleday, 1961. Pages 198-217.
    This classic description of the French movement
makes brief references to the existential subject
matter of Pinter's early plays.

_____. The Theatre of the Absurd Reconsidered." In his
Reflections: Essays on the Modern Theatre. Garden
City, N.Y.: Doubleday, 1969. Pages 183-91.

Evans, Gareth Lloyd. "Pinter's Black Magic." Manchester
Guardian, 20 September 1965, p. 8.

Feldman, Heinz. "Harold Pinter." In Englische Literatur
der Gegenwart in Einzeldarstellung. Ed. H. W.
Drescher. Stuttgart, 1970. Pages 431-57.
    This is a general description of the play-
wright's career with plot summaries and biography.

Feynman, Alberta E. "The Fetal Quality of the 'Character' in Plays of the Absurd." Modern Drama, 9
(1966), 18-25.
    In a bright, witty essay Feynman notes that
Pinter's characters are not "developed" in the
traditional sense. She worries too much, perhaps,
about what the characters "do" and too little
about what they "are."

Fitzgerald, Marion. "Playwriting Is Agony, Says Hugh
    Leonard." Irish Digest, 79 (January 1964), 34-36.
    Leonard says he admires the plays of Harold
    Pinter.

Fisher, Peter. "Versuch uber das scheinbar absurde
    Theater." Merkur, 19, ii (1965), 151-63.
    Pinter makes a fine example of an Englishman
    who employs the non-sequiturs, ellipses and other
    stylistic devices of the continental absurd tradi-
    tion.

Franzblau, Abraham N. "A Psychiatrist Looks at 'The
    Homecoming.'" Saturday Review, 8 April 1967,
    p. 58.

Fraser, G. S. The Modern Writer and His World. New York:
    Praeger, 1964. Pages 238-42.
    Fraser examines Pinter's "demotic stylized" dia-
    logue, real-life settings and characters, and the
    threatening atmospheres which make his plays sini-
    sterly familiar. In particular, Fraser delves into
    The Caretaker, comparing it to Beckett's Waiting
    for Godot and outlining possible Freudian and
    Christian interpretations.

Free, William J. "Treatment of Character in Harold Pin-
    ter's The Homecoming." South Atlantic Bulletin,
    34, iv (1969), 1-5.
    Pinter pushes character as near to confusion as
    possible in his plays, forcing us to regard expe-
    rience from a new perspective. Ruth's unexpected
    behavior in The Homecoming is a good example of
    this technique.

Freedman, Morris. Essays on the Modern Drama. Boston:
    Heath, 1964.

_____. The Moral Impulse. Carbondale: Southern Illinois
    University Press, 1967. Pages 124-26.

Fricker, Robert. Das modern englische Drama. Gottingen:
    Vandenhoeck, 1964. Pages 166-70.
    Fricker ends the book with Pinter, whom he con-
    siders basically an absurdist.

Gale, John. "Taking Pains with Pinter." The Observer,
    10 June 1962, p. 19.

Gale, Steven H. Butter's Going Up: A Critical Analysis
    of Harold Pinter's Work. Durham: Duke Press,
    1977.
    This is a brilliant thematic analysis of Pin-
    ter's plays through Old Times. It contains a

valuable chronology.

Gallagher, Kent G. "Harold Pinter's Dramaturgy." Quarterly Journal of Speech, 52 (1966), 242-48.
        Examination of Pinter's "unusual and unexpected
  devices" in The Caretaker explains their creation
  of a sense of "hyper-reality." This added to
  realism creates an absurd microcosmos in which unexpected distortion becomes acceptable, and comedy
  bears a burden of savagery."

Ganz, Arthur. "A Clue to the Pinter Puzzle: The Triple
  Self in The Homecoming." Educational Theatre
  Journal, 21 (1969), 180-87.
        Ganz disagrees with Lahr and Schechner who find
  Pinter is deliberately obtuse; he then analyzes
  The Homecoming to demonstrate Pinter's clarity.

_____, ed. Pinter: A Collection of Critical Essays.
  Englewood Cliffs, N.J.: Prentice-Hall, 1973.
        This is a useful "Twentieth-Century Views" col-
  lection of essays on Pinter, most of which have
  been printed elsewhere.

Gascoigne, Bamber. "Cult of Personality." Spectator,
  29 (June 1962), 859.

_____. "Pulling the Wool." Spectator, 27 (January 1961),
  106.

_____. Twentieth-Century Drama. London: Hutchinson,
  1962. Page 206.

Gassner, John. "Broadway in Review." Educational Theatre Journal, 13 (1961), 289-97.
        Gassner sees The Caretaker as an allegory of
  man's mutual dependence in an alien environment.

_____. "Foray into the Absurd." In his Dramatic Sound-
  ings. New York: Crown, 1968. Pages 503-07.
  Reprints "Broadway in Review." Educational Theatre Journal, 13 (1961), 294-96.
        See above, "Broadway in Review."

_____. "Osborne and Pinter." In his The World of Con-
  temporary Drama. New York: American Library Association, 1965. Pages 21-33.
        This is a very brief analysis and plot summary
  of the major works of Osborne and Pinter.

Geerts, Leo. "De Terreur van de alledaagse vervreemding.
  Beschouwing over Pinter." Dietsche Warande en
  Belfort (Antwerp), 1 (1969), 46-58.

Giachetti, Romano. "L'avanguardia mi irrita." La Fiera
    Litteraria, 21 (November 1968), 10.

Gillen, Francis. "All These Bits and Pieces: Fragmenta-
    tion and Choice in Pinter's Plays." Modern Drama,
    17 (1974), 477-87.
        Gillen explores the themes of "fragmentation and
    choice" in The Caretaker, Landscape, Silence, and
    Old Times. Gillen sees in each one character forced
    to choose between two essentially incomplete parts
    of his fragmented self. The choice itself lies be-
    tween "the concrete, physical or the material" and
    "the incomprehensible, the spiritual, or the un-
    touchable."

_____. "'. . . Apart from the Known and the Unknown':
    The Unreconciled Worlds of Harold Pinter's Charac-
    ters." Arizona Quarterly, 26 (1970), 17-24.
        This is an examination of Tea Party and The Home-
    coming. Gillen sees the major characters in these
    plays as possessed by a dual vision of the world:
    the tangible world of physical existence and a world
    of idea, glimpsed but not verifiable by "instinctual
    criteria for reality."

Goetsch, Paul. "Das englische Drama seit Shaw." In Das
    englische Drama. Ed. J. Nunning. Darmstadt, 1973.
    Pages 403-507.
        Since Shaw, Goetsch finds a much greater concern
    in English drama for confronting social issues.
    Pinter's complaints about society are not specific
    but he portrays an alarming, threatened world.

_____. English Dramatic Theories, IV: Twentieth Century.
    Tubingen, 1972. Pages 118-24.
        Pinter is listed as one of the major English
    writers since John Osborne. His enigmatic plots
    and elliptical verbal style is noted.

_____. "Harold Pinter: Old Times." In Das englische
    Drama der Gegenwart. Ed. H. Oppel. Berlin, 1975.
        This is an interesting study of memory and illu-
    sion in Old Times.

Goldstone, Herbert. "Not So Puzzling Pinter: The Home-
    coming." Theater Annual, 25 (1969), 20-27.
        Goldstone analyzes The Homecoming in terms of
    "eroticism or sexual desire." This underlies the
    actions of all the characters. Ruth seeks it and
    thus accepts Max's proposition while the men all
    fear it and create a less threatening view of women
    and sexuality.

Goodman, Florence J. "Pinter's The Caretaker: The Lower
    Depths Descended." Midwest Quarterly (Pittsburg,
    Kansas), 5 (1964), 117-26.
        The relationships in The Caretaker have the ele-
    ments of a Sartrian nightmare. Pinter's view of man
    is shaped by existential thought, his techniques are
    influenced by the absurdists.

Gordon, Lois. "Harold Pinter--Past and Present." Kansas
    Quarterly, 3, ii (1971), 89-99.
        The psychological approach of Gordon's disserta-
    tion and booklength study seems further verified by
    recent developments in Pinter's plays, especially
    Old Times.

_____. Stratagems to Uncover Nakedness: The Dramas of
    Harold Pinter. Columbia: University of Missouri
    Press, 1969.
        Gordon uncovers the elaborate defense mechanism
    with which Pinter's characters hope to protect them-
    selves, and she perceives the often unconscious
    feelings which they would attempt to deny. Her
    Freudian approach clarifies the enigmatic behavior
    of certain characters.

Gottfried, Martin. A Theater Divided: The Postwar Ameri-
    can Stage. Boston: Little, Brown, 1967. Pages
    288-95.
        An overview and brief analysis of the major plays
    through The Homecoming. Gottfried sees Pinter as a
    realistic playwright, "and the special tone of his
    work is achieved by his presentation of the impos-
    sible in the guise of the actual."

Gray, Wallace. "The Uses of Incongruity." Educational
    Theatre Journal, 15, iv (1963), 343-47.
        Pinter uses three basic types of incongruity in
    his works to depict the paradoxical quality of exis-
    tence.

Gross, John. "Amazing Reductions." Encounter, 23 (Sep-
    tember 1964), 50.

Gupta, Manju Dutta. "Recent Experimental Drama." Bulle-
    tin of the Department of English (Calcutta Univer-
    sity), 4, i (1968-1969), 13-32.

Guthke, Karl S. "Die metaphysische Farce im Theater der
    Gegenwart." Deutsche Shakespeare-Gesellschaft West.
    Jahrbuch, 1970, 49-76.
        Along with Stoppard and Beckett, Pinter is a dra-
    matist who sees the perverse humor in man's control
    by an arbitrary fate. The bitter comedy of Shake-
    speare's King Lear is in this tradition.

Habicht, Werner. "Der Dialog und das Schweigen im 'Theater des Absurden.'" <u>Die Neueren Sprachen</u>, N.S. 16, ii (1967), 53-66.
   Habicht compares Ionesco, Beckett, and Pinter in their approach to absurdism. Ionesco shows us the horrors of conformity and Beckett is concerned with the paradoxes of existence. Pinter illustrates man's basic separation from his community.

_____. "Theatre der Sprache. Bermerkungen zu einigen englischen Dramen der Gegenwart." <u>Die Neueren Sprachen</u>, 7 (July 1963), 302-13.
   Habicht provides some background on English "nonsense-literature," alluding to Edward Lear and Lewis Carroll. He shows that N. F. Simpson derives materials from this tradition and Pinter also, to a lesser extent.

Hafley, James. "The Human Image in Contemporary Art." <u>Kerygma</u>, 3, iii (1963), 25-34.
   Hafley points out relationships between absurdism in literature and abstract expressionism in paintings.

Hall, John. "British Drama in the Sixties--A note from London." <u>Texas Quarterly</u>, 10 (Summer 1967), 15-19.
   A flamboyant essay discusses, briefly, Pinter, Fry, Bolt, Arden, Osborne, Wesker, Peter Shaffer, and Charles Wood. Hall feels that Pinter is the most important of these.

Hall, Peter. "Directing Pinter." <u>Theatre Quarterly</u>, IV, xvi, (1974-1975), 4-17.
   Hall discusses "his own approach to directing Pinter, and the problems and rewards the plays have for actors and directors alike."

_____. "Is the Beginning the Word?" <u>Theatre Quarterly</u>, II, vii (1973), 5-11.
   In a condensed version of Hall's 1971 Herbert Read Lecture, he considers the varied and mutable relationships between actor, director, playwright, audience, and text in the theatre. Brief mention of Pinter is included.

Hall, Rodney. "Theatre in London." <u>Westerly</u>, 3 (October 1964), 57-60.
   Hall gives a balanced synopsis of <u>The Birthday Party</u> which he feels exemplifies both the best and the worst in the new drama.

Hare, Carl. "Creativity and Commitment in the Contemporary British Theatre." <u>Humanities Association Bulletin</u>, 16, i (1965), 21-28.

Hare examines the attitudes toward social commitment and their effect on the plays of Osborne, Wesker, Arden, and Pinter. Hare feels Osborne and
Wesker are committed to "the reform of the social
system and the assertion of the individual" while
Arden and Pinter show the dangers both of commitment
and withdrawal from it respectively.

Hasler, Jörg. "Bühnenanweisungen und Spiegeltechnik bei
Shakespeare und im modernen Drama." Deutsche Shakespeare Gesellschaft West Jahrbuch, 1970, 99-117.
Shakespeare's dialogue indicated what acting and
gestures were appropriate in a scene, whereas Pinter and Beckett use elaborate stage directions to
replace references in the dialogue.

Hayman, Ronald. Harold Pinter. Contemporary Playwrights.
London: Heinemann, 1968. 2d ed. London: Heinemann, 1969. [2d edition is expanded to include discussions of Landscape, Silence, and Night.]
This is an analysis of the radio dramas of Beckett and Pinter and the unique attributes of radio
as a medium.

_____. "Landscape without Pictures: Pinter, Beckett,
and Radio." London Magazine, 8 (July 1968), 72-77.
Hayman discusses the influence of Beckett and the
experience of writing for radio in Pintar's Landscape.

Hays, H. R. "Transcending Naturalism." Modern Drama,
5, i (1962), 27-36.
This is a brief analysis/summary of The Birthday
Party, The Room, The Dumb Waiter, The Caretaker.
Hays sees Pinter as transcending naturalism, using
realistic settings as "deception concealing a world
of chaos and madness." Pinter has a keen ear for
everyday speech patterns and for realistic details
but beneath the surface of the "ordinary" lies a
terrifying abyss.

Heilman, Robert B. "Demonic Strategies: The Birthday
Party and The Firebugs." Sense and Sensibility in
Twentieth-Century Writing: A Gathering in Memory of
William Van O'Connor. Ed. Brom Weber. Carbondale
and Edwardsville: Southern Illinois University Press;
London: Feffer & Simons, 1970. Pages 57-74.
This is a lengthy and thoughtful analysis of the
similarities in point of view and theme between Max
Frisch's The Firebugs and The Birthday Party. He
sees both plays as presenting a pair of "demonic"
invaders to "mark alternative extremes possible to
the melodrama of social disaster: the destruction of
the individual by oppressive order . . . and the

elimination of order by the destructive instinct
. . . ."

Henkle, Roger B. "From Pooter to Pinter: Domestic Comedy and Vulnerability." Critical Quarterly, 16 (1974), 174-89.
 Henkle offers an intriguing contrast and comparison of Pinter's plays with a domestic comedy of the late nineteenth century, a series in Punch entitled Diary of a Nobody. Pinter has altered the approach to anxieties and attitudes of domestic comedy while retaining the form.

Henry, Patrick. "Acting the Absurd." Drama Critique, 6, i (1963), 9-19.
 An actor gives his interpretation and approach to a Pinter character. This proves to be revealing, especially when one considers that Pinter is himself an actor.

Hewes, Henry. "The British Bundle." Saturday Review, 11 September 1971, pp. 20, 54.
 See Nichols above.

  ——. "Odd Husband Out." Saturday Review, 4 December 1971, pp. 20, 22.
 This is a brief analysis of Old Times and discussion of the London and New York performances.

  ——. "Probing Pinter's Play." Saturday Review, 8 April 1967, p. 56.

Hilský, Martin. "The Two Worlds of Harold Pinter's Plays." Acta Universitatis Carolinae. Philologica 3 (1969). Prague Studies in English XIII. Ed. Bohumil Trnka and Zdeněk Stríbrný. Praha: Univ. Karlova, 1969. Pages 109-15.
 Hilský posits a unity in Pinter's plays from The Room to The Caretaker in theme and in "a certain gradation, a sort of logical staircase with The Caretaker on top."

Hinchliffe, Arnold P. The Absurd. Critical Idiom Series. London, 1969. Pages 82-85.
 This is a general study of the genre including an overview of Pinter's work through Landscape.

  ——. Harold Pinter. (TEAS 51.) New York: Twayne, 1967.
 This Twayne series biography provides useful biographical data, extensive plot summaries and a useful survey of criticism. Hinchliffe's interpretations of the plays and his discussions of language are sophisticated and thorough.

_____. Harold Pinter. New York: St. Martin's, 1975.
This is an elaboration of the biography with
more emphasis on interpretation and the inclusion
of more recent plays.

_____. "Mr. Pinter's Belinda." Modern Drama, 11 (1968),
173-79.
This is an exploration of the role and characterization of women in The Homecoming, The Collection,
The Lover, Tea Party, A Slight Ache, and A Night
Out. Hinchliffe is particularly concerned with
sexuality in Pinter's female characters and the reaction of the male characters to them.

Hirschberg, Stuart. "Pinter's Caricature of Howard's End
in The Homecoming." Notes on Contemporary Literature, 4, iv (1974), 14-15.
Hirschberg suggests, without elaboration, that
The Homecoming "is patterned after E. M. Forster's
novel Howard's End in a fairly straightforward and
systematic fashion."

Hoefer, Jacqueline. "Pinter and Whiting: Two Attitudes
Toward the Alienated Artist." Modern Drama, 4
(1962), 402-08.
Hoefer considers The Birthday Party and Whiting's
Saint's Day plays about artists. Whiting views the
artist as a predatory figure, whereas Pinter sees
him as the victim of society.

Hollis, James R. Harold Pinter: The Poetics of Silence.
Pref. Harry T. Moore. Carbondale: Southern Illinois University Press; London: Feffer & Simons,
1970.
This is a survey and critical discussion of Pinter's major plays, focusing particularly on the
"playwright's relationship to and utilization of
language." Hollis includes an introductory section
on modern drama in general.

Hughes, A. "They Can't Take That Away from Me; Myth and
Memory in Pinter's Old Times." Modern Drama, 17
(1974), 467-76.
Hughes offers a reading which begins with the assumption that "to alter one's memory is to change
the past." Hughes sees Deeley and Kate as creating
Anna, who then assumes reality, and the rest of the
play presents attempts by all three to change the
past by changing their memories of it.

Hughes, Catherine. "Pinter Is as Pinter Does." Catholic
World, 210 (December 1969), 124-26.
Hughes provides a thoughtful, but limited, analy-
sis of Silence and Landscape. She concentrates on

communication and silence.

Hunt, Albert. "Around Us . . . Things Are There."
Encore, 8, vi (1961), 24-32.
This is a lengthy plea for what the author calls
"poetic realism" in the theatre, divorced from naturalism in that it rejects illusion in favor of
"physical reality." Hunt includes an analysis of
Arden's Serjeant Musgrave's Dance in these terms and
a brief mention of The Birthday Party.

_____. "Pinter and Coward." New Society (1976), 696.

Hutchings, Patrick. "The Humanism of a Dumb Waiter."
Westerly, 1 (1963), 56-63.
The Dumb Waiter is analyzed thematically and
structurally. Hutchings feels the play is a metaphor for the estrangement of man from his society,
the impersonality and brutality of a profit-oriented
bureaucracy.

Imhof, Rüdiger. "Pinter's Silence: The Impossibility of
Communication." Modern Drama, 17 (1974), 449-60.
This is an interpretive examination of the characters in Silence. Imhof sees Pinter as portraying
"the essential qualities of the characters" as well
as their interrelationship. Each of them is attempting to communicate, "to establish a true relationship," but they can only communicate their own
problems and concerns and cannot hear the other
characters.

Itzin, Catherine. "The Pinter Enigma." Theatre Quarterly, 4, xiii (1974), 95.

Jiji, Vera M. "Pinter's Four Dimensional House: The
Homecoming." Modern Drama, 17 (1974), 433-42.
Jiji examines ritual and myth in The Homecoming.
Pinter has not only used "unconscious processes"
for motive and action but also has "put on stage the
very language and thought processes of the unconscious." He has consistently reversed the audience's expectations of the ritual presented.

Jones, D. A. N. "Silent Censorship in Britain." Theatre
Quarterly, I, i (1971), 22-28.
This is an interesting examination of the rela-
tionship between economics, politics, and morality
in the success or failure of a production. The
Birthday Party is mentioned briefly.

Kastor, Frank S. "Pinter and Modern Tragicomedy."
Wichita State University Bulletin: University
Studies (Kansas), 46 (August 1970), 1-13.

The center of Pinter's vision is a room in which
two people are alone, but not together. The realism
of his characters, settings, and dialogue contrasts
with the uncertainty and menace of the absurd universe beyond the room.

Kathane, Eric. "Pinter et le realisme irreal." L'Avant-
Scene, 15 April 1967, p. 9.

Kaufman, Michael W. "Actions That a Man Might Play:
Pinter's The Birthday Party. Modern Drama, 16
(1973), 167-78.
Kaufman offers an analysis of the meaning of
ritual and games, particularly the actual game of
blind man's buff, which subdue and conceal "the chaotic world of human emotions." Game-playing emerges
as both concealment for and protection from those
emotions.

Kaufman, Stanley. "Stanley Kaufman on Theatre: Landscape
and Silence." New Republic, 25 April 1970, p. 20.

Kennedy, Andrew K. "Old and New in London Now." Modern
Drama, 11 (1969), 445-46.
See Nichols above.

Kerr, Walter. "The Caretaker." In his The Theatre in
Spite of Itself. New York: Simon and Schuster,
1963. Pages 116-19.
Kerr analyzes the play as a vision of "a world
wholly opaque, wholly impermeable, and . . . wholly
hollow," amd he proposes two levels of appreciation:
total identification or a wish to know the worst of
society.

_____. Harold Pinter (CEMW27.) New York: Columbia
University Press, 1967.
Kerr sets out to prove that Pinter is not only an
existentialist but "the only playwright who writes
existentially."

_____. "The Hey, Wait a Minute Theater." In his Thirty
Plays Hath November. New York: Simon and Schuster,
1969. Pages 29-41.
Kerr uses The Birthday Party as an example of a
trend in theatre: leaving nothing out, selecting
nothing. Kerr feels "the theatre, like everything
else in life, comes under two commands and a question. Say it. Show it. What is it? Pinter is
asking an audience to go beyond a plot and instead
pay close attention to everything that happens."

_____. "The Moment of Pinter." In his Thirty Plays Hath
November. New York: Simon and Schuster, 1969.

Pages 41-46. [Reprints "Put-Off--Or Turned On--By
Pinter?" New York Times, 15 October 1967, II:1.]

_____. "The Theater Is the Victim of a Plot." New York
Times, 25 June 1967, VI:10.

Kershaw, John. "The Caretaker." In his The Present Stage.
London: Collins, 1966. Pages 70-87.
Kershaw links Pinter to the Absurd, does not see
him as a "problem" writer. Pinter's psychological
insights in The Caretaker are profound; Pinter is
concerned with the "time when reality must be faced."

_____. "Harold Pinter, Dramatist" and "The Language of
Silence." In The Present Stage. London: Collins,
1966. Pages 70-78, 79-87.
Kershaw reviews many possible approaches to Pinter's work. He particularly notes the importance
of what is not said in various scenes, as a clue to
understanding their underlying tensions.

Kesting, Marianne. "Harold Pinter." In Panorama des
zeitgenossischen Theaters. Munich, 1969. Pages
243-48.
Pinter is one of fifty-eight playwrights Kesting
discusses in this book. With reference to The
Lover, The Room,The Dumb Waiter, The Dwarfs and
others she explores a paradox: Pinter is so realistic he seems unbelievable.

Kitchin, Laurence. "Backwards and Forwards." Twentieth
Century, 169 (January 1961), pp. 168-69.
Kitchin offers a look at contemporary drama in
Britain. Some commentary on Pinter and Arden is
included, but Kitchin discusses no one playwright
in depth.

_____. "Compressionism. The Form." In his Drama in the
Sixties. London: Faber and Faber, 1966. Pages 45-
53.
This contains a brief mention of Pinter as "one
of the best of all practitioners" of compressionism,
yet still beginning to break out of the form.

_____. Mid-Century Drama. 2d ed. London: Faber and
Faber, 1962. Pages 119-22.
Kitchin admires Pinter's ability to compress action, to intensify feelings and emotions. He compares him to Chekhov. In general he admires the
staging techniques, use of dialect and other verbal
innovations of the new English realists.

_____. "Realism in English Mid-Century Drama." World Theatre, 14, i (1965), 17-26.
Synge, O'Neill, Miller, Ibsen, and Gorki are all seen to be influences on the English realists. The mastery of dialect by Pinter and others as well as their perceptive insights into human nature qualify them as realists.

Kleinman, Neil. "Naming of Names." Midwest Monographs (University of Illinois), 1, i (1967), 4.

Klotz, Friedrich. "Jean Tardieu: Theatre de Chambre." Der Fremdsprachliche Unterricht, IV, xiii (1970), 69-83.
Jean Tardieu, early twentieth-century aesthete, theatre person and philosopher, is seen to be a possible influence on Pinter.

Klotz, Günther. "Individuum und Gesellschaft im englischen Drama der Gegenwart: Arnold Wesker und Harold Pinter." Weimararer Beiträge, 19, x (1973), 187-91.
See Wesker below.

Knight, G. Wilson. "The Kitchen Sink." Encounter, 21 (December 1963), 48-54.
Knight places Pinter in the "Kitchen-Sink" school because of the playwright's naturalism, his use of dialect and early concentration on lower-class characters. Although Knight perceives Pinter's links to the absurdists he overlooks the uniqueness and brilliance of the author's techniques.

Kosok, Heinz. "Das moderne englische Kurzdrama." Neusprachliche Mitteilungen aus Wissenschaft und Praxis, 3 (1970), 131-41.

Kunkel, Francis L. "The Dystopia of Harold Pinter." Renascence, 21 (1968), 17-20.
Kunkel discusses The Birthday Party and The Homecoming as presenting a shared "portrait of modern society as degenerate." Both plays exhibit striking similarities in theme, language, and situation.

Lahr, John. "The Language of Silence." Evergreen Review, 13 (March 1969), 53-55, 82-90.
Lahr examines the use of silence in modern theatre, proposing that it is used to shock audiences into a reawakening of their senses. Pinter's Landscape is used and analyzed as an example.

_____. "Pinter and Chekhov: The Bond of Naturalism." Tulane Drama Review, 13, ii (1968), 137-45.
Pinter's acknowledged admiration for Chekhov has led Lahr to conjecture that in their verbal tech-

niques and use of setting, particularly, the two
playwrights are similar.

_____. "Pinter the Spaceman." Evergreen Review, 12
(June 1968), 49-52, 87-90.
This is a discussion of Pinter as exponent of the
new relationship between man and nature now being
explored in other arts and sciences: the basic ambiguity of life.

_____. "Pinter's Room: Who's There." Arts Magazine
(March 1967), 21-23.
Lahr explores Pinter's use of space.

_____. Up Against the Fourth Wall: Essays on Modern
Theater. New York: Grove Press, 1970. Pages 175-194.

_____, ed. Casebook on Harold Pinter's The Homecoming.
New York: Grove Press, 1971.
This is a good collection of essays, designed for
use by college students.

Lambert, J. W. "Introduction." In New English Dramatists 3. Ed. Tom Maschler. Harmondsworth: Penguin,
1961. Pages 7-10.
Lambert presents a broad critical analysis of
Willis Hall, John Arden, and Harold Pinter.

Lamont, Rosette C. "Pinter's The Homecoming: The Contest
of the Gods." Far Western Forum: A Review of Ancient
and Modern Letters, I, 1 (1974), 47-73.
Lamont examines The Homecoming in terms of myth.
Lamont concludes Pinter was asserting "that our
world, ruled for so many centuries by the brutality
of male ethics . . . is ready for the transformative
feminine psychic constellation," personified in Ruth
and Jessie.

Landstone, Charles. "From John Osborne to Shelagh Delaney." World Theater, 8 (1959), 203-16.
This article contains a brief mention of The
Birthday Party within a survey of British drama in
the 50s.

Lane, John F. "No Sex Please, I'm English: John Francis
Lane on the Pinter-Visconti Case." Plays and Play-
ers, 20, x (1973), 19-21.
Lane details the textual alterations made in the
Visconti production in Rome of Pinter's Old Times
and the ensuing controversy.

Langley, Lee. "Genius: A Change in Direction." Daily
Telegraph Magazine, 23 November 1973, p. 30.

Lechler, Hans-Joachim. "Harold Pinter's Sketch Last to
     Go." Der fremdsprachliche Unterricht, 4, xiii
     (1970), 29-37.

Leech, Clifford. "Two Romantics: Arnold Wesker and Har-
     old Pinter." Contemporary Theatre. Stratford-upon-
     Avon Studies 4. Ed. John R. Brown and Bernard
     Harris. London: Edward Arnold; New York: St. Mar-
     tin's Press, 1962. Pages 11-31.
          To understand Pinter and Wesker one must first
     know Coleridge and Wordsworth, their views of imagi-
     nation and experience.

Lesser, Simon O. "Reflections on Pinter's The Birthday
     Party." Contemporary Literature, 13, i (1972), 34-
     43.
          Lesser analyzes The Birthday Party both in itself
     and compared with Kafka's The Trial.

Levidova, I. "A New Hero Appears in the Theatre (Notes
     on Young Dramatists in England)." Inostrannaya
     Literatura, 1 (January 1962), 201-08.
          Pinter, like Wesker, is described as a playwright
     who lovingly portrays proletariat heroes.

Lewis, Peter. "Fascinated by Unsatisfactory People."
     Time and Tide, 21 June 1962, pp. 16-17.
          The Collection is discussed as a prototypical
     Pinter play.

Leyburn, Ellen D. "Comedy and Tragedy Transposed." Yale
     Review, 53, iv (1964), 553-62.
          Leyburn discusses the fusion of tragedy and come-
     dy in modern drama. She mentions Pinter briefly as
     a writer of comedies that are "concerned with the
     same ultimate questions . . . which in earlier peri-
     ods have led to the writing of tragedy."

Loney, Glenn. "Broadway in Review." Educational Theatre
     Journal, 19, iv (1967), 514.

_____. "Theatre of the Absurd: It Is Only a Fad." The-
     atre Arts, 46, xi (1962), 20, 22, 24, 66-68.
          Loney feels that the plays of the Absurdists do
     not have enough to offer to sustain the form. They
     have abandoned traditional form but offer only
     "sloppy writing," nihilism, and non-communication in
     return. Pinter, however, "seems more akin to the
     main currents in theatre tradition."

Lubbren, Rainer. "Robbe-Grillet, Pinter, und 'Die blaue
     Villa in Hongkong.'" Die neue Rundschau, 78, i
     (1967), 119-26.

Lumley, Frederick. New Trends in 20th Century Drama. New York: Oxford University Press, 1967. Pages 266-73.
  Lumley's book provides an overview of Pinter's work, through The Homecoming. Lumley feels that Pinter "has no axe to grind, no significance is to be attached to his themes, nor do they mask any abstract idea."

Macneice, Louis. Varieties of Parable. Cambridge: Cambridge University Press, 1965. Pages 121-23.
  Macneice compares Beckett, Kafka, and Pinter, quoting liberally from Esslin. He deals primarily with The Birthday Party and The Caretaker.

Mannes, Marya. "Just Looking, Thanks." Reporter, 13 (October 1960), 48.

Mander, Gertrud. "Die jungen englischen Dramatiker." Neue deutsche Hefte, 83 (1961), 104-30.
  Pinter is considered one of the most important British dramatists. His plays are not political-- rather they are in the continental tradition of the absurd.

_____. "Wie langweilig is das Orinare?" Theater Heute (February 1966), 4.

Manvell, Roger. "The Decade of Harold Pinter." Humanist, 132 (April 1967), 112-15.
  Within ten years after the start of the new English drama, Pinter has gained preeminence in a distinguished field.

_____. "Pinter Through French Eyes." Humanist, 84 (May 1969), 142-44.
  The French see Pinter primarily as a disciple of Beckett, very witty, and an existentialist in the Camus tradition.

Marowitz, Charles. Confessions of a Counterfeit Critic. London: Methuen, 1973. Pages 47-49, 163-65, 184-88.
  This contains reprints of some original reviews, and Marowitz analyzes The Caretaker, Landscape, Silence, and Old Times.

_____. "Notes on the Theater of Cruelty." Tulane Drama Review, 11 (Winter 1966), 152-56.
  Marowitz describes the tremendous impact of Artaud's writing--decades earlier--in the postwar stage. Pinter is one of many writers who seem to have been influenced by Artaud's theories.

_____. "'Pinterism' Is Maximum Tension through Minimum
Information." New York Times, 1 October 1967, VI,
pp. 36-37, 89-90, 92, 94-96.
    Marowitz illustrates the ways in which pauses and
silences at appropriate moments reveal character,
increase tensions,and add suspense.

Martineau, Stephen. "Pinter's Old Times: The Memory
Game." Modern Drama, 16 (1973), 287-97.
    Martineau gives an analysis of Old Times, which
he feels lacks the continuity and the outburst of
energy characterizing Pinter's best known plays.

Mast, Gerald. "Pinter's Homecoming." Drama Survey
(Minneapolis), 6 (1968), 266-77.
    This is an interesting analysis of the characters
in The Homecoming which seeks to answer criticism
that the ending is "unreal and unmotivated."

Matthews, Honor. The Primal Curse: The Myth of Cain and
Abel in the Theater. New York: Schocken Books,
1967. Pages 22-23, 198-201.
    See N. F. Simpson below.

Mayersberg, Paul. "Harold Pinter's The Collection."
Listener, 5 July 1962, p. 26.

McCrindle, Joseph, ed. Behind the Scenes. New York:
Holt, Rinehart, 1971. Pages 211-22.
    Pinter and his director Clive Donner discuss the
film production of The Caretaker.

McLaughlin, J. "Harold Pinter and PBL." America, 10
February 1968, p. 193.

McWhinnie, Donald. "Donald McWhinnie Interviewed by
Robert Reubens." Transatlantic Review, 12 (Spring
1963), 34-38.
    McWhinnie discusses his direction of The Caretaker,
the transfer of A Slight Ache from radio to stage,
and the demands Pinter's plays make on the actors.

Mennemeier, Franz. Das moderne Drama des Auslandes.
Dusseldorf: A. Bagel, 1961. Pages 159-171.

Messenger, Ann P. "Blindness and the Problem of Identity
in Pinter's Plays." Die Neueren Sprachen, 21
(1972), 481-90.
    In many of Pinter's plays blindness, light and
dark imagery, and problems of vision are associated
with physical or spiritual death. In addition, "The
ideas of sight and blindness, along with light and
darkness, are traditional metaphors for knowledge
and ignorance, which Pinter uses, again traditional-

166

ly, to image forth the problem of identity."

Milberg, Ruth. "1 + 1 = 1: Dialogue and Character Split-
ting in Harold Pinter." Die Neueren Sprachen, 23
(1974), 225-33.
A discussion of the "basic dialogue form" of
Pinter's best known plays as well as the themes of
lack of communication, the influence of the past,
illusion vs. reality, sexual games, and the fragmentation of the male characters.

Miller, Mary Jane. "Pinter as a Radio Dramatist." Modern Drama, 17 (1974), 403-12.
Miller examines the unique quality of Pinter's
radio plays: A Slight Ache, A Night Out, The
Dwarfs. She discusses similarities and differences
in Pinter's stage and radio drama and the particular
techniques used in radio.

Milne, Tom. "The Hidden Face of Violence." In the
Encore Reader. Ed. Charles Marowitz. London:
Eyre Methuen, 1965. Pages 115-24. Also in Modern
British Dramatists. Ed. John R. Brown. Englewood
Cliffs, N.J.: Prentice-Hall, 1968. Pages 38-46.
Reprinted from Encore, 7 (1960), 14-20.
Milne examines the comic theme of the nature of
violence in Whiting's Saint's Day, Pinter's The
Birthday Party, and Arden's Serjeant Musgrave's
Dance. Each of these plays "creates its own dis-
tinctive world, with a mood and logic of urgency,
directness and excitement," and each demands that
the audience examine their own lives and the soci-
ety in which they live.

Minogue, Valerie. "Taking Care of the Caretaker." Twentieth Century, 168 (September 1960), 243-48.
This is a thorough discussion of The Caretaker.
The characters seem assiduously to avoid communication.

Morgan, Ricki. "What Max and Teddy Come Home to in The
Homecoming." Educational Theatre Journal, 25
(1973), 490-99.
The cyclical pattern of The Homecoming is discussed here. Both Max and Teddy have been married
to whores, have three sons, provide for their families, and are left to cope on their own.

Morris, Kelly. "The Homecoming." Tulane Drama Review,
11, ii (1966), 185-91.
The classic theatrical devices of the homecoming
of a relative widely used by Ibsen and Strindberg
exist in Pinter's play as well--although Pinter
parodies some of the techniques. The power of one

family and modern confusion over sex roles add to
the complexity and power of The Homecoming.

Morrison, Kristen. "Pinter and the New Irony." Quarterly Journal of Speech, 55 (1969), 388-93.
    Morrison uses The Room and The Homecoming as
examples of Pinter's reversed irony: it is the audience who does not understand what is happening; the
characters do understand their situation. "In Pinter's irony, the spectator comes to fear that he may
himself be an unwitting victim."

Muir, Kenneth. "Verse and Prose." In Contemporary Theatre. Eds. John R. Brown and Bernard Harris. London: Edward Arnold, 1962. Pages 97-115.
    Pinter "uses dialogue superficially colloquial to
express neurosis, madness, and terror."

Münder, Peter. Harold Pinter und die Problematik des
Absurden Theaters. Bern: Herbert Lang, 1976.
    A complete and extensive survey of Pinter's
career and plays from The Room through Old Times,
including critical comments and a bibliography of
secondary sources, is presented by Münder.

Murphy, Marese. "Pinter and Visconti." Drama, 109
(Summer 1973), 45.

Murphy, Robert P. "Non-Verbal Communication and the
Overlooked Action in Pinter's The Caretaker."
Quarterly Journal of Speech, 58 (1972), 41-47.
    Murphy sees Davies as the "gratuitous victim" of
a concerted, planned game, cruelly carried out by
Aston and Mick. Murphy's reading is based largely
on stage directions.

Nelson, Hugh. "The Homecoming: Kith and Kin." In Modern
British Dramatists. Ed. John R. Brown. Englewood
Cliffs, N.J.: Prentice-Hall, 1968. Pages 145-63.
    Nelson explores the biblical allusions in the
play, the parable of the prodigal son and the story
of Ruth, and the influence of Shakespeare's Troilus
and Cressida. He notes that the central movement of
the play is the process of Ruth's self-discovery and
that an important conflict is the assertion of
"man's primitive nature" against family values.

"News from the Universities." The Times, 8 September
1970, p. 10.

Nicoll, Allardyce. English Drama: A Modern Viewpoint.
New York: Barnes and Noble, 1968. Pages 140-44.
    Nicoll finds Pinter a technically adept play-
wright, but he criticizes the characters as too like

each other and finds the conclusion of The Homecoming "almost incomprehensible."

Nightingale, Benedict. "Taking Bloody Liberty." New Statesman, 18 July 1969, p. 83.

Nollau, Michael. "Texterfahrung als Selbsterfahrung: die Lekture von Harold Pinters Fernsehspiel The Basement and seines Vortrages 'Writing for the Theatre' in Klasse 12." Die Neuren Sprachen, 73, N.S. 23, vi (1974), 495-511.

Novick, Julius. "Mr. Pinter's Memory Play." Humanist, 32, ii (1972), 37.
    Novick mentions that Pinter is "obsessed" by two themes: the subjectivity of reality and the struggle for power in human relationships. He praises the New York production of Old Times and the subtlety of Pinter's style, but even so he finds Pinter's view "limited."

Nyszkiewicz, Heinz. "The Dumb Waiter/The Caretaker." Zeitgenossische englische Dichtung, Bd. 3. Frankfurt, 1968, pp. 210-33.

O'Casey, Sean. "The Bald Primaqueera." Blasts and Benedictions: Articles and Stories. London: Macmillan; New York: St. Martin's Press, 1967. Pages 70-73.
    O'Casey rails out against Ionesco, Pinter, and Artaud for their overemphasis on human cruelty. He appears to take literally dramatic events which were probably meant to be symbolic or metaphoric.

Odajima, Yushi. "Pinter Notes." Eigo Seinen (Tokyo), 115 (1969), 416-17. In Japanese.

Oliver, Edith. "The Bum in the Attic." New Yorker, 14 October 1961, p. 162.

Oliver, William. "Between Absurdity and the Playwright." In Modern Drama: Essays in Criticism. Ed. T. Bogard and W. I. Oliver. New York: Oxford, 1965. Pages 3-19.
    Oliver's essay is essentially a long re-definition of Absurdist drama. Pinter is mentioned briefly, with Albee, as choosing "to write in a far more realistic vein than did the first masters of the form" since such a form "accomplishes some, if not all, of the intents of the original absurdists without resorting to tedious expressionistic symbols."

Orley, Ray. "Pinter and Menace." Drama Critique, 11,
iii (1968), 124-48.
Orley feels Pinter's plays deal with the terror
and menace of existence. In the earlier plays he
concentrates on dark forces that affect man from
without, in the later dramas, forces within the
human psyche.

Pallavicini, Roberto. "Aspetti della drammaturgia con-
temporanea." Aut Aut, 81 (May 1964), 68-73.
Pallavicini finds Pinter rather boring and complains that the playwright's works are too subjective and not accessible to people outside the theatrical profession.

Parker, R. B. "The Theory and Theatre of the Absurd."
Queen's Quarterly, 73, iii (1966), 521-41.
This is a lengthy discussion of Pinter, Beckett,
Ionesco, and Genet who are all seen to present the
alienation of existential philosophy but not the
positive action role advocated by Camus.

Peel, Marie. "Violence in Literature." Books and Bookmen, 17, v (1972), 20-24.
Peel believes there is probably no way of telling
whether there is more or less violence in the world
today than before. But she feels that the passivity in the face of violence shown by Pinter and
others is unhealthy.

Pesta, John. "Pinter's Usurpers." Drama Survey (Minneapolis), 6 (1967), 54-65.
Pesta has observed that in most of Pinter's early
plays a threatening, predator "usurper" upsets the
balance of life for the more timid characters.

Petrulian, Catrinel. "Între realism şi absurd--Harold
Pinter." Revista de Istorie şi Theorie Literara,
21 (1972), 533-39.
Pinter has not aligned himself altogether with
the absurdists or the naturalists. His ambiguity,
his dramatic tensions depend upon his holding a
stance somewhere between the two.

Pinter's Optics: "Get thee Glass Eyes." (Mid M. Ser. 1
No. 1) Urbana: University of Illinois Department
of English, 1967.

"Pinterview." Newsweek, 23 July 1962, p. 69.

Powlick, Leonard. "A Phenomenological Approach to Harold
Pinter's A Slight Ache." Quarterly Journal of
Speech, 60 (1974), 25-32.
This is a subjective reading of the play. A

Slight Ache reflects the "perceptions and attitudes" of Edward, and the language, "in its connotative, phonemic, and reverberational aspects," allows the audience to experience Edward's world.

Prickett, Stephen. "Three Modern English Plays." *Philologica Pragensia*, 10, i (1967), 12-21.
      This article considers Jellicoe's *The Knack*, Arden's *Serjeant Musgrave's Dance*, and Pinter's *The Caretaker* as being influenced by authors from without England. All three juxtapose naturalistic and symbolic or ritual action.

Prideaux, Tom. "The Adventurous Play--Stranger to Broadway." In *The Discovery of Drama*. Ed. Thomas E. Sanders. Glenview, Ill.: Scott, Foresman, 1968. Pages 624-27. Reprinted from *Life*, 3 March 1967, p. 6.

Quigley, Austin E. "*The Dwarfs*: A Study in Linguistic Dwarfism." *Modern Drama*, 17 (1974), 413-22.
      Quigley sees the primary concern of the play, around which all other concerns locate, as the difficulty between perceiving an environment and verbally expressing that perception in a form understood by others. He posits "linguistic dominance" as Pinter's central conflict throughout his work.

_____. *The Pinter Problem*. Princeton, N.J.: Princeton University Press, 1975.
      Quigley, using the linguistic theories of Wittgenstein and others, brilliantly demonstrates that language is a weapon to Pinter's characters who are engaged in a life-and-death struggle.

"The Reaction Against Realism." *Times Literary Supplement*, 30 June 1961, p. 400.

Richards, Michael. "Harold Pinter." In *Englische Dichter der Moderne*. Ed. R. Suhnel and D. Riesner. Berlin, 1971. Pages 578-87.

Richardson, Jack. "English Imports on Broadway." *Commentary*, 43 (June 1967), 73-75.
      Richardson criticizes *The Homecoming* and Peter Shaffer's *Black Comedy*. He finds Pinter's play incomprehensible and without coherence, writing "in Harold Pinter, we have a writer who puts together loose fragments of highly actable scenes and then hopes that some part of life will conform to them."

Rickert, Alfred E. "Perceiving Pinter." *English Record*, 22, ii (1971), 30-35.
      Rickert does not consider Pinter a traditional

dramatist because of his concentration on individual rather than social problems. The article deals with communication, conflict, and the desire to control and its relationship to personal identity.

"The Road to Sidcup: The Caretaker." New Statesman, 67 (1964), 423.

Robertson, Roderick. "A Theater of the Absurd: The Passionate Equation." Drama Survey, 2 (June 1962), 24-43.

Roger, Ian. "The Moron as Hero." Drama, 59 (Winter 1960), 36-39.
    Roger attacks what he sees as the trend toward using characters of below normal intelligence in theatre. Pinter's The Caretaker and N. F. Simpson in general are given as examples. His primary requirement for drama seems to be that "the centre of the stage must of necessity be held by a character who is possessed of supra-normal abilities."

Roland, Alan. "Pinter's Homecoming: Imagoes in Dramatic Action." Psychoanalytic Review, 61 (1974), 415-28.
    This is a fascinating study of The Homecoming. Especially interesting is Teddy's passivity, interpreted in terms of his being an obliging older brother. He curiously imitates the pattern of his father's life.

Roll-Hansen, Diderik. "Harold Pinter og det absurde drama." Samtiden, 74 (September 1965), 435-40.
    In Norwegian.
    This article discusses the beginning of the absurdist movement in Europe, especially in France and Suggests possible influences on Pinter's early work.

Rosador, Kurt T. "Pinter's Dramatic Method: Kullus, The Examination, The Basement." Modern Drama, 14, ii (1971), 195-205.
    This is a study of these minor works which permit insights into the situations which most often stimulate Pinter's imagination, the battle for position, between two or more characters confined to a room.

_____. "Pinter: The Homecoming." In Das englische Drama. Ed. Dieter Mehl. Dusseldorf: A. Bagel, 1970. Pages 319-33.
    Rosador describes the happenings in The Homecoming and discusses critical appraisal of the work. He then discusses the Freudian and existential elements in the play that make it such a challenging enigma.

172

Rosenberg, James. "European Influences." American Theatre. New York: St. Martin's Press, 1967. Pages 59-60.
    Rosenberg, discussing O'Neil, compares dialogue in The Caretaker and The Birthday Party with that in O'Neill's Yank. He finds O'Neill's dialogue "a form of dramaturgical carpentry," while Pinter's is "verbal and dramatic art."

Roy, Emil. British Drama Since Shaw. Carbondale: University of Southern Illinois Press, 1972. Pages 115-23.

Ryan, Stephen P. "The London Stage." America, 106, xii (1961), 956-58.
    Ryan connects Pinter with the theatre of the absurd, a frequent assessment in the 1960s.

Sainer, Arthur. The Sleepwalker and the Assassin: A View of the Contemporary Theatre. New York: Bridgehead Books, 1964. Pages 99-102.

Salem, Daniel. "La blessure peuplée de Pinter." Les Langues Modernes, 67 (1973), 84.

_____. "Le gardien: Analyse d'un personnage [Davies] de [Harold] Pinter." Les Langues Modernes, 67 (1973), 67-71.
    Salem provides an interesting character study of Davies in The Caretaker.

_____. Harold Pinter, Dramaturge de l'ambiguite. Paris: Denoël, 1968.
    This is a fine study of Pinter, emphasizing the richness that is gained by his carefully worked out ambiguities.

Salmon, Eric. "Harold Pinter's Ear." Modern Drama, 17 (1974), 363-75.
    Salmon offers an examination of Pinter's use of language, seemingly naturalistic yet able to portray "the strange life that moves below the surface." Both within the plays and chronologically between plays, the language moves "from closely-observed naturalistic speech to a highly-charged and allusive, stylised prose." Salmon cites some points of comparison with Synge.

Saurel, Renée. "Pinter, Arden, Weingarten." Les Temps Modernes, 247 (1966), 1110-19.
    See Arden above.

Schechner, Richard. "Puzzling Pinter." <u>Tulane</u> <u>Drama</u> <u>Review</u>, 11, ii (1966), 176-84.
One new aspect of Pinter's drama is that it requires the audience to complete its meaning. We cannot receive his message passively; we must involve ourselves in the whole dramatic process.

Scheehen, Peter. "Theatre of the Absurd: A Child Studies Himself." <u>English Journal</u>, 58, iv (1969), 561-65.
Scheehen discusses absurdist drama as a means of "interesting" students in "the variables of human nature." He gives his method of teaching <u>The Dumb Waiter</u>.

Schenker, Ulrich. "Harold Pinter's Caretakers." <u>Neue Zürcher Zeitung</u>, 15 August 1971, p. 39.

Schiff, Ellen F. "Pancakes and Soap Suds: A Study of Childishness in Pinter's Plays." <u>Modern Drama</u>, 16 (1973), 91-101.
Schiff finds that Pinter's characters seem childlike in that they often lack any past, they fear to leave their nest-like rooms, and they exhibit a delightful literalness, naive curiosity, and a host of "juvenile dreads."

Schlegelmilch, Wolfgang. "Der Raum des Humanen: Zu Harold Pinter's <u>The Caretaker</u>." <u>Die Neueren Sprachen</u>, 13 (July 1964), 328-33.
This is an examination of the room as symbol in <u>The Caretaker</u>. It symbolizes the derelict state of Aston's inner life, Mick's loss of inner life, and Davies' lost identity.

Schrey, Helmut. "Das zeitgenossische englische Drama in Schule und Fersehen." <u>Der fremdsprachliche Unterricht</u>, Jg. 4, xiii (1970), 2-14.

Schwarze, Hans-Wilhelm. "Orientierungslosigkeit und Betroffensein: Spielelement in Harold Pinter's <u>The Birthday Party</u>." <u>Literatur in Wissenschaft und Unterricht</u> (Kiel), 7 (1974), 98-114.

Simon, John. "Theatre Chronicle." <u>Hudson Review</u>, 25 (1972), 83-87.
Simon criticizes <u>Old Times</u> as being "even emptier than the usual Pinter product." Like Albee, Pinter is linguistically <u>nouveau riche</u> while his famed "silences" merely stretch a sixty minute play to seventy.

Singh, Mohindar. "Harold Pinter: A Reappraisal." <u>Indian Journal of English Studies</u>, 10 (1969), 81-95.
Singh feels Pinter presents a higher degree of

realism than the more traditional "well-made play."
His plays present a vision of life, depicting the
horrors of society and the truth about human beings.

Sinko, Gregorz. "Atara i Mloda Anglia." Dialogue, 60, iv
(April 1961), 97-99. In Polish.
    Sinko makes a strong case for the influence of
Kafka on Pinter's work.

Smallwood, Clyde G. "Harold Pinter." In his Elements of
Existentialist Philosophy in the Theatre of the Absurd. Dubuque, Iowa: William C. Brown, 1966.
Pages 140-45.
    The shape of Pinter's plays is open-ended, in a
sense, existential. His characters cling to numer-
ous illusions but find no refuge in a violent, de-
humanizing world.

Smith, Cecil. "Pinter: the Compulsion of Playwriting."
Los Angeles Times, Calendar Sec., 3 December 1967,
1:19.

Smith, Frederick N. "Uncertainty in Pinter: 'The
Dwarfs.'" Theatre Annual, 26 (1970), 81-96.
    The Dwarfs, based on Pinter's "unfinished, unpub-
lished, semi-autobiographical novel . . . is in a
sense a diary of Pinter's encounter with Sartrean
existentialism." Thus, in a Pinter play, "the mys-
teriousness of atmosphere, the tenuousness of character, and fragmentation of world-view are not theatrical tricks . . . but . . . rest soundly on the
author's preconceptions concerning the uncertain
nature of reality."

Smith, R. D. "Back to the Text." In Contemporary Theatre. Eds. John R. Brown and Bernard Harris. London: Edward Arnold, 1962. Pages 117-37.
    Smith condemns critics for "labelling" theatrical
productions, whose "tests" are not those of the author, in that he lacks control of all features.
Examining Pinter, Beckett, and Ionesco, Smith claims
they elude such thematic labels as "Non-communication" or "pessimism."

Sprague, Claire. "Possible or Necessary?" New Theatre
Magazine (Bristol), 8, i (1967), 36-37.
    This is a brief discussion of The Birthday Party.

States, Bert O. "The Case for Plot in Modern Drama."
Hudson Review, 20 (Spring 1967), 49-61.
    States, disagreeing with J. R. Brown's enthusiasm
for Pinter, deplores the lack of clarity in matters
of plot and characterization in the works of Pinter
and other modern playwrights. He obviously feels
that too much subtlety is affectation.

_____. "Pinter's _Homecoming_: The Shock of Nonrecognition." _Hudson Review_, 21 (1968), 474-86.
States examines _The Homecoming_ "as a fiction about a group of people so _different_ from us, while in certain obvious respects _resembling_ us." Pinter is an "ironist . . . committed to the search of a more and more exterior point of view" and he is perhaps akin to Poe, whose imagination "is not only anti-social but anti-human."

Stein, Karen F. "Metaphysical Silence in Absurd Drama." _Modern Drama_, 13, iv (1971), 423-31.
Silence is a symbol of emptiness for the absurdist, and Pinter's _A Slight Ache_ and _The Birthday Party_ show its varied use.

Storch, R. F. "Harold Pinter's Happy Families." _Massachusetts Review_ (University of Massachusetts), 8 (1967), 703-12.
Storch argues that "Pinter's plays affect us because they are about the middle-class family, both as sheltering home longed for and dreamed of, and as many-tentacled monster strangling its victim." He examines _The Birthday Party_, _The Caretaker_, _A Slight Ache_, _A Night Out_, and _The Homecoming_.

Styan, J. L. _The Dark Comedy_. 2d ed. Cambridge: Cambridge University Press, 1968. Pages 224-50.
Styan considers Pinter's major works through _The Homecoming_, with short sections devoted to Pinter's style, language, themes, and characters. Pinter, he feels, "practises a new illogicality, yet one pregnant with the logic of feeling that belongs to the subtextual world of tragicomedy."

_____. "Pinter: Penny Plain or Tuppenny Colored." _CEA Critic_, 34 (January 1972), 40.

_____. "The Published Play After 1956. II." _British Book News: A Guide to Book Selection_, 301 (1965), 601-05.
Styan enthusiastically endorses the works of Arden and Pinter. The former he calls a "new realist" and the latter he considers an absurdist.

Susini, C. "Le Lieu et la Parole dans les Théâtre de Harold Pinter." _Recherches Anglaises et Américaines_, 5 (1972), 3-34.
Susini concentrates on Pinter's fascination with place and names in his dramas.

Sykes, Alrene [sic]. _Harold Pinter_. New York: Humanities, 1970.
Sykes treats each of Pinter's works through

<u>Landscape</u> in terms of the media for which they were
written and traces both development of theme and
technique.

_____. "Harold Pinter's Dwarfs." <u>Komos</u>, 1 (1967), 70-75.
Sykes attempts to identify the dwarfs as repre-
sentations of the dissolving relationship between
Pete, Mark, and Len, and finds precise correspon-
dences between this radio play and Beckett's novel
<u>Watt</u>. This is an intriguing, well-supported essay.

Tabachnick, Stephen E. and William Baker. "Reflections
on Ethnicity in Anglo-American Jewish Fiction."
<u>Jewish Quarterly</u>, 21:1-2 (1973), 88-93.
See Wesker below.

Tarn, Adam. "Die Magie des Absurden." <u>Theater Heute</u>, 10
(1965), 3.

Taubman, Howard. "Shared Quicksand." <u>New York Times</u>, 9
December 1962, II:5.

Taylor, John R. <u>Anger, and After</u>. London: Eyre Methuen,
1962. Pages 233-61.
In recognition of Pinter's importance Taylor de-
notes a whole chapter to his work, from his first
play through <u>Landscape</u>. He dwells on the techniques
which create ambiguity.

_____. "British Drama of the Fifties." <u>World Theatre</u>,
11, iii (1962), 241-54.
Pinter is classified as a non-realist, at the
center of English theatrical activity with Osborne
and Arden.

_____. <u>Harold Pinter</u>. (WRW212.) London: Longmans,
1969.
The Longmans' series biography surveys Pinter's
work up to <u>Landscape</u> and <u>Silence</u> and explores his
thematic preoccupations (menace, need, etc.).

_____. "A Pinter Power Struggle." <u>Plays and Players</u>
(August 1975), 34.

_____. "Pinter Pointers." <u>Times Literary Supplement</u>,
1 July 1965, p. 552.

_____. <u>The Rise and Fall of the Well-Made Play</u>. New
York: Hill and Wang, 1967. Pages 162-64.
After the revolution in stage language attributed to Pinter and others, the intellectual, structured dialogue of the well-made play rings false.
Furthermore, Pinter charges us to participate in
his plays. We "feel" our way through events.

_____. "A Room and Some Views. Harold Pinter." In his
The Angry Theatre. New York: Hill and Wang, 1962.
Pages 231-61.
    Taylor comments, "Instead of regarding Pinter as
the purveyor of dramatic fantasy he is usually taken
for, we might equally regard him as the stage's most
ruthless and uncompromising naturalist." The Room,
The Dumb Waiter, The Birthday Party, A Slight Ache
are of a type, the "comedy of menace," akin to
Hitchcock. With his sketches and television plays,
Pinter enters a period of "new directness and simplicity," while "the desire for verification" has
moved from audience to stage.

_____. "What Happened to the New Dramatists?" Plays and
Players, 11, xi (1964), 8.

Tener, Robert T. "Uncertainty as a Dramatic Formula."
Humanities Association Bulletin (Canada), 24 (1973),
175-82.
    Tener states that, unlike Ionesco and Beckett,
"Pinter stresses the idea that language in its
daily, conversational use is illogical, or nonsensi-
cal, and frequently ritualistic. At this level it
often communicates by suggestion men's primitive
urges or biological impulses." In The Lover, The
Homecoming, and The Caretaker "Pinter reveals the
semantic uncertainty which underlies experience."

Thompson, Marjorie. "The Image of Youth in the Contemporary Theater." Modern Drama, 7 (1965), 443-45.
    In dealing with the concern of "young people and,
in particular, their predicament in the world to-
tay," Thompson alludes, in passing, to Pinter.

Thomson, Philip. The Grotesque. London: Eyre Methuen,
1972. Pages 29-32.

Thornton, Peter C. "Blindness and the Confrontation with
Death: Three Plays by Harold Pinter." Die Neueren
Sprachen, 17 (1968), 213-23.
    The Room, The Birthday Party, and A Slight Ache
deal with "the confrontation of a human being with
the object of his hidden or repressed fears, through
the increasingly subtle manipulation of the motif of
blindness." Our mortal nature is of concern in The
Room and A Slight Ache, our social nature in The
Birthday Party.

Trewin, John C. Drama in Britain, 1951-1965. London:
Longman, 1965. Pages 54-65.
    Trewin's evaluation of Pinter is generally hos-
tile. He finds his plays boring, repetitious, without substance.

_____. "Guessing Game." Illustrated London News, 4 July 1964, p. 28.

Trilling, Ossia. "The New English Realism." Tulane Drama Review, 7 (1962), 184-93.
Trilling notes Pinter's anti-establishment views, his anger with the class structure and with monolithic institutions (such as the military) which threaten human values.

_____. "The Young British Drama." Modern Drama, 3 (May 1960), 168.

Trussler, Simon. The Plays of Harold Pinter: An Assessment. London: Gollancz, 1973.
Trussler examines each of Pinter's works, major and minor, through Old Times. This is an extremely thorough study which includes a chronology and cast lists. He feels that Pinter is "a consummately skillful craftsman who has very little sense of his own art."

Tutaev, David. "The Theater of the Absurd . . . How Absurd?" Gambit, 2 (1968), 68-70.
Tutaev sees absurdism as a romantic, even sentimental, aberration which will be short-lived. He does not seem to connect the movement to existentialism.

Tynan, Kenneth. "Dramatists in Perspective. The Observer, 15 September 1963, p. 27.

_____. Tynan on Theatre. London, 1964.
Tynan was originally concerned over a certain paranoiac quality in Pinter's work, but he has become increasingly impressed with Pinter's stature and range.

Uhlmann, Wilfred. "Neurotische Konflikte und triebgesteuertes Sozialverhalten in den Stücken Harold Pinters." Literatur in Wissenschaft und Unterricht (Kiel), 5 (1972), 299-312.

Vamos, Laszlo and Gyorgy Lengyel. "Laszlo Vamos and Gyorgy Lengyel, Interviewed by Paul Neuberg." Transatlantic Review, 18 (Spring 1965), 107-15.
Vamos and Lengyel do not understand the current popularity of Pinter whom they consider decadent, needlessly obscure, and boring.

Verkein, Lea. "Van Broadway naar Piccadilly." Vlaamse Gids, 45 (July 1961), 492-95.
Brief description (in Flemish) of a number of productions in London, including The Caretaker.

179

Vidan, Ivo. "Komedija nespokojstva." _Forum_ (Zagreb), 9 (1963), 462-73.

Volker, Klaus. "Groteskformen des Theaters." _Akzente_, 4 (August 1960), 321-39.

Vos, Josef De. "Harold Pinter: Praten tegen het niets." _Ons Erfdeel_ (Rekkem), 16, iv (1973), 118.

Wager, Walter. "Harold Pinter." _The Playwrights Speak_. Ed. Walter Wager. New York: Delacorte, 1967. Pages 171-78.
     Wager provides excerpts from Lawrence Bensky interview in _The Paris Review_ (January 1967) to be reprinted in _Writer at Work_ as well.

Walker, Augusta. "Magnificent, Yes--and Now I Know Why." _Evening Standard_, 16 July 1964.

_____. "Messages from Pinter." _Modern Drama_, 10 (1967), 1-10.
     Walker believes that Pinter offers two levels of meaning in his plays. On one he dissects interpersonal relationships in a psychologically convincing manner; on the other he creates allegories of universal experience.

Wardle, Irving. "Comedy of Menace." In _The Encore Reader_. Ed. Charles Marowitz. London: Eyre Methuen, 1965. Pages 86-91. Reprinted from _Encore_, 5 (September-October 1958), 28-33.
     Nigel Dennis, David Compton, N. F. Simpson, and Pinter are writers of "comedies" as well as being "non-naturalists." Wardle comments on _The Birthday Party_: "It is in the relationships between the groups--not how they behave in isolation--that the play's farce resides."

_____. "Holding up the Mirror." _Twentieth Century_, 173 (Autumn 1964), 34-43.
     This is a general essay in which Pinter, among others, is pictured as a playwright attempting to shock audiences into an awareness of contemporary wrongs.

_____. "New Waves on the British Stage." _Twentieth Century_, 172 (Summer 1963), 57-65.
     Wardle pronounces Pinter one of the most significant and enduring new playwrights in England, who is contributing to the "vital development" of the theatre.

_____. "Revolt Against the West End." _Horizon_, 5, iii (1963), 26-33.
     See Osborne above.

_____. "There's Music in That Room." In The Encore
Reader. Ed. Charles Marowitz. London: Eyre
Methuen, 1965. Pages 129-32. Reprinted from Encore, 7 (July-August 1960), 32-34.
    Wardle adds another voice to those who admire the
poetic or musical quality of Pinter's language and
relate it to Chekhov's influence.

Warner, John M. "The Epistemological Quest in Pinter's
The Homecoming." Contemporary Literature, 11
(1970), 340-53.
    Warner notes that The Homecoming describes man's
plight in the godless world of science and reason.
Each character is concerned with "knowing," and
Warner analyzes them as archetypes: Max as "a degenerate patriarch" associated with "the sacred
meal," and Ruth, who "like her biblical namesake
. . . seeks a home among her husband's people."

Wellwarth, George. Teatro de Protesta y Paradoja.
Barcelona: Lumen, 1966.

_____. The Theatre of Protest and Paradox. New York:
New York University Press, 1964. Pages 197-211,
221, 233.
    Wellwarth connects Pinter with the absurdists.
He notes Pinter's extensive use of allusion and he
generally praises the writer's originality and pro-
fessionalism. Pinter has rebelled against pseudo-
realism and tired stage conventions.

Wendt, Ernst. "Burgerseelen und Randexistenzen: uber die
Dramatiker Harold Pinter und Franz Xavier Kroetz."
In Moderne Dramaturgie. Frankfurt, 1974. Pages 91-
117.

Williams, Raymond. "The Birthday Party: Harold Pinter."
In his Drama from Ibsen to Brecht. London: Chatto
and Windus, 1968. Pages 322-25.
    Williams feels that Pinter's plays represent the
"domestication, in an English idiom," of the world
of Kafka and Ionesco. He presents the normality of
everyday life without any significance: "a naturalism at once confirmed and emptied of content."

Winegarten, Renee. "The Anglo-Jewish Dramatist in Search
of His Soul." Midstream, 12, viii (1966), 40-52.
    See Wesker below.

Worsley, T. C. "A New Dramatist, or Two." New Statesman, 55 (1958), 692-94.
    This brief article is a prophetic notice of Pin-
ter's potential.

_____. "A New Wave Rules Britannia." Theatre Arts, 5
(October 1961), 17-19.
      Pinter among others has a key role in an impor-
tant dramatic renaissance.

Worth, Katherine J. "Harold Pinter." In Revolution in
   Modern English Drama. London, 1972. Pages 86-100.
      Worth writes that "Pinter is the conjuror who
comes into the realist tradition, takes over the
well-worn material . . . and works a dazzling trans-
formation act with it." While indebted to Beckett,
Pinter, with his interest in "the revelation of character," is even more Chekhovian, indebted as well to
Coward. "Quietness" and "secrecy" are key elements
in his plays; hence the appropriateness of the
"closed" situation. "Pinter's drama might be called
all sub-text . . . the action poised between inner
and outer reality," best demonstrated in his use of
ritual, akin to Eliot's.

Wray, Phoebe. "Pinter's Dialogue: The Play of Words."
   Modern Drama, 13, iv (1971), 418-22.
      Faced with the "devaluation" of words, Pinter,
like others, experiments with language. In a scene
from The Birthday Party, "language is distorted into
a non-language," while "The Homecoming is structured
by its language, its silences counterpointing non-
communicative language."

Wright, Ian. "Shooting the Caretaker." Manchester
   Guardian, 20 February 1963, p. 7.

Ziegler, Klaus. "Das moderne Drama als Spiegel unserer
   zeit." Der Deutschunterricht, 13 (1961), 5-24.

Zolotow, Maurice. "Young Man with Scorn." New York
   Times, 17 September 1961, II:1.

III. DISSERTATIONS

Ben-Zvi, Linda. "The Devaluation of Language in Avant-
   Garde Drama." Dissertation Abstracts International
   33:1158A (Oklahoma, 1972.)
      Ben-Zvi discusses "the collapse of discursive
language as a communicative tool" in the dramas of
Ionesco, Beckett, and Pinter, examining Pinter's
"Silence as Communication" and his "Poetry of
Imagery."

Brigg, Peter A. "The Understanding and Uses of Time in
   the Plays of John Boynton Priestly, Samuel Beckett,
   and Harold Pinter." Dissertation Abstracts International 32:6964A (Toronto, 1972).

182

Brigg writes: "Harold Pinter differs from Priestly and Beckett in being only peripherally aware
of time as a problem. The present is Pinter's main
sphere of action."

Burkman, Katherine. "The Dramatic World of Harold Pinter:
Its Basis in Ritual." Dissertation Abstracts International 30:434A (Ohio State, 1968).
  Burkman applies "myth criticism" to Pinter, using
Frazer for a "metaphorical clue" to Pinter's "vic-
tim-victors" who are threatened, first externally,
then internally. Pinter's women become fertility
goddesses.

Canny, Mildred R. "Patterns of Human Interaction in the
Plays of Harold Pinter." Dissertation Abstracts International 31:6204A (Wisconsin, 1970).
  "To create an understanding of the fusion of
realistic and poetic qualities" in Pinter, Canny
examines "the patterns of characters' interactions
in the sixteen published stage plays [proving] that
they are organically structured in that each unit of
character interaction functions both as an individual transaction in a developing human relationship
and as an image of the completed dramatic form."
Canny desires "to integrate the seemingly desparate
details of Pinter's drama."

Conlon, Patrick O. "Social Commentary in Contemporary
Great Britain, as Reflected in the Plays of John
Osborne, Harold Pinter, and Arnold Wesker." Dissertation Abstracts International 29:3713A (Northwestern, 1969).
  Conlon notes: "Pinter's works, discussed in
Chapter IV, portray the contemporary Briton's piti-
ful defenses against a suffocating world of violence
and frustration."

Dillon, Perry C. "The Characteristics of the French Theatre of the Absurd in the Plays of Edward Albee and
Harold Pinter." Dissertation Abstracts International 29:257A (Arkansas, 1968).
  Dillon states: "Harold Pinter's plays, like
Albee's, tend to become progressively more realistic,
but he is closer to French Absurdists than Albee."
Dillon discusses Pinter's use of mise en scène, dialogue, character, and themes as Absurdist.

Dohmen, William F. "Possession of People or the Past:
Competition for Dominance in Pinter's Recent Drama."
Dissertation Abstracts International 34:5165A (Vir-
ginia, 1974).
  Dohmen has written a study of "battle for posi-
tions . . . the question of dominance and subser-

vience," as Pinter put it. "The territorial struggle" in early plays is well documented, "but inadequate attention has been given to their more recent
forms."

Elliot, Susan M. "Fantasy behind Play: A Study of Emotional Responses to Harold Pinter's The Birthday
Party, The Caretaker, and The Homecoming." Dissertation Abstracts International 34:5963A (Indiana,
1974).
    Elliot has studied the effect of Pinter's plays
on audiences and critics and has gained insights into human behavior as well as Pinter's dramatic techniques.

Feldstein, Elayne P. "The Evolution of the Characters of
Harold Pinter." Dissertation Abstracts International 36:7748 (New York University, 1974).
    This is a sophisticated study of Pinter's charac-
ters, noting his growing power to create personality
with subtle phrasing, gestures, pauses.

Fields, Suzanne. "Levels of Meaning in Structural Patterns of Allegory and Realism in Selected Plays of
Harold Pinter." Dissertation Abstracts International 32:2087A (Catholic University, 1971).
    Fields analyzes The Room, The Birthday Party, The
Dumb Waiter, The Caretaker, A Slight Ache, demonstrating that Pinter is "a traditional playwright,
and the antecedents for the specific plays under
discussion relate to traditions of medieval allegory
and Chekhovian realism."

Flakes, Nanette S.B. "Aesthetics of Modern Play Direction: Non-Realistic Drama from Pirandello to Pinter." Dissertation Abstracts International 34:896A
(Minnesota, 1973).
    Flakes applies "the elements of the new aesthet-
ics and the director's use of them" to plays, "developing the progress of non-realistic drama from
Pirandello . . . to Pinter as a progress toward a
more exclusive use of aesthetics."

Gale, Steven H. "Thematic Change in the Stage Plays of
Harold Pinter." Dissertation Abstracts International 31:3546A (Southern California, 1970).
    Gale believes Pinter writes a cluster of plays
around a single theme, then moves on to incorporate
earlier ideas into new areas of exploration.

Garber, Stephen M. "Open and Closed Sequences in the
Plays of Harold Pinter." Dissertation Abstracts
International 34:312A (Illinois: Urbana-Champaign,
1973).

Garber notes: "The plays of Harold Pinter through .The Homecoming show him developing from a writer of open sequences to a writer of closed sequences." Sequence is defined as "the viewer perceiving the materials in a specific, predetermined order," while closed means "the artist has defined completely within the limits of his work the relationships which exist between all the work's parts."

Hancock, Jim R. "The Use of Time by Absurdist Playwrights: Ionesco, Genet, and Pinter." Dissertation Abstracts International 33:5876A (Minnesota, 1973).
    This is a study of the use of time by absurdists in which all share seven aspects of treating time.

Herin, Miriam M. "An Analysis of Harold Pinter's Use of Language as Seen in The Birthday Party, The Caretaker, The Homecoming, and Old Times." Dissertation Abstracts International 34:1913A (South Carolina, 1973).
    Herin writes: "At the center of our modern crisis lies a failure of language, i.e., the inability of language to apprehend the essence of experience or to communicate that essence." Pinter's dialogue recreates modern "estrangement and non-communication," while his "technical devices and linguistic experiments" make the theatre "speak to our times."

Higgins, David M. "Existential Valuation in Five Contemporary Plays." Dissertation Abstracts International 32:4612A (Bowling Green, 1972).
    Higgins has analyzed "the problems and consequences of existential valuation" in Genet's The Balcony, Beckett's Waiting for Godot, Pinter's The Homecoming, Miller's The Price, and Albee's Box-Mao-Box. "In the section on The Homecoming, which centered upon mind-body dissociation, it was found that the unity, surety, and metaphysical structure suggested by the honorific term, 'home,' were illusory."

Hunt, Joseph A. "Interaction Process Analysis of Harold Pinter's The Homecoming: Toward a Phenomenological Criticism of Drama." Dissertation Abstracts International 32:4159A (New Mexico, 1972).
    Hunt devises a new critical approach to drama, based on "the field of social-psychology, specifically to Robert Hales' . . . 'Interaction Process Analysis.' . . . The play was analyzed into over 3,000 unit acts--both verbal and non-verbal--and each act was scored according to its process content (...) and according to who initiated the act and who received it. . . . The results are tabulated by computer and schematic diagrams . . . are drawn. . . . The critic is able to examine relational pat-

185

terns among the characters."

Jennings, Ann S. "The Reactions of London's Drama Crit-
     ics to Certain Plays by Henrik Ibsen, Harold Pinter
     and Edward Bond." Dissertation Abstracts Interna-
     tional 34:2067A (Florida State, 1973).
         Jennings analyzes The Birthday Party, The Care-
     taker, and The Homecoming to demonstrate "the pro-
     cess by which plays that are initially rejected by
     drama critics become standard dramas within a cul-
     ture." See Bond above.

Jones, Paul D. "The Intruder in the Drama of Harold
     Pinter: A Functional Analysis." Dissertation Ab-
     stracts International 32:4758A (Syracuse, 1972).
         Jones groups fifteen plays and five revue sketch-
     es according to their use of the intruder motif:
     "Mystery-Mystification, Cyclical-Circular, Menace-
     Threat, Escape-Frustration, and Fantasy-Memory."

Pease, Nicholas B. "Role, Ritual and Game in the Plays
     of Harold Pinter." Dissertation Abstracts Interna-
     tional 32:3324A (Southern California, 1971).
         Using Interaction Ritual, by Erving Goffman, and
     Games People Play,by Eric Berne, Pease "concentrates
     on the premise that character is situationally de-
     fined," that, rather than "archetypal or Freudian
     images . . . a struggle for dominance in personal re-
     lationships" is the key to Pinter's symbolism.

Pierce, Roger N. "Three Play Analyses." Dissertation
     Abstracts International 30:2660A (Iowa, 1970).
         Pierce analyzes Chekhov's Three Sisters, Buchner's
     Woyzeck, and Pinter's The Homecoming. He uses the
     "principle of hierarchy" on Pinter, an attempt to
     "perceive how it (speech) functions in each of the
     larger wholes such as scenes, acts, etc.," conclud-
     ing that the "basic plot is the rebirth in Ruth of
     Max's dead wife Jessie."

Prentice, Penelope A. "An Analysis of Dominance and Sub-
     servience as Technique and Theme in the Plays of
     Harold Pinter." Dissertation Abstracts International
     32:7000A (Loyola: Chicago, 1972).
         The Dumb Waiter is closely analyzed by Prentice
     for its revelation of themes of "dominance and sub-
     servience," followed by The Birthday Party, The Room,
     Landscape, Silence, and Night. Prentice believes that
     "if man strives for dominance . . . he is sure to de-
     stroy the possibility of fruitful relations and ul-
     timately himself."

Powlick, Leonard. "The Terror of Temporality: The Phe-
nomenology of Change in Six Early Plays of Harold
Pinter." Dissertation Abstracts International
35:1668A (Pittsburgh, 1974).
   Powlick examines The Room, The Birthday Party, A
Night Out, A Slight Ache, Tea Party, and The Dwarfs.
"The plays are a projection of the consciousness of
the characters within the plays. . . . In each case,
the character has become aware of his temporality
. . . forced to accept the fact of his temporal
change. In existential terms, the character is
forced to surrender his familiar identity in order
to take on a new one."

Quigley, Austin E. "The Dynamics of Dialogue: The Plays
of Harold Pinter." Dissertation Abstracts International 33:6928A (California: Santa Cruz, 1973).
   To resolve critical disputes over Pinter's work,
Quigley discovers "an erroneous theoretical position
(...) to be implicit in many of the critical approaches." Analyzing The Room, The Caretaker, and
Landscape, he discovers critics have "an inadequate
understanding of the complexity of linguistic meaning."

Rogers, Rodney O. "Harold Pinter: Essays on the Meta-
physics of His Theatre." Dissertation Abstracts International 35:2295A (Virginia, 1974).
   Rogers states: "Three related essays elucidate a
single thesis: Pinter's drama illustrates . . . the
idea that man by the very nature of the human condi-
tion is metaphysically isolated from the world he
must inhabit."

Rusinko, Susan. "Stratagems of Language in the Poems and
Plays of Harold Pinter: A Study of Text, Sub-Text,
and Conscious Sub-Test." Dissertation Abstracts International 32:6451A (Pennsylvania State, 1972).
   According to Rusinko, "In this study, overt silences are considered as text, unspoken silences as
sub-text, and the continued reference or irrevocable
word as conscious sub-text," three divisions based
on Pinter's statements. "This study is concerned
with the nature and function of the language techniques" of Pinter.

Sanders, Walter E. "The English-Speaking Game-Drama."
Dissertation Abstracts International 30:5001A
(Northwestern, 1970).
   Sanders asserts that Beckett, Albee, and Pinter
"are game-dramatists in the sense of using game as
the central principle of both structure and theme of
their plays." Sanders looks at The Birthday Party
and The Homecoming.

Schneider, Ruth M. "The Interpolated Narrative in Modern Drama." Dissertation Abstracts International 34: 6605A (S.U.N.Y.: Albany, 1974).
See Hampton above.

Stephens, Suzanne S. "The Dual Influence: A Dramaturgical Study of the Plays of Edward Albee and the Specific Dramatic Forms and Themes Which Influence Them." Dissertation Abstracts International 34:342A (Miami, 1973).
According to Stephens, "Chapter three is devoted to a study of plays by Ionesco, Beckett, and Pinter in order to illustrate the technical methods used by absurdist playwrights to embody their peculiar philosophies."

Talley, Mary E. "The Relationship of Theme and Technique in Plays of Harold Pinter." Dissertation Abstracts International 33:1744A (Vanderbilt, 1972).
Talley studies "the correspondence between the thematic emphasis of Pinter's work and the design of his dramatic technique" in The Room, A Slight Ache, The Birthday Party, The Caretaker, and The Homecoming. The thematic emphasis is "the liberation which accompanies confrontation with the "unknown,'" and is paralleled in Pinter's denial of "verification" via characterization, symbol, and language.

Towey, Denis J. "Form and Content in Selected Plays of Harold Pinter." Dissertation Abstracts International 34:3609A (New York University, 1973).
Towey examines The Dumb Waiter, The Homecoming, Silence, Old Times, concluding that "for the most part Pinter's work grows in its realization of the capabilities of form. Contents increasingly have little life outside of the plays. . . ."

Wagner, Marlene S. "The Game-Play in Twentieth-Century Absurdist Drama: Studies in a Dramatic Technique." Dissertation Abstracts International 32:4637A (Southern California, 1972).
Wagner examines Albee, Beckett, Genet, and Pinter, using Schechner's Tulane Drama Review (Summer 1966) article on drama as "a performance activity" and Berne's Games People Play on the nature of "games" for theoretical basis. The Collection, The Lover, The Basement "center around games of evasion and . . . illustrate the necessity for deceptiveness (...) in order to maintain human relationships."

Wycisk, Max M. "Language and Silence in the Stage Plays of Samuel Beckett and Harold Pinter." Dissertation Abstracts International 33:4442A (Colorado, 1973).

Wycisk contrasts and compares the use of language and silence in Pinter and Beckett, finding "Pinter's plays are characterized by conflict, often purely linguistic conflict, while Beckett's move in a world in which language is completely divorced from action."

IV. REVIEWS

THE BASEMENT

The Times, 21 February 1967, p. 8.

Sunday Times, 26 February 1967, p. 50.

BIRTHDAY PARTY

The Times, 20 May 1958, p. 3.

Sunday Times, 25 May 1958, p. 11.

Sunday Times, 15 June 1958, p. 11.

The Times, 23 March 1960, p. 16.

Sunday Times, 27 March 1960, p. 23.

Sunday Times, 24 July 1960, p. 31.

The Times, 19 June 1964, p. 18.

Sunday Times, 21 June 1964, p. 33.

New York Times, 1 October 1967, II:1.

New York Times, 4 October 1967, p. 40.

New York Times, 15 October 1967, II:1.

New York Times, 17 January 1968, p. 39.

The Times, 21 May 1970, p. 11.

THE CARETAKER

The Times, 31 May 1960, p. 4.

Sunday Times, 5 June 1960, p. 25.

New York Times, 15 October 1961, II:1.

New York Times, 31 January 1964, p. 16.

The Times, 26 October 1966, p. 14

The Times, 3 March 1972, p. 11.

The Times, 9 November 1973, p. 17.

THE COLLECTION

The Times, 12 May 1961, p. 19.

Sunday Times, 14 May 1961, p. 48.

Sunday Times, 17 June 1962, p. 44.

Sunday Times, 24 June 1962, p. 35.

New York Times, 27 November 1962, p. 44.

New York Times, 9 December 1962, II:5.

THE DUMB WAITER

The Times, 22 January 1960, p. 6 [With The Room.]

The Times, 9 March 1960, p. 4. [With The Room.]

The Times, 11 August 1961, p. 11. [With The Room.]

Sunday Times, 13 August 1961, p. 32. [With The Room.]

New York Times, 9 December 1962, II:5.

Sunday Times, 16 December 1973, p. 36.

THE DWARFS

The Times, 3 December 1960, p. 10.

Sunday Times, 25 December 1960, p. 32.

New York Times, 29 January 1968, p. 63.

The Times, 18 July 1972, p. 11.

THE HOMECOMING

The Times, 4 June 1965, p. 15.

New York Times, 4 June 1965, p. 38.

New York Times, 6 January 1967, p. 29.

New York Times, 26 February 1967, II:8.

The Times, 26 April 1968, p. 9.

New York Times, 13 July 1969, II:8.

LANDSCAPE

Sunday Times, 28 April 1968, p. 53.

The Times, 18 October 1973, p. 17.

The Times, 3 July 1969, p. 13. [With Silence.]

The Times, 4 July 1969, p. 7. [With Silence.]

Sunday Times, 6 July 1969, p. 52. [With Silence.]

New York Times, 13 July 1969, II:8. [With Silence.]

New York Times, 25 July 1969, p. 34. [With Silence.]

New York Times, 3 April 1970, p. 43. [With Silence.]

New York Times, 12 April 1970, II:3. [With Silence.]

THE LOVER

The Times, 29 March 1963, p. 15.

Sunday Times, 31 March 1963, p. 39.

New York Times, 6 January 1964, p. 35.

A NIGHT OUT

The Times, 2 March 1960, p. 130.

The Times, 25 April 1960, p. 160.

The Times, 22 July 1960, p. 16.

THE ROOM

New York Times, 17 June 1965, p. 24.

New York Times, 13 July 1969, II:8.

A SLIGHT ACHE

The Times, 30 July 1959, p. 8.

Sunday Times, 2 August 1959, p. 14.

The Times, 19 January 1961, p. 16.

Sunday Times, January 22, 1961, p. 33.

New York Times, 17 June 1965, p. 24.

The Times, 26 April 1973, p. 14.

The Times, 18 October 1973, p. 17.

Sunday Times, 21 October 1973, p. 27.

New York Times, 10 December 1964, p. 62. [With The
    Room.]

TEA PARTY

The Times, 26 March 1965, p. 15.

Sunday Times, 28 March 1965, p. 26.

New York Times, 16 October 1968, p. 40. [With The
    Basement.]

New York Times, 3 November 1968, II:7. [With The
    Basement.]

The Times, 18 September 1970, p. 6. [With The Base-
    ment.]

ANTHONY SHAFFER

Born Liverpool, Lancashire, May 15, 1926.

Anthony Shaffer, identical twin of Peter Shaffer, shares with his brother an interest in well-constructed, carefully plotted, yet highly theatrical plays. Sleuth is Anthony Shaffer's most unqualified success to date. In it two male protagonists, a detective writer and his prey, become involved in a struggle-to-the-death game playing. On the surface a polished whodunit, Sleuth is, in fact, a kind of metaphor for the relationship of the actor to his audience. The suspense of the play is most intense when the audience is aware of being manipulated by the playwright and the actors.

PRIMARY SOURCES

I. STAGE

The Savage Parade. Staged London 1963.

Sleuth. Staged London and New York 1970. New York: Dodd, Mead, 1970.

_____. London: Calder and Boyars, 1971.

Murderer. Staged London 1976.

II. FILM

Black Comedy, 1970

Fourbush and the Penguins, 1970.

Frenzy, 1972.

Play with a Gypsy, 1970.

III. TELEVISION

Pig in the Middle.

IV. FICTION

How Doth the Crocodile? with Peter Shaffer (as Peter
    Anthony). London: Evans, 1961.

_____, with Peter Shaffer. New York: Macmillan, 1957.

Withered Murder, with Peter Shaffer. London: Gollancz,
    1955.

_____, with Peter Shaffer. New York: Macmillan, 1956.

Woman in the Wardrobe, with Peter Shaffer (as Peter
    Anthony). London: Evans, 1952.

SECONARY SOURCES

I. CRITICISM

"Death of a Bloodsport." Harper's Bazaar, November 1970,
    p. 22.

Glenn, J. "Anthony and Peter Shaffer's Plays: The Influ-
    ence of Twinship on Creativity." American Imago, 31
    (Fall 1974), 270-92.
        Glenn analyzes Equus, "confirm[ing] that the two
    main characters interact like and display the traits
    of twins." He finds "similar situations" in White
    Lies, The White Liars, and The Public Eye. Glenn's
    analysis deals with "the unconscious meaning to the
    author" and "how this may differ from his conscious
    intent," forcing him to adapt established forms and
    conventional public symbols to his own use." "It is
    quite likely that many people who watch the plays
    . . . react to the author's latent imagery. . . .
    Their wish to possess a twin is rekindled . . . .
    The disguised oedipal underlay, putting the rivalry
    in a more tolerable form."

_____. "Twins in Disguise: A psychoanalytic essay on
    Sleuth and the Royal Hunt of the Sun." Psychoana-
    lytic Quarterly, 43 (1974), 288-302.
        Thematically this article emphasizes the same
    theories of twinship and their relationship to the
    Shaffer brothers' plays that Glenn discusses in the
    article above. Here with slightly more technical
    language Glenn uses Sleuth and Royal Hunt as the

194

starting point for his analysis, demonstrating that in each play two male protagonists, each a half-person, maintain a tense, love-hate relationship.

Kennedy, Veronica. "A Possible Source for the Opening of Sleuth." Armchair Detective, 7 (1974), 175.

Taylor, J. R. "The Legacy of Realism." In The Second Wave. New York: Hill and Wang, 1971. Pages 199-200.
  Taylor gives very brief notice to Sleuth, which he describes without great conviction as a commercial success and a tour de force.

II. REVIEWS

SLEUTH

   The Times, 13 February 1970, p. 15

   New York Times, 13 November 1970, p. 25.

   New York Times, 22 November 1970, II:18.

   New York Times, 16 October 1971, p. 23.

   New York Times, 26 September 1972, p. 43.

PETER SHAFFER

Born Liverpool, Lancashire, May 15, 1926

Like his twin brother Anthony, Peter Shaffer creates
plays in which two male characters exist in a symbiotic
relationship. He, too, seems to view all life in terms
of theatrical motifs. Although Peter Shaffer is better
known and a more prolific playwright, the talents and
achievements of the brothers are comparable. They both
have the facility to delight theatre audiences with a
virtually bottomless bag of theatre tricks; at the same
time their ideas are serious and involving. Equus may
well be one of the most popular plays to come out of the
whole dramatic movement. In it the inherently dramatic
nature of psychotherapy is explored and the stage becomes
a space for healing the modern psyche. Furthermore,
Equus explores the conflict between the Apollonian and
Dionysian views of art in a way that calls to mind a
whole history of western theatre.

PRIMARY SOURCES

I. STAGE

The Battle of Shrivings. Staged London 1970.

Black Comedy. Staged Chichester 1965; London 1966; New
    York 1967. Included in Black Comedy, Including
    White Lies. London: Samuel French, 1967.

_____, Including White Lies: Two Plays. New York: Stein
    and Day, 1967. As The White Liars, Black Comedy:
    Two Plays. London: Hamish Hamilton, 1968.

_____. The Best Plays of 1966-1967. Ed. Otis L. Guern-
    sey, Jr. New York: Dodd Mead, 1967.

_____. Plays and Players, 15 (April 1968).

_____. Adapted by Barillet and Gredy. L'Avant Scene,
    397 (February 1968).

197

_____. Modern Short Comedies from Broadway and London. Ed. Stanley Richards. New York: Random House, 1970.

Equus; a play. Staged London 1973; New York 1975. London: Deutsch, 1973.

_____; and, Shrivings; 2 plays. New York: Atheneum, 1974.

Sketch in The Establishment. Staged New York 1963.

Five Finger Exercise. Staged London 1958; New York 1959. London: Hamish Hamilton, 1958.

_____. Toronto: William Collins, 1958.

_____. New York: Harcourt Brace, 1959.

_____. The Best Plays of 1959-1960. Ed. Louis Kronenberger. New York: Dodd, Mead, 1961.

_____. Theatre Arts, 45 (February 1961), 27-56.

_____. Three Plays. London: Penguin Books, Harmondsworth, 1968.

_____. Great Scenes from the World Theater. Ed. James L. Steffensen, Jr. New York: Discus Books, 1968.

It's about Cinderella. Staged London 1969.

The Merry Roosters Panto, with the Theatre Workshop. Staged London 1963.

The Private Ear and the Public Eye. Staged London 1962; New York 1963. London: Hamish Hamilton, 1962.

_____. New York: Stein and Day, 1964.

L'Oeil Anonyme. Adapted by Barillet and Gredy. L'Avant Scene, 397 (February 1968).

The Royal Hunt of the Sun; a drama in 2 acts (acting ed.). New York; Samuel French, 1964.

_____. Plays and Players. Ed. Clive Barnes. Vol. 11, no. 4. London: Hansom Books, 1964.

_____: A Play Concerning the Conquest of Peru. Staged Chichester and London 1964; New York 1965. London: Hamish Hamilton, 1965.

_____. New York: Stein and Day, 1965.

_____. New York: William Collins, 1965.

_____. London: Longmans, 1966.

_____. Plays of the Sixties, Vol. I. Ed. J. M. Charlton. London: Pan Books, 1966.

_____. The Best Plays of 1965-1966. Ed. Otis L. Guernsey, Jr. New York: Dodd, Mead, 1966.

_____. Literary Cavalcade. Ed. Jerome Brondfield. New York: Scholastic Magazines, Inc.

Shriving; a play in 3 acts. London: Deutsch, 1974.

A Warning Game. Staged New York 1967.

The White Lies/Black Comedy. Plays and Players 1966-1969. London: Plays and Players, 1969.

White Lies. Staged New York 1967. Included in Black Comedy Including White Lies, 1967; as The White Liars. Staged London 1968. London: Samuel French, 1967.

The White Liars. Plays and Players, 15 (April 1968).

_____. Best Short Plays of the World Theatre, 1958-67. Ed. Stanley Richards. New York: Crown, 1968.

II. FILM

Follow Me! 1972.

Lord of the Flies, with Peter Brook, 1963.

The Pad (and How to Use It), 1966.

III. RADIO

The Prodigal Father, 1957.

IV. TELEVISION

The Balance of Terror, 1957.

The Salt Land, 1955.

V. FICTION

How Doth the Little Crocodile? With Anthony Shaffer (as
   Peter Anthony). London: Evans, 1951.

_____. With Anthony Shaffer. New York: Macmillan,
   1957.

Withered Murder. With Anthony Shaffer. London: Gollancz, 1955.

_____. With Anthony Shaffer. New York: Macmillan, 1956.

Woman in the Wardrobe. With Anthony Shaffer (as Peter
   Anthony). London: Evans, 1952.

VI. NON-FICTION

Shaffer and Peter Hall, Peter Brook, and Michel St.-Denis.
   "Artaud for Artaud's Sake." [A discussion.] Encore,
   11 (May-June 1964), 20-31.

[About Equus]. Vogue, February 1975, pp. 136-37.

Shaffer, Peter. "Cannibal Theater." Atlantic, October
   1960, pp. 48-50.

"Gilbert's Insubstantial World." Time and Tide, 5 April
   1962, p. 25.

"Labels Aren't for Playwrights." Theatre Arts, February
   1960, pp. 20-23.

"Liszt's Embryonic Inventions: Faust Symphony." Time
   and Tide, 12 April 1962, p. 24.

"The Pity Was Distilled: War Requiem." Time and Tide, 7
   June 1962, pp. 23-24.

"Rituals at the G and S Club." Time and Tide, 4 January
   1962, p. 28.

"What We Owe Britten." Sunday Times, 18 November 1973,
   p. 35.

VII. INTERVIEW

Pree, Barry. "Peter Shaffer, Interviewed by Barry Pree."
   Transatlantic Review, 14 (Autumn 1963), 62-66.
      Shaffer discusses Five Finger Exercise, Private
   Ear and Public Eye, Royal Hunt (which was not yet
   produced), his place within modern theatre and

playwrights, and his views on the creation of theatre.

SECONDARY SOURCES

I. CRITICISM

Brustein, Robert. The Third Theatre. London: Jonathan
    Cape, 1969.
        In "Peru in N.Y." Brustein is dismayed by New
    York's "reproduction" of London's Royal Hunt. "Un-
    derneath the tumult and the swirl lie a very conven-
    tional set of liberal notions about the noble savage
    . . . . By the end of the play, in fact, the whole
    brutal struggle has degenerated into a fraternal
    romance between a lissome young redskin and an aging
    lonely paleface . . . , a relationship which is il-
    luminated less by Artaud than by Leslie Fiedler."

Buckley, T. "Write Me, Said the Play to Peter Shaffer."
    New York Times Magazine, 13 April 1975, pp. 20-21.
        Buckley reports on an extended interview he had
    with Shaffer concerning Equus. He recounts Shaffer's
    description of the writing of Equus--the problem he
    had with character portrayal. Giving a plot summary,
    Buckley then describes the production history. He
    reports on the psychoanalytic community's reaction.
    A history of Shaffer's career concludes with his
    discussing his LSD trips and his "many contradictory
    selves."

Downer, Alan. "Total Theatre and Partial Drama: Notes
    on the New York Theatre, 1965-66." Quarterly Jour-
    nal of Speech, 52 (October 1966), 225-36.
        Downer surveys a number of plays in addition to
    Shaffer's, seeing Weiss' Marat/Sade as perhaps its
    closest analogue in "total theatre." With a good
    deal of plot summary, Downer views Pizarro "as an
    old man . . . permitted, with superb irony, to re-
    cover both his capacity to dream and to feel at the
    climax of the most cynical act of his life."

Glenn, Jules. "Anthony and Peter Shaffer's Plays: The
    Influence of Twinship on Creativity." American
    Imago, 31 (Fall 1974), 270-92. See Anthony Shaffer
    above.

Glenn, J. "Twins in Disguise: A psychoanalytic essay on
    Sleuth and The Royal Hunt of the Sun. Psychoanalyt-
    ic Quarterly, 43 (1974), 288-302.
        See Anthony Shaffer, above.

Hayman, Ronald. "Like a Woman They Keep Going Back to." Drama, 98 (Autumn 1970), 57-64.
  Hayman discusses Mortimer, Shaffer, and Bolt as a group whose "careers can be seen in terms of oscillation between the same extremes . . . for all of them, Naturalism has been like a woman they could neither marry nor abandon." Hayman looks briefly (one paragraph each) at Black Comedy, Five Finger Exercise, Private Ear and Public Eye, focusing on Royal Hunt, which was "seriously overrated." He thinks Shaffer's "courage in jettisoning naturalism admirable," but views Royal Hunt as disunified.

New York Times, 13 April 1975, VI:20.

Nightingale, Benedict. "Some Immortal Business." New Statesman, 13 February 1970, p. 227.
  In a sarcastic fablesque style, Nightingale attacks Shaffer's The Battle of Shrivings as "the worst play since Tiny Alice." Shaffer's "mistake was to make a debate and polemic, anti-Catholic, indeed anti-Sky and pro-Earth, of implications that could have lain doggo within . . . Royal Hunt." While Black Comedy is "one of the funniest farces in the language," the rest of Shaffer's early plays are simplistically divided "into Them and Us."

Pennel, Charles. "The Plays of Peter Shaffer: Experiment in Convention." Kansas Quarterly, 3 (1971), 100-09.
  Pennel feels critics do not take Shaffer seriously enough, that Shaffer "makes conventional theatrical devices serve his unconventional purpose," and that, duped by "the smooth, realistic surface," critics ignore the "real drama." Pennel examined Five Finger Exercise, Private Ear and Public Eye, and Royal Hunt to prove his point.

"Playwrights Twisty Road Toward Success." Life, 21 March 1960, p. 97.

Salem, Daniel. La Révolution Théâtrale Actuelle en Angleterre. Paris: Denoël, 1969. Pages 131, 132-35, 175.
  Salem offers a brief survey of Shaffer's work with plot summaries of Five Finger Exercise and Royal Hunt of the Sun.

"Showman Shaffer." Time, 11 November 1974, p. 117.

Simons, Piet. "Equus: Verslag van een beleving." Ons Erfdeel (Rekkem), 18, i. 125-26. [In Dutch.]
  Simons concentrates on Shaffer's deft exploitation of the illusion and reality theme in the theatre. The psychiatrist is a conjurer who can help Alan bring his fantasy world to life.

Taylor, John Russell. "Peter Shaffer." In Anger and
    After. London: Eyre Methuen, 1962. Pages 227-30.
    Taylor offers an introduction to Shaffer's work
    and analyzes Five Finger Exercise, which he calls
    psychologically penetrating and "theatrical in the
    best possible sense."

_____. Peter Shaffer. Harlow: Longman, 1974. 34 pp.
    One of the brief Longman series biographies,
    competently handled by Taylor, who also provides
    plot summaries of Shaffer's plays and critical reac-
    tions to them.

Vandenbrouke, Russell. "Equus: Modern Myth in the Mak-
    ing." Danske Folkemaal (Copenhagen), 12, 129-33.

Webb, Wil. "Committed to Nothing but the Theatre."
    Guardian, 27 August 1959, p. 4.

Winegarten, Renee. "The Anglo-Jewish Dramatist in Search
    of His Soul." Midstream, 12 (October 1966), 40-52.
    Winegarten discusses Pinter and Shaffer as "Anglo-
    Jewish dramatists," finding their "Anglo-Jewish sen-
    sibility" limited. Shaffer's Royal Hunt, indebted
    to Artaud, has as its main concern the hypocrisy of
    Christians--"always likely to arouse the atavist in
    the Jewish writer"--although "the play is not spe-
    cifically anti-Christian so much as against all or-
    ganized religion."

Wulf, Herwig. "Peter Shaffer: Five Finger Exercise
    (1958)," in Fehse, Klaus-Dieter and Norbert Platz,
    eds. Das zeitgenössiche englische Drama: Einfuhrung,
    Interpretation, Dokumentation. Frankfurt: Athenäum,
    1975. Pages 71-85.
    Wulf reevaluates criticism on Shaffer, explores
    his brilliant theatricality and his psychological
    insights.

II. DISSERTATIONS

Lawson, Wayne P. "The Dramatic Hunt: A Critical Evalua-
    tion of Peter Shaffer's Plays." Dissertation Ab-
    stracts International, 34:7374A-75A. Ohio State
    University, 1974.
    Lawson calls Five Finger Exercise a successful
    "well made play." The Public Eye, The Private Ear,
    Black Comedy, and White Lies he praises for Shaf-
    fer's "use of farce and his excellent dialogue and
    character development." The Royal Hunt he calls
    "total theatre," and Shrivings "A commercial and
    dramatic failure." He concludes: "Peter Shaffer
    [is] a playwright who refuses to be labelled."

Mitch, Albert. "A Study of Three British Dramas Depict-
    ing the Conquest of Peru." Dissertation Abstracts
    International, 30:4595A-6A. Northwestern University,
    1969.
        Mitch analyzes Davenat, Sheridan, and Shaffer,
    concluding that, while superior to its analogues,
    Royal Hunt "follows the traditional bias of present-
    ing the Peruvians as persecuted innocents and the
    Spaniards as bloodthirsty and rapacious." "These
    three plays appear to reflect a similar conviction
    that the story of the conquest should utilize all
    the technical resources of theatre." Pizarro's dif-
    fering presentation is also analyzed.

III. REVIEWS

BATTLE OF SHRIVINGS

    New York Times, 7 February 1970, p. 23.

BLACK COMEDY

    New York Times, 29 July 1965, p. 19.

    New York Times, 13 February 1967, p. 42.

    New York Times, 26 February 1967, II:1.

EQUUS

    New York Times, 17 August 1973, p. 11.

    New York Times, 2 September 1973, II:1.

    Harper's Bazaar, October 1974, p. 133.

    New York Times, 25 October 1974, p. 26.

    New York Times, 3 November 1974, II:1.

    Newsweek, 4 November 1974, p. 60.

    New Yorker, 4 November 1974, p. 123.

    Time, 4 November 1974, p. 119.

    Newsweek, 11 November 1974, p. 121.

    Nation, 16 November 1974, pp. 506-07.

    America, 30 November 1974, p. 349.

    New Republic, 7 December 1974, p. 18+.

New York Times, 15 December 1974, II:1.

Saturday Review, 25 January 1975, pp. 2, 54.

National Review, 31 January 1975, pp. 114-15.

Commentary, February 1975, pp. 77-78.

Vogue, February 1975, pp. 136-37.

Sports Illustrated, 3 March 1975, p. 9.

New York Times Magazine, 13 April 1975, pp. 20-21.

Commonweal, 25 April 1975, pp. 78-79.

Dance Magazine, May 1975, pp. 48-50.

Newsweek, 8 March 1976, p. 70.

FIVE FINGER EXERCISE

New York Times, 3 December 1959, p. 45.

New York Times, 13 December 1959, II:3.

THE PRIVATE EAR

New York Times, 10 October 1963, p. 51.

THE PUBLIC EYE

New York Times, 10 October 1963, p. 51.

THE ROYAL HUNT OF THE SUN

New York Times, 8 July 1964, p. 40.

Illustrated London News, 8 August 1964, p. 208.

Encounter, 23 (September 1964), 50.

London Magazine, 4 (October 1964), 60-65.

Encore, 12 (March-April 1965), 44-45.

New York Times, 27 October 1965, p. 36.

New York Times, 14 November 1965, II:1.

WHITE LIES

New York Times, 13 February 1967, p. 42.

New York Times, 26 February 1967, II:1.

N. F. SIMPSON

Born London, January 29, 1919

N. F. Simpson (N.[orman] F.[rederick] Simpson) is
the oldest playwright included in this book. He was a
schoolteacher by profession long before he became a playwright and was middle-aged when in 1956 he shared third
prize with Ann Jellicoe and Richard Beynon in a playwriting competition. His characters, situation, and comic
techniques all seem very English, but his basic method of
composition and his philosophy are more akin to the
French absurdists' approach than to other English New
Wave writers. Still, a rumbling anger underscores the
sometimes bitter humor, and an obsession with the arbi-
trary class divisions and traditions of his country
determine to some extent his heavy reliance on the non
sequitur. He is important because he related England to
the continent's absurdist movement and contributed to the
range of Royal Court's repertory and the vitality of the
movement in its early years.

PRIMARY SOURCES

I. STAGE

Always or More. Staged London 1961.

Can You Hear Me? In One to Another by N. F. Simpson,
    John Mortimer, and Harold Pinter. London, 1960.

The Cresta Run. Staged London 1965. London: Faber and
    Faber, 1966; New York: Grove Press, 1967.

_____. In Plays and Players Plays, 1966-1969. London,
    1969.

The Form. Staged London 1961. Acting edition. London
    and New York: Samuel French, 1961.

_____. In Three with John Mortimer and Harold Pinter.
    London: Samuel French, 1961.

_____. In The Hole and Other Plays and Sketches. London: Faber and Faber, 1964.

Gladly Otherwise. In One to Another by N. F. Simpson, John Mortimer, and Harold Pinter. London: Samuel French, 1960.

_____. In The Hole and Other Plays and Sketches. London: Faber and Faber, 1964.

The Hole. Staged London 1958. London: Samuel French, 1958.

How Are Your Handles? (includes Gladly Otherwise, Oh, The Other Side of London.) First staged London 1971.

Oh. Staged London 1961.

_____. In The Hole and Other Plays and Sketches. London: Faber and Faber, 1964.

On the Avenue [contributor]. Staged London 1961.

One Blast and Have Done. Staged London 1961. In The Hole and Other Plays and Sketches. London: Faber and Faber, 1964.

One Over the Eight [contributor]. Staged London 1961.

One to Another [contributor with John Mortimer and Harold Pinter]. Staged London 1959. New York: Samuel French, 1960.

One Way Pendulum. Staged London 1959; New York 1961.

_____. Acting edition. New York: Samuel French, 1960.

_____. London: Faber and Faber, 1960.

_____. New York: Grove Press, 1961.

_____. In The Drama Bedside Book. Ed. H. F. Rubenstein. New York: Atheneum, 1966.

_____. In The New British Drama. Ed. Henry Popkin. New York: Grove Press, 1964.

Playback 625 [with Leopoldo Maler]. Staged London 1970.

A Resounding Tinkle. Staged London 1957. London: Faber and Faber, 1958; New York: Samuel French, 1958.

_____. In Observer Plays. London: Faber and Faber, 1958; New York: Samuel French, 1958.

_____. In New Directions; Five One-Act Plays in the
Modern Idiom. Ed. Alan Durband. London, 1961.

_____ (shortened version). In The Hole and Other Plays
and Sketches. London: Faber and Faber, 1964.

_____. In Post-war Drama: Extracts from Eleven Plays.
Ed. John Hale. London: Faber and Faber, 1966.

Was He Anyone? Staged London 1972. London: Faber and
Faber, 1973.

You, Me and the Gatepost. Staged Nottingham
1960.

II. TELEVISION

At Least It's a Precaution Against Fire. In Some Tall
Tinkles. London: Faber and Faber, 1968.

The Best I Can Do by Way of a Gate-Leg Table Is a Hundred-
weight of Coal. In Some Tall Tinkles. London:
Faber and Faber, 1968.

Charley's Grants (series), 1970.

Elementary, My Dear Watson, 1973.

Four Tall Tinkles (includes At Least It's a Precaution
Against Fire, We're Due in Eastbourne in Ten Minutes, In A Pint with Friends Under A, Haystack on
the River, We're A Bit Above Sea-level for that Sort
of Thing), 1967.

Make a Man, 1966.

Silver Wedding, 1974.

Some Tall Tinkles (includes We're Due in Eastbourne in
Ten Minutes, The Best I Can Do . . . , At Least It's
a Precaution Against Fire). London: Faber and
Faber, 1968.

Thank You Very Much, 1971.

Three Rousing Tinkles (includes The Father by Adoption of
One of the Former Marquis of Rangoon's Natural
Granddaughters, Those Are Mr. Heckmonwick's Own Per-
sonal Pipes They've Been Lagged Once Already, The
Best I Can Do By Way of a Gate-Leg Table Is a Hun-
dredweight of Coal), 1966.

We're Due in Eastbourne in Ten Minutes. In Some Tall
    Tinkles. London: Faber and Faber, 1968.

World in Ferment (series), 1969.

III. FILM

Diamonds for Breakfast, 1968.

One Way Pendulum, 1964.

IV. RADIO

A Resounding Tinkle, 1959.

Six Sketches for Radio, 1974.

Something Rather Effective, 1972.

SECONDARY SOURCES

I. CRITICISM

Angus, William. "Modern Theatre Reflects the Times."
    Queen's Quarterly, 70 (Summer 1963), 255-63.
        This is a survey of the definitions of drama
    through the ages and a look at the "abominable"
    humanity which the Theatre of the Absurd portrays,
    with a focus on Pinter and Beckett. Angus claims
    that Simpson makes a "travesty of our contemporary
    society" in the "logical nonsense" of One Way Pen-
    dulum, A Resounding Tinkle, and The Hole.

Berveiller, Michel. "Tableaux de Londres." Revue de
    Paris, 67 (April 1960), 119-24.
        Berveiller tells of a charming conversation he
    had at the Simpsons over a cup of tea. Not exactly
    an interview. Berveiller recalls talk of Ionesco,
    Bergson, and Kafka and concludes that Simpson's
    orientation is very French.

Churchill, Caryl. "Not Ordinary, Not Safe." Twentieth
    Century, 168 (November 1960), 443-51.
        There is a passing reference to Simpson: "Simp-
    son's passers-by fill the hole with their own vi-
    sions."

Cook, David. "Of the Strong Breed." Transition, 3
    (March-April 1964), 38-40.
        This is essentially a review of Wole Soyinka's

Three Plays which mentions a link with the writings
of Brecht, Miller, Pinter, Simpson, and Ionesco, but
does not explore the link with Simpson.

Dennis, Nigel. *Dramatic Essays*. London: Weidenfeld and
Nicolson, 1962.

Diller, Hans-Jürgen. "N. F. Simpson's *A Resounding
Tinkle* als philosophische Satire." *Die Neueren
Sprachen*, 16 (1967), 357-61.
Diller insists Simpson's work is not nihilistic
or truly absurdist because the playwright is deliberately satirizing man's selfishness and inhumanity.
His works are really a Christian plea for the virtue
of charity, and his title, *A Resounding Tinkle*, alludes to the biblical warning, "[if I] have not
charity, I am become as sounding brass, or a tin-
kling cymbal."

Esslin, Martin. "Pinter and the Absurd" (contains references to N. F. Simpson). *Twentieth Century*, 169
(February 1961), 176-85. See full-length study below.

_____. *Theatre of the Absurd*. Garden City, N.Y.:
Doubleday, 1969. Pages 258-65, 402-03.
Esslin finds Simpson's highly intellectual, spontaneous, loosely constructed plays full of "nonsense
and satire mingled with parody" but with a "serious
philosophical intent." *The Hole* explores the "rela-
tivity of our vision of the world, according to the
individual's preoccupations, obsessions, and circum-
stances." *One Way Pendulum* is a brutal attack on
the cruelty of middle class society. Its characters, absorbed as they are in their own private
fantasy world, make little contact with each other.

Fothergill, C. Z. "Echoes of *A Resounding Tinkle*: N. F.
Simpson Reconsidered." *Modern Drama* 16 (1974),
299-306.
Fothergill examines Simpson's humor in *A Resounding Tinkle* and *One Way Pendulum*, and claims that
Simpson is "neither absurdist nor, . . . a powerful
social critic." Simpson's humor derives from systematically deranged characters, paradoxes, puns,
literal metaphors, and rituals without content.

Gilliat, Penelope. "Schoolmaster from Battersea."
Guardian, 10 April 1960, p. 14.

Habicht, Werner. "Theater der Sprache, Bemerkungen zu
einigen englischen Dramen der Gegenwart." *Die
Neueren Sprachen*, N.S. 12 (July 1963), 302-13.
This contains references to Pinter, Osborne, and

Wesker as well as Simpson. A Resounding Tinkle and
One Way Pendulum are analyzed in detail as manifes-
tations of the absurdist movement in England.

Lumley, Frederick. New Trends in 20th Century Drama.
    Oxford: Oxford University Press, 1967. Pages 300-
    03.
        Lumley provides brief "plot" summaries and com-
    ments on A Resounding Tinkle, One Way Pendulum, The
    Hole, and The Cresta Run. Lumley finds that "in-
    verted logic is the key to his dramatic method" and
    claims that language, rather than character, carry
    the plays.

Marowitz, Charles. "New Wave in a Dead Sea." X, A Quar-
    terly Review, 1 (October 1960), 270-77.
        Marowitz criticizes the lack of form and content
    in Simpson's plays. He finds him odd but not humor-
    ous.

O'Casey, Sean. "The Bald Primaqueera." In Blast and
    Benedictions, Articles and Stories. London:
    Macmillan, 1967.
        O'Casey offers a rather irrelevant comment on the
    elephant in the garden in A Resounding Tinkle.

Smith, R. D. "Back to the Text." In Contemporary Thea-
    tre. Ed. J. R. Brown and Bernard Harris. London:
    Edward Arnold, 1962.
        Simpson is closer to the social plays of Osborne
    and Wesker than to the Absurdist tradition, writing
    as he does from "the satirist's position of intel-
    lectual and moral normality. . . In his A Resounding
    Tinkle, The Hole, and One-Way Pendulum we see a
    lightweight inspiration, supported by considerable
    technical virtuosity, working a number of fashion-
    able themes for satire (bourgeois family life, per-
    sonal obsessions, emotional insecurity, freak phi-
    losophies) with a coruscation of verbal tricks."

Styan, J. L. The Published Play After 1956. London:
    Cambridge University Press, 1968. Page 166.

Swanson, Michele. "One Way Pendulum: A New Dimension in
    Farce." Drama Survey, 2 (February 1963), 322-32.
        Swanson explores One Way Pendulum as a farce in a
    new dimension, "derived from the theory of the ab-
    surd: that farce is reality and that the incredible
    and the improbable are not only legitimate but the
    true course of things, that not only incidents are
    isolated and meaningless; man himself is." Swanson
    discusses the arbitrary identities and the conform-
    ity of the characters and the verbal play, and re-
    views the London and New York productions. Although

close to the absurdist tradition, Simpson does not
share its despair.

Taylor, John Russell. *Anger and After*. London: Eyre
Methuen, 1963. Pages 58-64.
    In this harsh review of *A Resounding Tinkle*, *The
Hole*, and *One Way Pendulum*, Taylor claims that Simpson's plays are academic, contain no deep messages,
plot or character differentiation, and, totally
based on the non sequitur, are not particularly
funny.

Tynan, Kenneth. *Curtains*. London: Longmans Green, 1961.
Pages 198-200, 209-11, 218, 232.
    Tynan says seeing Simpson is like hearing a
Benchley lecture or looking at a Thurber cartoon or
a good show. Simpson's humor has an international
flavor, and he is "the most gifted comic writer the
English stage has discovered since the War."

Velde, Paul. "The Stage." *Commonweal*, 28 April 1967,
pp. 176-77.
    This is a passing mention of Simpson's *A Resound-
ing Tinkle* and *The Hole*, "full of paradox, displace-
ments of space and time, and the whole bag of current tricks by which the best of the new drama is
teaching us to see again."

Verkein, Lea. "Van Broadway near Piccadilly." *Vlaamse
Gids*, 45 (July 1961), 492-95.
    Verkein surveys the current English theatre and
notes the parallels between Simpson's work and the
French absurdists.

Wellwarth, George. "N. F. Simpson: Parallel to Logic."
Theatre of Protest and Paradox. New York: New York
University Press, 1964. Pages 212-20.
    This highly complimentary article looks at the
"parallel reality that runs alongside our reality
and clowns at it" in Simpson's *A Resounding Tinkle*,
The Hole, and *One Way Pendulum*.

Worth, Katherine. "Avant Garde at the Royal Court Theatre: John Arden and N. F. Simpson." In W. A. Armstrong, *Experimental Drama*. London: Bell, 1963.
Pages 204-23. See Arden above.

II. DISSERTATIONS

Galassi, Frank Stephen. "The Absurd Theatre of Joe Orton
and N. F. Simpson." *Dissertation Abstracts International* 32:5930A (New York University, 1972).
    "This study of the plays of Joe Orton and N. F.

Simpson undertakes to demonstrate that the two contemporary English playwrights have articulated a
message of social and political satire which they
have cast within a dramatic farcical medium." Both
Orton and Simpson deal mostly with the middle class
and probe such subjects as the law, psychiatry,
business organization, and organized pleasure. "The
farcical characters of Orton and Simpson and the
situations which they experience are products of
such incongruity, antithesis, and mystification, in
comparison to the ordinary and everyday world, that
they begin to exist and function according to the
laws and behavior of a totally absurd universe."

III. REVIEWS

THE CRESTA RUN

The Times, 28 October 1965, p. 8.

THE FORM

The Times, 19 January 1961, p. 16.

THE HOLE

The Times, 3 April 1958, p. 3.

New York Times, 4 April 1961, p. 42.

ON THE AVENUE

The Times, 22 June 1961, p. 17.

ONE OVER THE EIGHT

The Times, 6 April 1961, p. 8.

ONE TO ANOTHER

The Times, 16 July 1958, p. 8.

ONE WAY PENDULUM

The Times, 23 December 1959, p. 9.

New York Times, 19 September 1961, p. 38.

PLAYBACK 625

The Times, 20 October 1970, p. 13.

A RESOUNDING TINKLE

    The Times, 2 December 1957, p. 3.

    New York Times, 4 April 1961, p. 42.

WAS HE ANYONE?

    The Times, 12 July 1972, p. 13.

TOM STOPPARD

Born Zlin, Czechoslovakia, July 3, 1937

   The recent English playwright with the most interesting background is Tom Stoppard, who, born a Czech, was
moved to Singapore when he was one year old, and to England when he was nine. If Pinter is the Shakespeare of
the new drama, then we might call Stoppard its Ben Jonson.
No one would have predicted in the 1950s and early 1960s
that a playwright so literary, so dependent on words for
dramatic impact would be a successful writer for the contemporary stage. One can say in retrospect that Rosencrantz and Guildenstern Are Dead was early proof that the
non-verbal culture of the past decade was a temporary
aberration and that, contrary to McLuhan, the typographic
page was far from dead. In fact, if Stoppard's stagger-
ing talents have one limitation, it may be that his plays
can be almost as much fun to read as to see. His verbal
skills are so prodigious one needs to scan each passage
close-up in order to discover its density and complexity.
Still, Stoppard's plays are enormously entertaining and
he is especially admired by the young. Initially, he
parodied many of Beckett's techniques; and Stoppard's
philosophical speculations, which are at the core of
every work, seemed fashionably existential and despairing.
More recent works, especially Jumpers and Travesties,
have been more affirmative in spirit and in method they
bear a kinship to T. S. Eliot's metaphysical dramas.
Stoppard is so adept at parody--and Travesties is the
supreme example of his parodic talents--that one might
overlook the evolution of a distinctive personal style.
Stoppard's plays, because of their intellectual content
and verbal richness, require superior acting talents, but
they reward any audience longing for substance, style,
and humor.

PRIMARY SOURCES

I. STAGE

After Magritte. London: Faber and Faber, 1971.

_____. New York: Grove Press, 1972.

_____. London: Samuel French, 1973.

Dirty Linen and New-Found-Land. In The Real Inspector Hound and After Magritte. New York: Grove Press, 1975.

_____. Staged London, Washington, New York 1976.

_____. Ambiance/Almost Free Playscript. London, 1976.

"Dogg's Our Pet." Staged 1971.

Enter a Free Man. (For previous versions see "A Walk on the Water" below.) London: Faber and Faber, 1968.

_____. London: Faber and Faber, 1969.

_____. New York: Grove Press, 1972.

_____. London: Samuel French, 1973.

"The Gamblers." Staged Bristol 1965.

"The House of Bernarda Alba." Adaptation of the play by Lorca; staged London 1973.

Jumpers. London: Faber and Faber, 1972.

"The Preservation of George Riley." See "A Walk on the Water" below.

The Real Inspector Hound. London: Faber and Faber, 1968.

_____. New York: Grove Press, 1969.

_____. London: Samuel French, 1970.

_____. London: Samuel French, 1973.

_____. In The Real Inspector Hound and After Magritte. New York: Grove Press, 1975.

Rosencrantz and Guildenstern Are Dead. London: Faber and Faber, 1967.

_____. New York: Grove Press, 1967.

_____. Evergreen Review, 12 (March 1968), 47-72.

_____. The Best Plays of 1967-1968. Ed. Otis L. Guernsey, Jr. New York: Dodd, Mead, 1968.

_____. London: Samuel French, 1970.

Tango. Adaptation of the play by Slawomir Mrozek, translated by Nicholas Bethel. London: Cape, 1968.

Travesties. New York: Grove Press, 1975.

"A Walk on the Water." Televised 1963; staged Hamburg
1964. Revised as "The Preservation of George
Riley." Televised 1964. Revised as Enter a Free
Man. London: Faber and Faber, 1968.

II. TELEVISION

"Another Moon Called Earth." Televised 1967.

"The Engagement." Televised, NBC-TV (U.S.A.), 8 March
1970.

"Neutral Ground." Televised, ITV, 11 December 1968.

"One Pair of Eyes." Documentary, televised, BBC, 7
July 1972.

"The Preservation of George Riley." Televised 1964.

"A Separate Peace." Playbill Two. Ed. Alan Durband.
London: Hutchinson, 1969.

"Teeth." Televised 1967.

"A Walk on the Water." Televised 1963.

III. RADIO

Albert's Bridge. Plays and Players, 15 (October 1967),
21-30.

_____. London: Samuel French, 1969.

_____. London: Faber and Faber, 1970.

Albert's Bridge and If You're Glad, I'll Be Frank.
London: Faber and Faber, 1969.

Artist Descending a Staircase; and, Where Are They Now?
London: Faber and Faber, 1973.

"The Dissolution of Dominic Boot." Broadcast, BBC, 1965.

If You're Glad, I'll Be Frank. See Albert's Bridge and
If You're Glad, I'll Be Frank above.

"M Is for Moon Among Other Things." Broadcast, BBC, 1965.

"Where Are They Now?" See <u>Artist</u> <u>Descending</u> <u>a</u> <u>Staircase</u> above. Broadcast, BBC, 18 December 1970.

IV. FILM

"The Romantic Englishwoman," 1975.

V. FICTION

<u>Introduction</u> <u>2</u>, <u>With</u> <u>Others</u>. London: Faber and Faber, 1964.

<u>Lord</u> <u>Malquist</u> <u>and</u> <u>Mr</u>. <u>Moon</u>. London: Anthony Blond, 1966.

_____. London: Anthony Blond, 1968.

_____. New York: Knopf, 1968.

_____. New York: Balantine, 1969.

_____. London: Faber and Faber, 1974.

_____. New York: Grove Press, 1975.

"The Story." <u>Evergreen</u> <u>Review</u>, 13 (July 1968), 53-55.

VI. NON-FICTION

"Doers and Thinkers: Playwrights and Professors." <u>Times</u> <u>Literary</u> <u>Supplement</u>, 13 October 1972, p. 1219.

"'I'm Not Keen on Experiments.'" <u>New</u> <u>York</u> <u>Times</u>, 8 March 1970, II:17.

"In Praise of Pedantry." <u>Punch</u>, 14 July 1971, pp. 62-63.

Review of <u>Orghast</u> by Ted Hughes. <u>Times</u> <u>Literary</u> <u>Supple-</u> <u>ment</u>, 1 October 1971, p. 1174.

"Something to Declare." <u>The</u> <u>Sunday</u> <u>Times</u>, 25 February 1968, p. 47.

"A Very Satirical Thing Happened to Me on My Way to the Theatre Tonight." <u>Encore</u>, 10 (March-April 1963), 33-36.

"The Writer and the Theatre: The Definite Maybe." <u>Author</u>, 78 (Spring 1967), 18-20.

"Yes We Have No Banana." The Guardian, 10 December 1971,
    p. 10.

VII. INTERVIEWS

"Ambushes for the Audience: Toward a High Comedy of
    Ideas." Theatre Quarterly, 4 (May-July 1974), 3-17.
    Stoppard is asked some penetrating questions by
    the journal's editors and answers openly and articu-
    lately. He discusses his early background, his
    education, and his first play, A Walk on the Water.
    The philosophy behind Rosencrantz and Guildenstern
    Are Dead is explored as well as Stoppard's approach
    to problems of stage craftsmanship. His strong
    aversion to totalitarian governments, especially
    fascism and Marxist/Leninism, his career as theatre
    critic, and his preferences in the modern theatre
    are covered in detail.

Gale, John. "Writing's My 43rd Priority." The Observer,
    17 December 1967, p. 4.

Gordon, Giles. "Tom Stoppard." Transatlantic Review, 29
    (Summer 1968), 17-25. Reprinted in Behind the
    Scenes. Ed. Joseph F. McCrindle. New York: Holt,
    Rinehart and Winston, 1971.
    This is an excellent interview. Stoppard speaks
    fluently and seriously about Rosencrantz and Guil-
    denstern, Enter a Free Man, the lack of the personal
    element in his writing, and the work of his contem-
    poraries.

Gussow, Mel. "'Jumpers' Author Is Verbal Gymnast." New
    York Times, 23 April 1974, p. 36.

_____. "Stoppard Refutes Himself, Endlessly." New York
    Times, 26 April 1972, p. 54.

Halton, Kathleen. "Young British Playwright Here for Re-
    hearsal." Vogue, 15 October 1967, p. 112.

Harper, Keith. "The Devious Road to Waterloo." The
    Guardian, 12 April 1967, p. 7.

"Interview with Tom Stoppard." Jumpers Program. London:
    The National Theatre, 1972, p. 11.

Leech, Michael. "The Translators: Tom Stoppard." Plays
    & Players, 20 (April 1973), 36-37.
    Stoppard discusses problems in translating and
    adapting Lorca's The House of Bernarda Alba. He
    sees adapting a text as including "what is under-

stood in the original." "I try to make a line work
as it should work."

Norman, Barry. "Tom Stoppard and the Contentment of In-
    security." The Times, 11 November 1972, p. 11.

Sullivan, Dan. "Young British Playwright Here for Re-
    hearsals of 'Rosencrantz.'" New York Times, 29
    August 1967, p. 27.

"Tom Stoppard: Playwright, Novelist." New Yorker, 4 May
    1968, pp. 40-41.
        Stoppard discusses Rosencrantz and Guildenstern,
    Enter a Free Man, and his novel. This is a brief
    interview, of little value.

Watts, Janet. The Guardian, 21 March 1973, p. 10.

SECONDARY SOURCES

I. CRITICISM

Anderson, Michael. "The Unnatural Scene: Plays about
    Plays." New Theatre Magazine, 8 (Spring 1968),
    28-31.
        Anderson considers Rosencrantz and Guildenstern
    and Günter Grass's The Plebians Rehearse the Upris-
    ing as "refinements" of the play within a play: the
    "play about a play." He finds Grass's play "the
    more interesting of the two." Stoppard writes with
    "wit, subtlety and a feeling for theatrical effect,"
    but the play contains "many weaknesses."

Asmus, Walter D. "Rosencrantz and Guildenstern Are
    Dead." Shakespeare-Jahrbuch (Heidelberg), 106
    (1970), 118-31. In German.
        Asmus ponders the question of the seriousness of
    Rosencrantz and Guildenstern Are Dead. Unlike Bond,
    who called the play "a crass little metaphysical
    exercise," Asmus feels Stoppard may be on the verge
    of making a significant philosophical statement.
    The article contains elaborate parallels between
    Hamlet and Stoppard's play, especially passages
    dealing with theatrical metaphors.

Babula, William. "The Play-Life Metaphor in Shakespeare
    and Stoppard." Modern Drama, 15 (Winter 1972),
    279-81.
        This is a somewhat inconclusive essay comparing
    the life-play metaphor as it applies to the leading
    characters in both Hamlet and Rosencrantz and
    Guildenstern.

Barker, Clive. "Contemporary Shakespearean Parody in
British Theatre." Shakespeare-Jahrbuch (Heidelberg),
105 (1969), 104-20.
This is a sociological and socialist analysis of
Osborne's Look Back in Anger, Rosencrantz and Guildenstern and Garson's MacBird as parodies of Shakespeare. He finds all parody of Shakespeare disgust-
ing and regards Stoppard's play as a "petty bourgeois tragedy."

Bennett, Jonathan. "Philosophy and Mr. Stoppard." Philosophy, 50 (January 1975), 5-18.
This intriguing essay examines the philosophical
content of Jumpers and Rosencrantz and Guildenstern.
Bennett finds the philosophical content of the
former "academic"; it has no relation to structure,
and Stoppard simply plays with the concepts:
"he has nothing to say about [them]." Rosencrantz
and Guildenstern seriously treats such concepts:
"the central one is the concept of reality, and
grouped around it are identity, memory, activity,
and death." The play's strength derives from the
importance of the concepts and "from the sheer
pertinacity and complexity and depth of the concep-
tual exploration."

Berlin, Normand. "Rosencrantz and Guildenstern Are Dead:
Theater of Criticism." Modern Drama, 16 (December
1973), 269-77.
Berlin argues for viewing Stoppard's Rosencrantz
and Guildenstern as criticism in dramatic form and
also believes that the audience acts as critic during the performance. ". . . Stoppard is most successful when he functions as a critic of drama and
when he allows his insights on the theatre to lead
him to observations on life."

Bondy, François. "Tendenzen des neuen Theatres, I: Rede
auf einer Dramaturgentagung." Merkur, 24:270 (October 1970), 963-71.
Bondy notes the appearance of several lavish contemporary productions of Shakespearean plays and believes the popularity of Rosencrantz and Guildenstern Are Dead is another tribute to the Bard.

Brustein, Robert. "Waiting for Hamlet." New Republic,
4 November 1967, pp. 25-26. Reprinted in The Third
Theatre. New York: Knopf, 1969. Pages 149-53.
This is an analysis of Rosencrantz and Guildenstern: "a noble conception which has not been en-
dowed with any real weight or texture." Includes
brief plot summary, discussion of thematic and character problems.

Callan, Anthony. "Stoppard's Godot: Some French Influ-
    ences on Post-War English Drama." New Theatre Maga-
    zine, 10 (Winter 1969), 22-30.
    Callen discusses the influence of Ionesco and
Beckett on modern British playwrights and compares,
at length, common elements of plot, theme, character, and language in Rosencrantz and Guildenstern
and Waiting for Godot. He sees Stoppard's originality in the "brilliant" grafting of Beckett and
Shakespeare, and feels the play's "complexity" con-
tributes to "one of the richest dramatic achievements
of the post-war period" but is also a "source of
some of its weaknesses."

Carroll, Peter. "They Have Their Entrances and Their
    Exits: 'Rosencrantz and Guildenstern Are Dead.'"
    Teaching of English, 20 (1971), 50-60.

Cushman, Robert. "The Moon Is on the Other Foot."
    Jumpers Program. London: The National Theatre,
    1972.

Downer, Alan. "Old, New, Borrowed and (a Trifle) Blue:
    Notes on the N.Y. Theatre, 1967-68." Quarterly
    Journal of Speech, 54 (October 1968), 199-211.
    Downer considers seven plays from the 1967-68
Broadway season, including Rosencrantz and Guildenstern. A brief analysis, plot summary, and discussion of the New York production are included.

Gardner, C. O. "Correspondence: Rosencrantz and Guilden-
    stern Are Dead." Theoria, 34 (1970), 83.
    Response to the Lee article.

Gianakaris, C. J. "Absurdism Altered: Rosencrantz and
    Guildenstern Are Dead." Drama Survey, 7 (1969),
    52-58.
    Gianakaris sees Rosencrantz and Guildenstern as
reconciling "the disparities between drama anchored
to personal/social responsibility and that pledged
to the stripping of hackneyed illusions." He explores affinities to absurdist drama and points out
ways in which Stoppard's play diverges from the absurdist view.

Guthke, Karl S. "Die metaphysische farce im Theatre der
    Gegenwart." Deutsche Shakespeare-Gesellschaft West.
    Jahrbuch (1970), 49-76.
    This is a general essay on metaphysical plays in
the absurdist tradition, such as Waiting for Godot,
The Chairs, Tiny Alice, and Rosencrantz and Guildenstern Are Dead. This last play addresses itself to
fundamental questions of existence. It explores the

nature of fate ("what is") and asks the question,
"But why."

Kalem, T. E. "Ping Pong Philosopher." Time, 6 May 1974,
    p. 85.

Kerr, Walter. "The Struggle to See: The Comedy That
    Kills." Thirty Plays Hath November. New York:
    Simon and Schuster, 1969. Pages 50-53.
        Kerr offers a favorable analysis of Rosencrantz
    and Guildenstern and its production. Kerr's only
    criticism of the play concerns its "overlength" and
    the fact that he sensed too much authorial presence.

Keyssar-Franke, Helene. "The Strategy of Rosencrantz and
    Guildenstern Are Dead." Educational Theatre Journal,
    27 (March 1975), 85-97.
        Keyssar-Franke discusses Rosencrantz and Guilden-
    stern in terms of Stoppard's "dramatic strategy,"
    the effect of the play on an audience. The audience
    is to be forced to a recognition that they can no
    more alter their fate than Rosencrantz and Guilden-
    stern could alter theirs. She examines the play
    minutely to determine the effect of each element in
    terms of Stoppard's strategy.

Lee, R. H. "The Circle and Its Tangent." Theoria, 33
    (1969), 37-43.

Levenson, Jill. "Views From a Revolving Door: Tom Stop-
    pard's Canon to Date." Queen's Quarterly, 78
    (Autumn 1971), 431-42.
        Here Stoppard is analyzed as a playwright of the
    Theatre of the Absurd, emphasizing similarities be-
    tween him and Beckett in theme, form, and character-
    ization. Levenson explores the plays (both radio
    and stage) through Real Inspector Hound and includes
    Stoppard's novel in an effective comprehensive study.

Mansat, A. "Rosencrantz et Guildenstern sont morts."
    Les Langues Moderne, 64 (1970), 396-400.
        Rosencrantz and Guildenstern is a bleak play be-
    cause it offers an extreme view of depersonaliza-
    tion. The protagonists are non-beings to start, and
    they cannot "die" in the usual sense since they do
    not exist. Like the absurdists, Stoppard depicts
    a world without purpose and without viable choices.

Nakanishi, Masako. "Tom Stoppard no Sekae-Kyoto to
    Genjitsu no Mondai." Oberon, 34 (1971), 53-71. In
    Japanese.
        Stoppard, like many modern dramatists, is ob-
    sessed with what is real and what is imagined--the
    illusion versus reality theme.

Quinn, James E. "Rosencrantz and Guildenstern Are Alive
    and Well in the Classroom." Missouri English Bulle-
    tin, 26 (October 1970), 16-19.

Taylor, John Russell. "British Dramatists--The New Ar-
    rivals: No. 4, Tom Stoppard." Plays & Players, 17
    (July 1970), 16-18, 78.
        This is a brief overview of Stoppard's work
    through After Magritte (1970). Taylor sees pattern
    or structure as one of Stoppard's primary concerns,
    coupled with completeness of effect. Stoppard
    recognizes the necessity for "intelligence and con-
    scious art in the shaping of his material."

_____. The Second Wave: New British Drama for the Seven-
    ties. New York: Hill and Wang, 1971.
        Reprint, with minor revision, of the article
    above.

Trussler, Simon. "Theatre Reviews: Second Generation
    London." The Drama Review, 12 (Winter 1968), 171-76.
        Trussler gives a highly appreciative analysis of
    Rosencrantz and Guildenstern. He sees the play as
    "perhaps, an attempt to conceive a plane of exis-
    tence on which the mythic quality of Hamlet becomes
    meaningful even as the nature of its immediate real-
    ity becomes ambiguous."

Weightman, John. "A Metaphysical Comedy." Encounter, 38
    (April 1972), 44-46.
        Weightman provides a thoughtful analysis of Jumpers.
    Although pleased with it, Weightman feels that
    "quite a few bits of this play have not been brought
    fully into intellectual or aesthetic focus." Stop-
    pard is a "Deist," who "has the makings of a tragic
    Deist," and who is also a "sentimentalist."

_____. "Mini-Hamlets in Limbo." Encounter, 29 (July
    1967), 38-40.
        This is an analysis of Rosencrantz and Guilden-
    stern. Weightman feels the "idea is brilliant and
    produces a certain amount of fun," but he has reser-
    vations. The play does not seem to be properly
    linked to Hamlet; and he finds a disturbing mix of
    "intellectual fooling around" and attempts at being
    "genuinely poetic," but "the poetry is spurious."

II. DISSERTATIONS

O'Malley, John F. "Caryl Churchill, David Mercer, and
    Tom Stoppard: A Study of Contemporary British
    Dramatists Who Have Written for Radio, Television,
    and Stage." Dissertation Abstracts International,

Florida State University, 1974.
   O'Malley examines the works of the three title
playwrights "in terms of their suitability for
radio, television, or stage," and attempts only to
illumine the "relationship between the media and the
playwright," not to compare the plays critically.

III. REVIEWS

AFTER MAGRITTE

   The Times, 10 April 1970, p. 16.

   Plays & Players, 17 (May 1970), 47.

   New York Times, 24 April 1972, p. 41.

   New York Times, 7 May 1972, II:3.

   Plays & Players, 20 (January 1973), 51.

ALBERT'S BRIDGE

   The Times, 13 July 1967, p. 8.

   New Theatre Magazine, 10 (Winter 1969), 32.

DIRTY LINEN

   Quarterly Theatre Review (Winter 1976), p. 46.

"DOGG'S OUR PET"

   The Times, 15 December 1971, p. 18.

   Punch, 12 January 1972, p. 58.

ENTER A FREE MAN

   The Times, 29 March 1968, p. 13.

   New York Times, 7 April 1968, II:8.

   Plays & Players, 15 (June 1968), 22-23.

   Newsweek, 31 August 1970, p. 77.

   Newsweek, 6 January 1975, p. 64.

   New Yorker, 6 January 1975, p. 50.

227

"THE HOUSE OF BERNARDA ALBA"

Plays & Players, 20 (May 1973), 42-43.

IF YOU'RE GLAD, I'LL BE FRANK

New Theatre Magazine, 10 (Winter 1969), 32.

JUMPERS

The Times, 3 February 1972, p. 13.

Plays & Players, 19 (April 1972), 34-37.

Sunday Times, 9 April 1972, p. 16.

New York Times, 9 August 1972, p. 24.

Nation, 13 August 1973, pp. 123-24.

Newsweek, 4 March 1974, p. 87.

Time, 11 March 1974, p. 103.

National Review, 29 March 1974, p. 377.

New York Times, 23 April 1974, p. 36.

New Yorker, 6 May 1974, p. 75.

Nation, 11 May 1974, p. 604.

America, 18 May 1974, p. 395.

Nation, 18 May 1974, pp. 637-38.

New Republic, 18 May 1974, pp. 18, 33.

Commentary, June 1974, pp. 79-80.

THE REAL INSPECTOR HOUND

The Times, 18 June 1968, p. 12.

New York Times, 8 July 1968, p. 45.

New York Times, 14 July 1968, II:4.

Plays & Players, 15 (August 1968), 12-15.

Modern Drama, 11 (February 1969), 437-39.

New York Times, 24 April 1972, p. 41.

New York Times, 7 May 1972, II:3.

New York Times, 16 October 1972, p. 46.

ROSENCRANTZ AND GUILDENSTERN ARE DEAD

The Times, 12 April 1967, p. 8.

New Yorker, 6 May 1967, pp. 179-80.

New York Times, 17 October 1967, p. 53.

New Yorker, 28 October 1967, p. 105.

New York Times, 29 October 1967, II:1.

Newsweek, 30 October 1967, pp. 90-92.

Saturday Review, 4 November 1967, p. 28.

Nation, 6 November 1967, pp. 476-77.

Commonweal, 10 November 1967, pp. 171-72.

Vogue, 15 November 1967, p. 72.

Reporter, 16 November 1967, pp. 39-40.

Commentary, December 1967, pp. 82-84.

National Review, 12 December 1967, pp. 1393-95.

Look, 26 December 1967, pp. 92-96.

Life, 9 February 1968, pp. 72-76.

Educational Theatre Journal, 20 (March 1968), 103.

Modern Drama, 11 (February 1969), 103.

Saturday Review, 5 July 1969, p. 20.

New Yorker, 4 March 1974, p. 70.

TRAVESTIES

Newsweek, 24 June 1974, p. 77.

Times Literary Supplement, 12 July 1974, p. 744.

New York Times, 19 October 1975, II:1.

New York Times, 31 October 1975, p. 21.

New Yorker, 10 November 1975, p. 135.

DAVID STOREY

Born Wakefield, Yorkshire, July 13, 1933

One can safely consider David Storey the most naturalistic playwright of the New Wave. The Russians who
admire his work especially consider him a Marxist, and
Lindsay Anderson, who has directed all his work, at least
partly shares this assumption. Surely his greatest sympathy lies with the working class, and he is faithful to
dialect and syntax of characters who represent working
men and women in his plays. But it is possible to regard
him as an apolitical neutral observer of life, recording
every sound of his world with precision and sensitivity.
Storey considers himself primarily a novelist, yet his
novels seem pedestrian compared to his dramatic achievements. Storey often concentrates on the peripheral moments of significant experiences, such as the prepara-
tions for and aftermath of a wedding ceremony or the
locker room activities before, during, and after a rugby
game. Once a professional rugby player himself, Storey
draws on his athletic experiences in his writings. He
has an astonishing sense of the possibilities and limits
of a stage. Due to their stark simplicity, his plays can
be somewhat dull to read, but, performed, they are
charged with tension and extremely absorbing.

PRIMARY SOURCES

I. STAGE

The Changing Room. Staged London 1971; New Haven, Conn.
1972; New York 1973. London: Cape, 1972.

_____. Sports Illustrated, 5 March 1973, pp. 70-83.

The Contractor. Plays and Players, 17 (December 1969),
63-86.

_____. Staged London 1969; New Haven, Conn. 1970.
London: Cape, 1970.

_____. The Contractor and In Celebration. Harmonds-
worth: Penguin Books, 1971.

_____. Plays and Players, 1971.

_____. Plays of the Year. Vol. 40. Ed. J. C. Trewin.
London: Elek Books, 1971.

_____. New York: Random House, 1971.

Cromwell. Staged London 1973. London: Cape, 1973.

Edward. Staged London 1973.

The Farm. Staged London 1973. London: Cape, 1973.

Home. Plays and Players, 17 (August 1970), 61-77.

_____. Staged London and New York 1970. London: Cape,
1970.

_____. Plays and Players, 17 (August 1970). Ed. Peter
Roberts. London: Hansom Books.

_____. New York: Random House, 1971.

_____. Plays of the Year. Vol. 41. Ed. J. C. Trewin.
London: Elek Books, 1972.

In Celebration. Plays and Players, 16 (June 1969).

_____. Staged London 1969. London: Cape, 1969.

_____. Plays and Players Plays 1966-1969.

_____. Plays of the Year. Vol. 38. Ed. J. C. Trewin.
London: Elek Books, 1970.

_____. The Contractor and In Celebration. London:
Penguin Books, 1971.

_____. London: Heinemann, 1973.

_____. New York: Grove Press, 1975.

Life Class. London: Cape, 1975.

The Restoration of Arnold Middleton. Staged Edinburgh
1966; London 1967. London: Cape, 1967.

_____. Plays of the Year. Vol. 35. Ed. J. C. Trewin.
London: Elek Books, 1968.

_____. New English Dramatists 14. Harmondsworth: Penguin Books, 1970.

II. FILM

"This Sporting Life," 1963.

III.' FICTION

Flight into Camden. London: Longmans, 1960.

_____. New York: Macmillan, 1960.

"Going Back Home." [Extract from Pasmore.] The Times, 30 September, 1972, p. 7.

Pasmore. London: Longmans, 1972.

_____. New York: Dutton, 1974.

Radcliffe. London: Longmans, 1963.

_____. New York: Coward-McCann, 1964.

This Sporting Life. London: Longmans, 1960.

_____. New York: Macmillan, 1960.

_____. London: Longmans, 1968.

_____. London: Longmans, 1970.

A Temporary Life. London: Longmans, 1973.

_____. New York: Dutton, 1974.

IV. NON-FICTION

"Commonwealth Art Today." Guardian, 3 November 1962, p. 5.

"A Gentle Dominance: William Coldstream." Guardian, 2 August 1962, p. 5.

"Journey Through a Tunnel." Listener, 1 August 1963, pp. 159-61.

"Marxism as a Form of Nostalgia." New Society, 15 July 1965, p. 23.

"Ned Kelly on Film." Guardian, 7 February 1963, p. 7.

"Nolan's Ark." New Statesman, 31 May 1963, pp. 840-41.

"Passionate Polemics." New Society, 26 January 1967, pp. 137-38.

"Robert Colquhoun." New Statesman, 12 October 1962, pp. 500-01.

"Shadows of the Ghetto." Guardian, 12 April 1972, p. 10.

"Slabs of State." Review of Merwyn Levy, Paintings of D. H. Lawrence.

"What Really Matters." Twentieth Century, 172 (Autumn 1963), 96-98.

"Writers on Themselves" [with others]. London: BBC, 1964.

V. INTERVIEWS

Ansorge, Peter. "The Theatre of Life." Plays and Players, 20 (September 1973), 32-36.
Storey outlines his empirical approach to writing for the theatre, and these remarks and others concerning both the novels and the plays are integrated into an essay in which Ansorge explores Storey's transition from novelist to playwright, and from idealist to pragmatist.

Gussow, Mel. "To David Storey a Play Is Holiday." New York Times, 20 April 1973, p. 14.

Hayman, Ronald. "Conversation with David Storey." Drama, 99 (Winter 1970), 47-53.
Storey describes his start in the theatre, his method of writing, his working relationship with Lindsay Anderson, and his own struggle to orient himself within a theatrical tradition in place of a literary one. He singles out the division between those who can make society work for them and those who can't as a recurring theme in his works.

_____. Playback. ["Essay-interviews"] London: Davis-Poynter, 1973.
Basically this is a reprint of the above article.

"Speaking of Writing." The Times, 28 November 1963, p. 15.

SECONDARY SOURCES

I. CRITICISM

Bentley, Phyllis. "Yorkshire and the Novelist." Essays
    by Divers Hands: Being the Transactions of The
    Royal Society of Literature, 33 (1965), 145-57.
        This is really an essay on Yorkshire and its
    influence on artists over the ages. Storey is
    simply noted in passing as a writer who carries on
    the district's literary tradition.

Bygrave, Mike. "David Storey: Novelist or Playwright?"
    Theatre Quarterly, 1 (April-June 1971), 31-36.
        Bygrave argues that Storey's novels are more im-
    portant than his plays. The novels are seen as
    didactic illustrations of outmoded social and apoca-
    lyptic theories, and the plays as dull reworkings of
    the same worn out material.

De Jongh, Nicholas. "Storey's Line." Guardian, 8 Octo-
    ber 1970, p. 10.

Duffy, Martha. "Ethics of Work and Play." [About The
    Changing Room.] Sports Illustrated, 5 March 1973,
    pp. 66-69.
        Duffy reviews the Broadway production of The
    Changing Room, describes the difficulties in staging
    it, and provides a brief biographical sketch of
    David Storey as well as his comments about the value
    of sports--life lived at its extremes.

Free, William J. "The Ironic Anger of David Storey."
    Modern Drama, 16 (December 1973), 307-16.
        According to Free, Storey is most like Pinter and
    Osborne, but differs from the former in his use of
    dramatic space--in which tension is released rather
    than built up--and from the latter in his ability to
    dramatize the meaning of his characters' lives in-
    stead of having characters rage about their lack of
    it. The article includes sensitive and detailed
    readings of In Celebration and The Contractor.

Hewes, Henry. "Theatre in '71." Saturday Review, 12
    June 1971, pp. 14-19.
        Hewes discusses the Drama Critics' selection of
    Home as best play of 1970. It was in competition
    with Hampton's The Philanthropist and Albee's All
    Over. Hewes attributes the success of the play to
    Ralph Richardson's acting ability.

Hunt, Albert.   "Too Far Above Ground."   New Society, 1
    May 1969, pp. 681-82.
        Set against society's neglect of miners and the
    deplorable conditions under which they are exploited
    and manipulated, Hunt feels that the "universal mes-
    sage" of In Celebration--living with the past--is
    trivial.

Kalson, Albert.   "Insanity and the Rational Man in the
    Plays of David Storey."   Modern Drama, 19 (June
    1976), 111-28.
        Kalson investigates the tormented protagonists of
    David Storey's plays.   Man seems doomed to isolation
    and defeat, but the rational man attempts to make a
    contribution, however meager, to his world rather
    than to resort to passivity or violence.

Kovalev, I.   "Stori govorit vxer' es."   Teatr (Warsaw), 8
    (1970), 161-62.
        This is a brief discussion of Storey as a natu-
    ralistic writer who has made effective use of the
    working class idiom on stage.

Peel, Marie.   "David Storey: demon [sic] and Lazarus."
    Books and Bookmen, 17 (March 1972), 20-24.
        Peel has provided an excellent survey of Storey's
    career, plays, and novels.   She believes The Chang-
    ing Room is his most complete literary effort so
    far.   She examines Storey's deterministic universe,
    his symbolic, almost allegorical use of names, and
    his odd mixture of tragedy and grudging optimism.

Pop, Mihai.   "Un 'furios' întîrziat" (an introduction).
    In Viaţa Sportiva [This Sporting LIfe].   Bucharest:
    Univers, 1972.   Pages 5-16.
        Storey is seen in this introduction as a latter
    day angry young man.

Roberts, Neil.   "Father and Children: David Storey's
    Recent Work."   Delta, 53 (1975), 12-19.
        Although Roberts is concerned with Storey's nov-
    els, his insights into Storey's views on education
    pertain to the plays as well.   He explores the
    domestic situation in Radcliffe, Pasmore, and A
    Temporary Life and concludes that too great an in-
    vestment of hope in children who are unwilling to
    fulfill their fathers' vision of a better life--the
    investment usually coming in the form of higher edu-
    cation--is not of mere sociological interest, but a
    situation central to the experience of our time.   He
    feels that Storey may be suggesting that certain
    spiritual needs are to be met in working for mate-
    rial goods, and not in some "great educated empti-
    ness."

Shrapnel, Susan. "No Goodness or No Kings." Cambridge
    Quarterly, 5 (Autumn 1970), 181-87.
        Shrapnel traces the changes in dramatic language
    in Storey's plays from a language commensurate to
    the exposure of domestic relations on a naturalistic
    level in Arnold Middleton and In Celebration, to a
    language which is purposefully incommensurate to the
    tragedy of human experience in The Contractor and
    Home. The Contractor succeeds because of its re-
    fusal to buttonhole its message, and Home because of
    its near perfect imitation of the texture of an
    everyday speech which is both mundane and in a way
    comforting to those who use it.

Taylor, John Russell. "British Dramatists--David Storey."
    Plays and Players, 17 (June 1970), 22-24.
        Taylor outlines a chronology of Storey's work as
    it was written, includes some of Storey's own re-
    marks about the advantages of working within a vari-
    ety of art forms--novels, plays, film, painting,
    etc.--and explains in some detail Storey's "method"
    of writing. He also summarizes the dramatic tech-
    nique of Arnold Middleton, In Celebration, and The
    Contractor, and praises Storey for his independence
    from fashion and his determination to follow his own
    vision.

_____. David Storey. Edited by Ian Scott Kilvert.
    Writers and Their Works, no. 239. Harlow: Long-
    man's, 1974.
        This Longman's pamphlet combines biography,
    criticism, and bibliography in a slender, useful
    study of Storey's work to date.

_____. The Second Wave. London: Eyre Methuen, 1971.
        This chapter includes essentially the same mate-
    rial as the Plays and Players article above.

"Thoughts on Contemporary Theatre." New Theatre Maga-
    zine, 7 (Spring 1967), 6-12.
        Storey is mentioned as one of many talented new
    English dramatists.

Worth, Katherine J. Revolutions in Modern English Drama.
    London: Bell, 1973.
        Worth comments on the naturalism in Storey's
    plays, so pure it is almost musical. She notes that
    the central event in each drama generally takes
    place off-stage and praises his sense of timing and
    craftsmanship.

II. DISSERTATION

Lockwood, Bernard. "Four Contemporary British Working-
Class Novelists: A Thematic and Critical Approach to
the Fiction of Raymond Williams, John Braine, David
Storey and Alan Sillitoe." Dissertation Abstracts,
28 (1967): 1081A (Wisconsin).
  Lockwood makes only a passing reference to a play
Storey had written (The Restoration of Arnold Middleton), which had not yet been produced at the
time he wrote this dissertation.

III. REVIEWS

THE CHANGING ROOM

The Times, 10 November 1971, p. 12.

New York Times, 13 December 1971, p. 52.

America, 8 April 1972, p. 379.

New York Times, 19 November 1972, p. 79.

New York Times, 3 December 1972,II:13.

Newsweek, 11 December 1972, p. 71.

Time, 18 December 1972, pp. 84-85.

New York Times, 7 March 1973, p. 37.

New York Times, 18 March 1973, II:1.

Newsweek, 19 March 1973, p. 86.

Nation, 26 March 1973, pp. 410-11.

Commonweal, 6 April 1973, p. 114.

New Republic, 14 April 1973, p. 22.

New York Times, 10 June 1973, II:1.

THE CONTRACTOR

Plays and Players, 17 (December 1969), 26-27.

The Times, 4 April 1970, p. 21.

The Times, 7 April 1970, p. 8.

New York Times, 17 August 1970, p. 32.

New York Times, 9 December 1971, p. 63.

New York Times, 18 October 1973, p. 66.

New York Times, 28 October 1973, II:3.

New Yorker, 29 October 1973, pp. 107-09.

America, 3 November 1973, p. 334.

Nation, 5 November 1973, p. 478.

Time, 5 November 1973, p. 84.

Saturday Review (World), 18 December 1973, p. 47.

New York Times, 9 April 1974, p. 83.

CROMWELL

New York Times, 9 September 1973, II:1.

New York Times, 11 September 1973, p. 55.

FLIGHT INTO CAMDEN

Minnesota Review, 1 (Spring 1961), 378-85.

Minnesota Review, 2 (Summer 1962), 546-57.

HOME

The Times, 18 June 1970, p. 8.

New York Times, 20 June 1970, p. 23.

New York Times, 17 August 1970, p. 32.

Plays and Players, 17 (August 1970), 30-33.

Nation, 21 September 1970, pp. 525-53.

New York Times, 18 November 1970, p. 41.

Newsweek, 30 November 1970, p. 98.

Time, 30 November 1970, p. 48.

Nation, 7 December 1970, p. 605.

New Republic, 12 December 1970, p. 20.

Saturday Review, 12 December 1970, p. 16.

239

Commonweal, 15 January 1971, pp. 373-74.

America, 16 January 1971, pp. 46-47.

IN CELEBRATION

    Plays and Players, 16 (June 1969), 26-29.

    Time, 10 June 1974, p. 106.

ARNOLD WESKER

Born Stepney, London, May 24, 1932

While Arnold Wesker and Harold Pinter were both
raised in the London Jewish community, Wesker has made
far greater use of Jewish traditions and attitudes in his
plays. Furthermore he has created a more truly proletarian drama than any of his contemporaries. The poor are
taken seriously in his works and possess a dignity and
determination that contrasts sharply with traditional
portrayals of the English working class--the good-natured,
ineffectual, congenitally lazy stereotypes that have ex-
isted for centuries in English literature. Wesker's
characters are not humorless. The music hall humor and
crude humor that Stoppard and Pinter have also employed
successfully in sophisticated dramas is present in Wesker,
too. Still, the emphasis of his plays is on a hard-won
survival in a caste system. His most famous plays form a
trilogy: Chicken Soup, Roots, and I'm Talking about
Jerusalem.

PRIMARY SOURCES

I. STAGE

Chicken Soup with Barley. In The Wesker Trilogy. Staged
     Coventry 1958; London 1958.

_____. In New English Dramatists. London: Penguin,
     1959.

_____. London: Evans Brothers, 1961.

Chips with Everything. Ed. Michael Marland, with an in-
     troduction by the author. Glasgow: Blackie & Son,
     1962. [Includes press reviews.]

_____. London: Cape, 1962.

_____. In Plays and Players (December 1962).

_____. New York: Random House, 1963.

_____. In New English Dramatists 7. Harmondsworth: Penguin, 1963.

_____. In Theatre Arts, 47 (October 1963).

_____. In The Best Plays 1963-1964. Ed. Henry Hewes. New York: Dodd, Mead, 1964. (Condensed version.)

_____. In America's Lost Plays. New York: Dodd, Mead, 1964.

_____. In Post-War Drama: Extracts from Eleven Plays. Ed. John Hale. London: Faber and Faber, 1966.

La Cuisine. (French translation of The Kitchen.) In L'Avant Scene du Théâtre, 385 (August 1967).

Des Frites, des Frites, des Frites . . . . In L'Avant Scene du Théâtre, no. 494 (May 1972).

The Four Seasons. Staged Coventry 1965; London 1965. London: Cape, 1966.

_____. In New English Dramatists 9. Harmondsworth: Penguin, 1966.

The Friends. London: Cape, 1970.

_____. In Plays and Players, 18 (October 1970).

I'm Talking About Jerusalem. In The Wesker Trilogy. Staged Coventry 1960; London 1960.

_____. Harmondsworth: Penguin, 1960.

_____. London: Evans Brothers, 1961.

The Journalists. In Dialog (Poland), March 1974.

_____. London: Writers and Readers Cooperative, 1975.

The Kitchen. In New English Dramatists 2. Harmondsworth: Penguin, 1960.

_____. Expanded version. London: Cape, 1961.

_____. Expanded version. New York: Random House, 1962.

_____. Harmondsworth: Penguin, 1964.

_____. In Three Plays. Harmondsworth: Penguin, 1968.

Menace. In The Jewish Quarterly (Spring 1963).

_____. In Six Sundays in January. London: Cape, 1971.

The Merchant. Staged Stockholm 1976.

The Nottingham Captain: A Moral for Narrator, Voices and
    Orchestra. Staged Wellingborough 1962. Music by
    Wilfred Josephs and David Lee. In Six Sundays in
    January. London: Cape, 1971.

The Old Ones. Staged London 1972. In Plays and Players,
    30 (October 1972).

_____. London: Cape, 1973.

The Old Ones by Arnold Wesker. Rev. ed. Ed. Michael
    Marland. London: Blackie & Son, 1974.

The Plays of Arnold Wesker. Volume 1. New York: Harper
    & Row, 1976. [Includes The Kitchen, Chicken Soup
    with Barley, Roots, I'm Talking About Jerusalem, and
    Chips with Everything.]

Les Quatre Saisons. (French translation of The Four Sea-
    sons.) In L'Avant Scene du Théâtre, 417 (January
    1969).

Roots. In The Wesker Trilogy. Staged Coventry 1969;
    London 1969.

_____. Harmondsworth: Penguin, 1959.

_____. London: Evans Brothers, 1961.

_____. In Audience, 8, i (Winter 1961), 83-100.

_____. In New British Drama. Ed. Henry Popkin. New
York: Grove Press, 1964.

_____. In The Drama Bedside Book. Ed. H. F. Rubinstein.
New York: Atheneum, 1966.

_____. London: Longmans, in association with Cape, 1967.

_____. In Twelve Modern Dramatists. Ed. Raymond Cowell.
London: Pergamon Press, 1967.

Their Very Own and Golden City. London: Cape, 1966.

_____. In Plays and Players, 13 (August 1966).

_____. In New English Dramatists 10. Harmondsworth:
Penguin, 1967.

_____. In Plays and Players Plays 1966-1969.

The Wedding Feast. Staged Stockholm 1974; Karl-Marx-
Stadt 1975; Leeds 1977.

The Wesker Trilogy: Plays. First staged as a trilogy
London 1960. London: Cape, 1960. [Includes
Chicken Soup with Barley, Roots, and I'm Talking
About Jerusalem.]

The Wesker Trilogy. New York: Random House, 1961.

_____. Harmondsworth: Penguin, 1964.

II. TELEVISION

Love Letters on Blue Paper, 1976.

Menace, 1963.

III. SCREENPLAY

The Kitchen, 1961.

IV. FICTION

"The Hill." In The Jewish Quarterly (Autumn 1958).
[Short story.]

Love Letters on Blue Paper: Three Stories. London: Cape,
1974. [Includes "The Man Who Became Afraid," "A
Time of Dying," and "Love Letters on Blue Paper."]

Love Letters on Blue Paper. New York: Harper & Row,
1975.

"The Man Who Would Never Write Like Balzac." Jewish
Quarterly (Spring-Summer 1975).

"Pools." The Jewish Quarterly (Winter 1958-59). [Short
story.]

"Time Parts the Memory." The Jewish Quarterly (Winter
1959-60). [Poem.]

V. COLLECTION

Six Sundays in January. London: Cape, 1971. [Includes
"Pools," The Nottingham Captain, Menace, "Six Sundays in January," and "The London Diary of Stockholm."]

VI. NON-FICTION

"Art and Action." Listener, 10 May 1962, pp. 806-08.

"Art Is Not Enough." Twentieth Century, 169 (February 1961), 190-94.

"Art--Therapy or Experience." Views No. 4 (Spring 1964), 44-47.

"Casual Condemnations: A Brief Study of the Critic as Censor." Theatre Quarterly, 1 (April-June 1971), 16-30.

"Centre 42. The Secret Reins." Encounter, 25 (March 1962), 3-6. (On John Osborne.)

"Christmas." The Sunday Times, 23 December 1974, p. 35.

"Cretinue of Critics; an Open Letter to Harold Hobson." Drama, no. 107 (Winter 1972), 55-56.

"A Crucial Question." The Jewish Quarterly (Autumn 1960), 43-45.

"Director's Introduction to the Report." In Annual Report 1961-1962 Forty two. London: Centre 42 Ltd., 1962. Pages 2-5.

"Discovery." The Transatlantic Review, 5 (December 1960), 16-18.

"East End My Cradle." The Observer Magazine, 24 November 1974, pp. 48-49, 51-52.

Fears of Fragmentation. London: Cape, 1970.

"From a Writer's Notebook." Theatre Quarterly, 2, vi (1973), 8-13.

"Green Room; the Playwright as Director." Plays and Players, 21 (February 1974), 10-12.

"House." Encounter, 27 (November 1966), 3-9.

Labour and the Arts: II; or, What, Then, Is to Be Done. Oxford: Gemini, 1960.

"Let Battle Commence." Encore (November 1958). Reprinted in The Encore Reader. Ed. Charles Marowitz. London: Eyre Methuen, 1965. Pages 96-103.

"Letter to a Killer" (open letter to all Irish terrorists). The Sunday Times, 13 October 1974, II:i.

245

"London's Jewish Immigrants of the Nineteenth Century."
The Times Educational Supplement, 7 March 1975,
p. 25.

"The Modern Playwright." Gemini/Dialogue, 3 (Spring
1960), 5-7.

The Modern Playwright; or, "O Mother, Is It Worth It?"
Oxford: Gemini, 1961.

"Resolution 42." New Statesman, 7 April 1961, p. 558.

"The Secret Reins." Encounter, 25 (March 1962), 306.

Text to Say Goodbye, You May Never See Them Again: Scenes
From Two East-End Backgrounds. Paintings by John
Albin. London: Cape, 1974.

"Theatre 1965: The Round House." The London Magazine, 5
(August 1965), 78-83.

"Vision! Vision! Mr. Woodcock." New Statesman, 30 July
1960, p. 153.

"Wesker on 42." The Observer Weekend Review, 7 July
1963, p. 19.

VII. INTERVIEWS

Bigsby, Christopher. "Arnold Wesker Talks to Professor
Christopher Bigsby." Cassette available at the
British Council, 65 Davies Street, London WIY2AA.

Dexter, John. "The Future of Centre 42." Challenge, 12
(October 1963), 2.

'Dramaturgii contemporani n-au decît o şansa pentru
supravieţuire!' Tribuna, 16 (January 1972), 15.

Gordon, Giles. "Arnold Wesker." Transatlantic Review,
21 (1966), 15-25.
    Gordon and Wesker mainly discuss the poor criti-
cal reception of The Four Seasons and its individual
rather than social focus. Wesker also presents his
views on subsidizing art.

Pomerance, Jill. "Question and Answer." New Theatre
Magazine (April 1960), 5-8.
    Wesker gives his personal view of several sub-
jects, including the potential of provincial repertory companies, the need for simplification in the

246

arts, a comparison of his theatrical ideas to those
of John Arden, and the artist's need for respect.
For him, the "New Drama" is not technically innovative; its importance lies, rather, in its concern
with contemporary social issues.

Rothberg, A. "Waiting for Wesker." Antioch Review, 24
    (Winter 1964-65), 492-505.
        This is a personal glimpse of the optimistic,
    lively and yet "melancholy driving, ambitious" play-
    wright in his Centre 42 office. Wesker briefly ex-
    plains his trilogy of plays, Chicken Soup With Bar-
    ley, Roots, and I'm Talking About Jerusalem, which
    deal with socialism in politics, love, and art. The
    article also provides a short history of Centre 42,
    the "cultural revolution" geared to involve the in-
    dividual and community in the arts, with a list of
    its activities which include photo exhibits, folk
    festivals, theatre activities, and poetry readings.

The Sunday Times, 29 June 1975, p. 27.

"The System and the Writer: Wesker Interviewed." New
    Theatre Magazine (Bristol), 11, ii (1971), 8-11.
        Wesker discusses "aspects of the present system
    of subsidy in the theatre, the drama inherent in the
    tension of ideas, and the different means which
    playwrights use to convey verisimilitude in their
    works."

Taëni, Rainer. "Interview with Arnold Wesker." Die
    Neueren Sprachen, 20 August 1971), 410-18.
        Wesker here discusses the English Arts Council,
    Center 42, his play, The Friends, violence, life in
    Cuba, and the political background to some of his
    plays.

Trussler, Simon. "His Very Own and Gold City." Ed. K.
    Morris. Tulane Drama Review, 11 (Winter 1966), 192-
    202.
        Wesker and Trussler discuss a broad range of sub-
    jects including the playwright's early impulses
    towards the stage; the rise and decline of the "New
    Wave drama" and its political commitment; the gene-
    sis, significance, and failure of Centre 42; the
    communal aspect of art; and the change in his use of
    language from his early plays to Four Seasons.

Wager, Walter, ed. The Playwrights Speak. New York:
    Delacorte Press, 1967. Pages 279-90.
        Wager provides a brief biography, focusing on
    Wesker's career as a playwright through the produc-
    tion of The Four Seasons, before he launches into
    this straightforward dialogue with Wesker on the

playwright's writing habits, political background,
and his move away from naturalism. Wesker also discusses in detail Centre 42 and his hopes for state-
subsidized art.

Wershba, Joseph. "A Cultural Rebel." New York Post, 28
October 1963, p. 36.

SECONDARY SOURCES

I. CRITICISM

Adereth, Max. "Sartre and Wesker: Committed Playwrights."
Comment, 5 (July 1964), 18-28.
   Sartre and Wesker, as committed writers, share an
intense awareness of modern problems and feel com-
pelled to awaken their audiences to responsible action in building a better civilization. The article
examines their respective evolutions as writers,
their similar belief in the need for human solidar-
ity, increased communication and responsibility, and
the dramatic techniques which each employs to help
their audiences maintain emotional distance from the
play.

Alvarez, A. "Wesker's Trilogy." New Statesman, 6 August
1960, p. 182.

Amis, Kingsley. "Not Talking About Jerusalem." Spectator, 12 August 1962, p. 190.

Anderson, Michael. "Arnold Wesker: The Last Humanist."
New Theatre Magazine (Bristol), 8, iii (1968), 10-27.
   Wesker's sympathetic portrayal of man's aspirations and failures, his "combination of the vision-
ary and the realist," and his tragic perspective
which reveals his belief in the dignity of man,
classes him as a humanist playwright. This article
discusses both the intimate connection between
political thought and the rhythms of human life,
and the need to combat failure and disappointment
"with the warmth and passion of argument" in Wesker's
trilogy, Chips With Everything, and Their Very Own
and Golden City.

"Arnold Wesker." Current Biography (February 1962), 456-
58.
   This is a general biography of Wesker's life with
emphasis on his career as a playwright and proletarian supporter. Both positive and negative critical opinions of his plays and talents are presented.
Lively and sincere, Wesker creates sharp images and

communicates emotion well; however, his plays are
often didactic, have flimsy plots and need editing.

Baillie, Martin and Roy Wilkie. "Wesker's Microcosm."
Glasgow Review, 1 (Spring 1964), 12-15.
The authors believe that Wesker's attack on the
establishment in Chips With Everything is unfair and
misleading.

Beaven, John. "Missionary in the Theatre." The New York
Times Magazine, 13 October 1963, pp. 28, 73-74, 76,
78.
Beaven discusses Wesker's crusade to bring culture to the masses through his plays and Centre 42,
with short comments on the trilogy and Chips. He
also looks at Wesker's working class background and
his political involvement.

Boys, Barry. "Theories Into Action." Encore, 8 (September-October 1961), 25-31.
Boys proclaims the need for both the vision of
writers like Brook and Artaud and the action of
those like Joseph, Littlewood, and Wesker in estab-
lishing a new theater in which the artist can "express himself significantly" without compromising
his ideals and at the same time can promote audience
awareness without didacticism. The article briefly
mentions Centre 42 and its financial and ideological
problems.

Breitback, Joseph. "Unakademische Betrachtungen zu
einem gut gemachten Stück." Deutsche Akademie für
Sprache und Dichtung, Darmstadt. Jahrbuch, 1969,
pp. 99-105.
Breitback provides a close reading of The Kitchen
which he finds an authentic commentary on modern in-
dustrial life.

Brezianu, Andrei. "Hora sarutuliu." Secolul, 20, ix
(1971), 132-34.

Brien, A. "Wesker Trilogy." Spectator, 5 August 1960,
p. 216.

Brown, John Russell. "Introduction." In Modern British
Dramatists. Ed. John Russell Brown. Englewood
Cliffs: Prentice-Hall, 1968. Pages 12-14.
Brown emphasizes the experimental in Wesker, par-
ticularly the film-like quality of The Kitchen and
Their Very Own and Golden City and the formalistic
and symbolistic elements in The Four Seasons. Brown
also briefly discusses the theme of cooperation in
Chips With Everything.

_____. Theatre Language: A Study of Arden, Osborne, Pinter and Wesker. London: Allen Lane, 1972, 158-189.
Brown chooses to study Pinter, Osborne, Arden and Wesker because of the wide attention they have all attracted, the scope of their experimentation, and their similar backgrounds as English dramatists of the same age. Rather than describing their careers and the content of their plays, Brown explores how each has "controlled theatrical reality in words, actions, and time, so that the plays say what the authors want to say now, to present audiences and in present theatrical conditions." He emphasizes Wesker's attempt to teach and to assert values through significant action, argument, and setting in The Kitchen, the trilogy, Chips With Everything, Their Very Own and Golden City, The Four Seasons, and The Friends.

Brown, E. Martin. "Theatre Survey." Drama Survey (October 1962), 183.

Brustein, Robert. "The Backwards Birds." New Republic, 19 October 1963, pp. 28, 30-31.
Brustein praises the intensity and "passionate sense of engagement" of the new English dramatists, but criticizes their outdated proletarianism and naturalism. He specifically condemns Osborne's lack of control and focus in Luther and Wesker's naive ideology and didacticism in Chips With Everything.

_____. Seasons of Discontent. New York: Simon & Schuster, 1965. Pages 48-49, 198-200.
Brustein views the exacting naturalism and naive theme of Roots as "theatrical primitivism." He finds Chicken Soup With Barley and I'm Talking About Jerusalem more complex in their treatment of politics and human nature and in their theme of the brutalization by mass culture. A reprint of "Backwards Birds" is also included.

Charles, Gerda. "East and West." The Jewish Quarterly (Winter 1960-1961), 5-7.

_____. "Elizabethan Age of Modern Jewish Literature." World Jewry (September 1961), 15-17.

Chiari, J. Landmarks of Contemporary Drama. London: Herbert Jenkins, 1965. Pages 115-18.
Chiari applauds Wesker's enthusiasm and courage but criticizes the predictability of Chips With Everything and the "poor construction, over-stressed didacticism, incoherence and melodramatic touches," and excessive naturalism of his trilogy. In The Kitchen Chiari feels Wesker has accurately portrayed

the tense atmosphere of a "closed, cooped world" and
claims it is the playwright's best work to date.

Churchill, Caryl. "Not Ordinary, Not Safe." Twentieth
Century, 168 (November 1960), 443-51.
    This diffused article generally complains about
current British drama with its safe attitudes and
small heroes. Churchill briefly mentions playwrights to illustrate the points of his lecture. He
uses Wesker's Chicken Soup With Barley to show that
an enthusiastic attitude toward life is possible in
drama.

Cohen, Mark. "Impersonal Hero." Jewish Quarterly
(Autumn 1962), 48.

_____. "The World of Wesker." Jewish Quarterly (Winter
1960-1961), 45

Coleman, Terry. "Centre 42 Needs £3/4m to Survive." The
Guardian, 30 January 1967, p. 3.

Coppieters, F. "Arnold Wesker's Centre Forty two: A Cultural Revolution Betrayed." Theatre Quarterly, 5
(June 1975), 37-51.
    This is an intricate history of Centre 42, from
its earliest conception to its failure, including
an analysis of "the personal, political, and practical reasons for its decline."

Cowell, Raymond. Twelve Modern Dramatists. Oxford:
Pergamon Press, 1968. Pages 103-05.

Curti, Lidia. "La nuova Gerusalemme di Arnold Wesker."
Annali Instituto Universitario Orientale, Napoli,
Sezione Germanica, 8 (1965), 221-60.
    Curti describes the Trilogy in detail, discusses
Centre 42, and concludes that Wesker's optimism
about creating a just society is his major strength.

D'Amico, Sandro. "Theatre." The London Magazine (October 1963), 72-76.
    D'Amico discusses the 1963 Italian theatre season
and the lack of fine Italian playwrights with a
brief and positive review of the Teatro Stabile of
Bologna production of Wesker's Chicken Soup With
Barley.

Dennis, Nigel. "What Though the Field Be Lost?" En-
counter (August 1962), 43-45.
    Dennis somehow ties in England's defeat by the
Brazilian soccer team with this satiric glance at
Chips With Everything. He criticizes Wesker's sim-

plistic view of social classes and lack of imagination.

Dexter, John. "Working with Arnold." Plays and Players (April 1962), 11.

Findlater, R. "Plays and Politics; Arnold Wesker's Trilogy." Twentieth Century, 168 (September 1960), 235-42.
    Findlater finds the Socialist politics of Wesker's trilogy shallow and confused. He claims that Wesker has transcended doctrines and ideologies in these plays through his strong affirmation of the dignity, love, and common humanity of his characters and audience.

Fletcher, John. "Arnold Wesker, John Arden, and Arthur Adamov." Caliban, 3, ii (1967), 153-56.
    Fletcher explores the success with which Arden, Adamov, and Wesker have clearly conveyed their political ideals in their plays, suggesting that Wesker's "poverty-stricken diction" causes him to fail where the "range and power" of their language enables Arden and Adamov to succeed.

Fraser, G. S. The Modern Writer and His World. New York: Praeger, 1965. Pages 233-38.
    Fraser believes Wesker is "a more politically and intellectually committed artist than Osborne." He has drawn on his personal experience as an East End Jew, a farm laborer, a cook, and an R.A.F. serviceman to achieve verisimilitude in his plays. Roots is his best play because it has "one tight and unified dramatic situation." Like Osborne he has "no literary distinction, but comes across well on the stage."

Gardner, Raymond. "Roots That Have Not Taken." The Guardian, 17 May 1969, p. 7.

Garforth, John. "Arnold Wesker's Mission." Encore, 10 (May-June 1963), 38-43.
    Commending Wesker's activity and concern, Garforth explores the playwright's emphasis on the need for "ordinary people" to think for themselves in Roots, I'm Talking About Jerusalem, Chips With Everything, and The Kitchen. However, Garforth feels that these plays tend to romanticize and condescend to the working class and to reinforce the prejudices of his typically middle class audiences.

Gascoigne, Bamber. Twentieth Century Drama. London: Hutchinson & Co., 1962. Pages 176-208.
    The "gap between idealism and practice is central"

252

to the three plays of Wesker's trilogy, which are united by "three different and, in general, disillusioning experiments in practical Socialism."

"Getting Down to the Roots." <u>N</u>. <u>Z</u>. <u>Listener</u>, 59, no. 1521 (1968), 11.

Grindin, James. <u>Postwar British Fiction</u>. Berkeley: University of California Press, 1962. Pages 235-37.
    Gindin claims that Wesker uses the political and social to delineate individuals, unlike the 1930 proletarian plays which used the individual to demonstrate political or social truths. Gindin also briefly explores the unresolved conflict between the "militant activist and the more passively limited" in Wesker's trilogy.

Goodman, Henry. "The New Dramatists, 2: Arnold Wesker." <u>Drama Survey</u> (Minneapolis), 1 (Fall 1961), 215-22.
    Goodman sees in Wesker traits of the American theatre of the 1930s: "a revolutionary ardor and innocence, a sense of being rooted in the times and directly mirroring the society and its distresses, and a talent for lyrical speech that is natural, fresh and of the character, with minor lapses into the conventional and 'Broadway.'" Goodman touches on language, character, and autobiographical elements in Wesker's plays and discusses theme in <u>The Kitchen</u> and the trilogy.

Gustavsson, Torgny. "Mannen mot strömmen: Ett samtal med Arnold Wesker." <u>Horisont</u>, 17, ii (1970), 57-64.

Habicht, Werner. "Theater der Sprache. Bermerkungen zu einigen englischen Dramen der Gegenwart." <u>Der Neueren Sprachen</u>, 7 (July 1963), 302-13.
    Habicht contrasts Wesker's use of language with N. F. Simpson's. He finds Wesker's more realistic dialogue less effective than Simpson's absurdist-influenced language. The latter conveys man's loss of values and disintegrating humanity more appropriately.

Hall, Stuart. "Beyond Naturalism Pure." <u>Encore</u>, 8 (November-December 1961), 12-19.
    Brief and unconnected glances at the post-naturalistic strains in Delaney's <u>Taste of Honey</u>, Wesker's <u>The Kitchen</u> and <u>Roots</u>, Osborne's <u>Look Back in Anger</u> and <u>The Entertainer</u>, and Arden's <u>Serjeant Musgrave's Dance</u> are included in this article.

Hare, Carl. "Creativity and Commitment in the Contemporary British Theatre." Humanities Association Bulletin, 16 (Spring 1965), 21-28.
Hare examines the attitudes of Osborne, Wesker,
Arden, and Pinter towards social commitment. He
finds that Osborne and Wesker are "intensely concerned with the reform of the social system and the
assertion of the individual," while Arden and Pinter
expose "subtly the bases of human relationship." He
charges Wesker with oversimplification because the
playwright attributes the success or failure of his
characters' commitment to the social system.

Hartley, Anthony. A State of England. New York: Harcourt, Brace and World, 1963. Pages 172, 186.
Hartley condemns Wesker's plea for trade-union
support of the arts and briefly discusses Wesker's
presentation in Roots of the intellectual's role in
society.

Hayman, Ronald. Arnold Wesker. Contemporary Playwrights
Series. London: Heinemann Educational, 1970.
Besides two interviews and a selected bibliography, this book provides play descriptions of and
summaries of critical reactions to The Kitchen, the
trilogy, Chips With Everything, Their Very Own and
Golden City, and The Four Seasons. In the first interview, Wesker talks about his life and the autobiographical strain in his writings, while in the
second, he and Hayman discuss particular snatches of
dialogue in his plays.

_____. Arnold Wesker. World Dramatists. New York:
Ungar, 1973.
This is a repeat of the above, with additional
chapters on The Friends, The Old Ones, and The
Journalists, and an index.

Heming, Gillian. "Arnold Wesker and the British Theatre."
Overland, no. 17 (April 1960), 36-37.
Heming discusses the concern, hope, and inspira-
tion evident in Chicken Soup With Barley and Roots,
two plays which sympathetically portray a communist
family.

Hughes, Ted. "Arnold Wesker: 'A Sort of Socialism.'"
Nation, 19 November 1960, pp. 402-04.
Hughes examines the love and the convincing and
moving realism which suffuse the three plays of the
trilogy and explains Wesker's special form of socialism. Wesker's socialist message, directed especially to the working class, "takes the form of a
desperate public exhortation--wake up and live."
This reveals Wesker's belief that only in a personal

commitment to action can "socialism fulfill any of
its aspirations."

Hunt, Albert. "Realism and Intelligence." Encore, 7
(May-June 1960), 12-17.
    In this article which basically explores the
plays of Arthur Miller, Hunt briefly compares
Beatie's traumatic awakening at the end of Roots to
Joe Keller's more gradually developed consciousness
revealed at the end of All My Sons.

Jones, A. R. "The Theatre of Arnold Wesker." Critical
Quarterly, 2 (Winter 1960), 366-70.
    Jones discusses the construction, the language
and the central position of politics in Wesker's
trilogy. He also claims that Wesker's "attitude is
not imposed upon the plays with distance and detachment but is allowed to evolve; to emerge gradually
and painfully through the actual development of the
play itself so that--in a sense--Wesker and his audience carry the burden of the dramatic experience
together and find its coherence as an artistic
statement simultaneously."

Jones, D. A. N. "Second Opinion: Arnold Wesker." The
Sunday Times Magazine, 29 October 1967, p. 54.

Jones, Mervyn. "Arnold Wesker's Epic." Encore, 7 (September-October 1960), 6-10.
    Jones briefly discusses the epic time-scale and
subject of Wesker's trilogy, and the interconnected-
ness of characters and themes of the three plays.

Kettle, A. "Quest for New Ways." Inostrannaja Literatura, no. 8 (August 1961), 182-88.
    Kettle praises John Braine's vivid Room at the
Top above all the other works of the angry movement.
Nevertheless, he mentions Wesker especially as a
meretorious playwright in this tradition.

Kitchin, Laurence. "Drama with a Message: Arnold Wesker."
In Experimental Drama. Ed. William A. Armstrong.
London: G. Bell, 1963. Pages 169-85.
    Kitchin dispenses with criticism of the New Wave
dramatists, claiming that modern critics are tied
to "restrictive notions about dramatic form." He
praises the emotional maturity of Chicken Soup, in
which political issues and characters are insepara-
ble. Kitchin also comments on Wesker's "command of
action in depth" and gives a perceptive analysis of
The Kitchen at four levels: "Documentary, character, conflict, and total statement or resolution."

_____. Mid-Century Drama. London: Faber and Faber, 1960. Pages 112-14, 215-18.

Kitchin finds that Wesker's naturalistic Roots "deals with this transitional phrase in which an old way of life, not without dignity amid its feudal superstitions, lies in decay at the mercy of mass-media values." Ignorance, rather than poverty, is the problem to be faced in Wesker's plays. Kitchin also summarizes an interview in which Wesker discusses his working class background, his promptings toward the theatre, and the problem of lack of communication.

_____. "Realism in English Mid Century Drama." World Theatre, 14 (January-February 1965), 17-26. See Arden above.

Kleinberg, Robert. "Seriocomedy in The Wesker Trilogy." Educational Theatre Journal, 21 (1969), 36-40.

Wesker's combination of the serious and comic are crucial to his "search for a workable definition of meaningful existence" in his trilogy. Kleinberg claims that such comic elements as stereotypes, dialect, and folk-manners, tend "simultaneously to lighten, intensify, and subvert the seriousness of situations."

Klotz, Günther. "Individuum und Gesellschaft im englischen Drama der Gegenwart. Arnold Wesker und Harold Pinter." Weimarer Meiträge, 19, x (1973), 187-91.

Although the 1950s opened up English drama to polemical onslaughts by angry writers, progressive drama is doomed, Klotz feels, in an imperialistic society where theatres are run for profit. Pinter and Wesker are both caught up in this conflict. Wesker defends the dignity of man but Pinter denies the social function of art and dooms his characters to submit to fate.

Knight, G. Wilson. "The Kitchen Sink: On Recent Developments in Drama." Encounter, 21 (December 1963), 48-54.

Knight directs a selective glance at several contemporary dramatists, including Pinter, Miller, Osborne, Wesker, Arden, etc., which focuses on the vitality, earthiness, and simplicity of key characters in their plays.

K[oolhass], A[nton]. "Drama." Delta (Amsterdam), 6, i. (1863), 51-52.

Koolhaas claims that the audience tends to identify with Wesker's "lazy farmers" in Roots rather than with Ronnie, the "scolding socialist," and that this is not Wesker's intention.

Kops, Bernard. "The Young Writer and the Theatre." *The Jewish Quarterly* (Summer 1961), 19-22.

Latham, J. "*Roots*: A Reassessment." *Modern Drama*, 8 (September 1965), 192-97.
    Latham explores the important role which the Bryants play in *Roots* and Wesker's handling of language.

Lee, Jennie. "Wesker's Centre 42." *Encounter* (August 1962), 95-96.
    This contains a letter written by one of the members of Centre 42 to enlist acceptance and optimism for Wesker's "poetic vision" in this endeavor.

Leech, Clifford. "Two Romantics: Arnold Wesker and Harold Pinter." In *Contemporary Theatre*. Ed. John Russell Brown and Bernard Harris. Stratford-upon-Avon Studies, 4. London: Arnold, 1962. Pages 11-31.
    Leech compares and contrasts the technique and attitudes of Pinter (in *The Birthday Party*, *The Caretaker*, *The Room*, *The Dwarfs*, *A Slight Ache*, *A Night Out*) and Wesker (in the trilogy and *The Kitchen*). Wesker creates an "atmosphere of actuality" in his somewhat rambling plays which plainly point out "what it means . . . to be fully alive." Pinter deals with extraordinary situations in his tightly constructed works. His message is darker and more subtle than Wesker's. Leech finds that both have a strong sense of contemporary issues and of the need for responsibility to others.

Leeming, Glenda. *Arnold Wesker*. Writers and Their Work, 225. Harlow: Longmans for the British Council, 1972.
    In this highly interesting and cohesive book, Leeming explores the major theme of fragmentation in Wesker's theories and plays, from *The Kitchen* to *The Friends*. Leeming finds that Wesker's characters are usually unaware of "how other unrecognized aspects of life are affecting them: fragmentation screens from them the connexions which explain why they so often suffer and are helpless."

_____ and Simon Trussler. *The Plays of Wesker: An Assessment*. London: Gollancz, 1971.
    In this thorough work, Leeming and Trussler closely examine the themes, characterization, structure and language of Wesker's plays from *The Kitchen* through *The Friends*. They also discuss *Fears of Fragmentation*, a collection of Wesker's lectures and essays, and provide a "chronology of Wesker's career as a playwright, a complete set of cast-lists of

London productions and revivals of his plays, and a
bibliography of work by and about the dramatist."

Leroy, Bernard. "Two Committed Playwrights: Wesker and
O'Casey." In Aspects of the Irish Theatre. Ed.
Patrick Rafroidi et al. Paris: Editions Univer-
sitaires, Publications de l'Université de Lille,
1972. Pages 107-17.
    Leroy discusses the similarities in themes, char-
acters, use of language, attitudes towards commitment, and personal background of Wesker and O'Casey.

Levidova, I. "A New Hero Appears in the Theatre."
Inostrannaya Literatura, 1 (January 1962), 201-08.
[In Russian.]
    Wesker, along with several of the other "angry"
writers, is responsible for introducing a new hero
to the English stage--the plebian hero.

Lumley, Frederick. New Trends in Twentieth Century
Drama. London: Barrie & Rockliff, 1967. Pages
273-79.
    Lumley mentions Wesker's attempts to bring aware-
ness and culture to the public through his plays and
Centre 42. He briefly discusses theme and character
in The Kitchen, the trilogy, and Chips With Everything, and the departure from naturalism in The Four
Seasons.

Mander, John. The Writer and Commitment. Philadelphia:
Dufour Editions, 1962. Pages 194-211.

Manet, Eduardo. "Arnold Wesker à la Havane." Les Lettres Nouvelles (September 1968), 108-15.
    Manet gives an account of Wesker's visit to
Havana in 1964, where he completed The Four Seasons.

Mannheimer, M. L. "Major Themes in Arnold Wesker's Play
The Friends." Moderna Språk (Stockholm), 66 (1972),
109-16.
    Mannheimer discusses such themes in The Friends
as (1) the "chaotic nature of our existence" and the
individual need to come to terms with it; (2) the
relations between individuals; and (3) the responsibility of the artist. For the most part, Mannheimer
finds the themes inconclusively explored.

_____. "Ordering Chaos: The Genesis of Arnold Wesker's
The Friends." English Studies, 56 (February 1975),
34-44.
    Mannheimer believes Wesker sees several solutions
to alienation and despair. First, the individual,
like Hester in The Friends, must accept life and
actively celebrate whatever good can be found.

Second, in assuming the role of artist, an individual must make a commitment to help others find solutions, social or philosophical, to human problems.

Marland, Michael, ed. Arnold Wesker. The Times Authors, 1. London: The Times, 1970.

Marowitz, Charles. "New Wave in a Dead Sea." X, A Quarterly Review, 1 (October 1960).
See Arden above.

_____. "Oh Mother, Is It Worth It?" Theatre Arts (May 1962), 21-22, 72-73.
This is basically an optimistic glance at the future of Centre 42, with a history of its germination. Marowitz, however, sees two major problems: (1) the patronizing attitude inherent in the desire to elevate the working class, and (2) the "assumption that working-class art is going to be superior to the best commercial art."

Matthews, Honor. The Primal Curse. New York: Schocken Books, 1967. Pages 193-94.
Matthews mentions Pip's betrayal of Charles, a working-class comrade, and consequently his "betrayal of the crusade for social justice" in Chips With Everything.

Murdoch, Brian. "Communication as a Dramatic Problem: Buchner, Chekhov, and Hofmannsthal and Wesker." Revue de Littérature comparée, 45 (1971), 40-59.
Murdoch examines aspects of the theme of non-communication in Buchner's Woyzeck, Chekhov's Three Sisters and The Cherry Orchard, Hofmannsthal's Der Schwierige and Chandos-Brief, and Wesker's Roots. Murdoch finds a developing optimism, culminating in Beatie's personal salvation through articulacy.

Nicoll, Allardyce. English Drama: A Modern Viewpoint. London: Harrap, 1968. Pages 126-48.
Nicoll makes brief mention of the effect of Wesker's desire for clarity, his interest in bettering the conditions of his fellow-beings, and the autobiographical elements in his plays. Nicoll claims that Wesker's plays reflect the playwright's "frank, open, and lively interest in the world around him."

O'Connor, Garry. "Arnold Wesker's The Friends: A Production Casebook." Theatre Quarterly, 1, ii (1971), 78-92.
Theatre Quarterly has printed "Extracts from a detailed diary kept by Garry O'Connor, who acted as Wesker's assistant director, on the planning of the production [of The Friends] and the progress of its

rehearsals." O'Connor bases his selections on the
question: "Should an author direct his own play?"

_____. "Wesker: A Voice Crying in the Wilderness."
Sunday Times Magazine, 10 May 1970, p. 38.

Oppel, Horst. "Arnold Wesker: The Chicken Soup Trilogy."
In Das moderne englische Drama: Interpretationen.
Ed. Horst Oppel. Berlin: Erich Schmidt, 1963.
Pages 345-71.
Oppel notes the theme of the Wandering Jew run-
ning throughout Wesker's work along with a preoccupation re the working class world. Taken together
these themes provide a kind of unity for the dense
and far-ranging materials of the trilogy. Oppel
points out characterizations which are not fully developed and plot contrivances, but he concludes that
Wesker's dramaturgy is rich in human experience. He
also mentions Wesker's fondness for the poets, D. H.
Lawrence and Dylan Thomas, and for the playwright,
John Osborne.

Page, M. "Whatever Happened to Arnold Wesker: His Recent Plays." Modern Drama, 11 (December 1968),
317-25.
From the simplicity and didacticism of The Kitch-
en and the trilogy, Wesker moved "through structural
experiments to greater self-knowledge and new linguistic attainment" in Chips With Everything, Four
Seasons, and Their Very Own and Golden City. Page
praises the ambitiousness of the three later plays,
but finds only Four Seasons truly successful, with
its poetic language, clarity and "subtle changes in
pace and tension." In Chips, the confused note,
multiple themes and uncertain style blur character
motivation and message. Golden City is loosely-
linked because of the time span, the frequent time
changes, and the cloudy character backgrounds and
relationships.

Peinert, Dietrich. "Chicken Soup with Barley: Unter-
suchungen zur Dramentechnik Arnold Weskers."
Literatur in Wissenschaft und Unterricht (Kiel), 3
(1970), 169-86.
Peinert praises Wesker's techniques. He observes
that Wesker's characters speak in an appropriate
idiom, that they provide us with information about
the past, that they hold our attention with their
concerns, and that their dialogue is naturalistic
and convincing.

Philpot, Terry. "Wesker's World." New Humanist, 90
(July 1974), 82.

Popkin, Henry. "Jewish Writers in England." Commentary
(February 1961), 135-41.
Popkin traces the previous dearth of Anglo-Jewish
writers to the British ideal of the Gentleman, the
pressure toward conformity, and the hostile images
of Jews in literature. However, "the present youth-
ful generation of Arnold Wesker, Dan Jacobson, Harold Pinter, Wolf Mankowitz, Dannie Abse and others"
have benefitted from the economic and social level-
ing of the welfare state and from the encouragement
of their American counterparts. Popkin finds that
Wesker deals most directly with Jewish subjects, and
with socialism and family life as necessary parts of
the Jewish scene." Popkin also mentions the presence of nostalgia and defensiveness in Jewish writers.

_____. "Nostalgia for a Lost World." Midstream, 6
(Autumn 1960), 102-05.
Popkin reveals the nostalgia and the respect for
a past community in this exploration of Wesker's
brand of socialism in Chicken Soup With Barley.

Pritchett, V. S. "A World of Kitchens." New Statesman
and Nation, 7 July 1961, p. 24.

Regina, Sister. "Arnold Wesker: Prophet and/or Dramatist?" Wisconsin Studies in Literature, no. 2
(1965), 75-80.
Sister Regina says that Wesker deals with the de-
basement of the working class, which is partly due
to the lethargy and passivity of the workers themselves. Wesker has the strength to see man's medioc-
rity and to contrast it with his potential, but so
far Wesker has lacked the artistic discipline to
make his prophetic optimism come to life.

Ribalow, Harold U. Arnold Wesker. (TEAS, 28.) New York:
Twayne, 1966.
In this thorough study of Wesker's works and life,
Ribalow attempts to "clarify Wesker's plays within
the patterns of recent British social, cultural, and
literary trends." He analyzes characters and themes
in Wesker's plays from The Kitchen through The Four
Seasons, discusses Pools, a short story, and Menace,
a little-known play, explores the effects of Wesker's
Jewishness on his life and writings, and provides a
history of Centre 42, a summary of critical articles
on Wesker, and a selected annotated bibliography of
criticism.

_____. "The Plays of Arnold Wesker." Chicago Jewish
Forum, 21 (1963), 127-31.

Rothberg, Abraham. "East End, West End: Arnold Wesker."
Southwest Review, 52 (Autumn 1967), 368-78.
   Rothberg rather harshly criticizes Wesker's autobiographical strain, his wordy leftist lectures, his
inability to fuse realistic and impressionistic impulses, and the contradictory political and dramatic
levels in The Kitchen and the trilogy.

Ryan, Stephen. "The London Stage." America, 27 October
1962, pp. 956-58.
   Ryan focuses on the New Wave playwrights associated with the English Stage Company and the stimu-
lating 1961-62 theatre season in London, with reviews of Osborne's The Blood of the Bambergs and
Under Plain Cover, Wesker's Chips With Everything,
Pinter's The Collection, and Whiting's A Penny for a
Song. Of Chips, Ryan claims that this frank attack
on the British military has masterly dialogue, an
important message, absorbing dramatic situations,
and a hero with dignity and integrity.

Ryapolova, V. "Arnold Uesker." Teatr, 6 (1968), 143-52.
   This is an overview of Wesker, noting his Jewish
proletarian background, his socialism, his brief
appearance in political theatre.

Seehase, Georg. "Abbild des Klassenkampfes." Zeitschrift für Anglistik und Amerikanistik, 16, iv,
(1969), 392-405.
   Seehase claims that in both the nineteenth and
twentieth centuries elements of working class culture can be seen in bourgeois literature and "proletarian literature proper." He calls Wesker a
twentieth century bourgeois writer who has great
sympathy for the working class.

Smith, Roger. "Rocking the Boat." Encore, 8 (January-
February 1961), 7-12.
   In this rousing article to encourage left-wing
theatre to expose the social systems of the modern
world, Smith commends Truffaut's 400 Blows and
Arden's The Happy Haven for their exposé of particular social worlds. He condemns Wesker in his trilogy for "structural and ideological sloppiness," an
"indifference to social and historical realities,"
and the failure to fully explore the sociological
significance of his family.

"Speaking of Writing. 4. Arnold Wesker." The Times, 12
December 1963, p. 13.

Spencer, Charles. "Arnold Wesker as a Playwright."
Jewish Quarterly (Winter 1959-60), 40-41.

Spender, Stephen. "A Literary Letter from London."
The New York Times Book Review, 20 November 1960.,
pp. 74-75.
   Spender finds the cinema, television, and theatre
most expressive of the contemporary voice and discusses the integrity of the new playwrights, like
Wesker, who explore socially significant subjects
and who attempt to establish a connection between
people who will fight for social and artistic values
in an indifferent and mechanized society.

"State of the Arts No Longer to Be 'Mean Joke.'" The
Guardian, 17 July 1964, p. 3.

Styan, J. L. The Dark Comedy. 2nd ed. London: Cambridge University Press, 1968. Page 166.

Tabachnick, Stephen E. and William Baker. "Reflections
on Ethnicity in Anglo-Jewish Writing." Jewish Quarterly, 21, i-ii (1973), 94-97.
   Tabachnick and Baker examine the way in which
Pinter, Wesker and Kops deal with their Jewish background through the themes and characters in their
plays: "Harold Pinter proves the most successful in
at once recapturing and universalizing personal
memories"; Wesker "presents a dramatic situation
which speaks to all former believers in 'truths,'
and to all men concerned with the situation of the
family," achieving artistic distance through the
perspective of time; Kops fails to transcend his
materials.

Taëni, Rainer. "Revolution oder Rebellion: Über Arnold
Weskers Die Freunde." Akzente, 18 (1971), 319-30.
   Taeni has provided an overview of Wesker's works,
but his interest here is a close reading of The
Friend.

_____. "Tendenzen des neuen Theaters, II: Theaterbrief
aus London." Merkur, 24 (October 1970), 971-78.
   Wesker is described as being one of the most
promising English dramatists but nothing specific
is said about his work.

_____. "Der Tod als Anstoss zur Revolution gegen das
Rebellieren: Zu Arnold Weskers Die Freunde."
Jahresring 71-72 (Stuttgart), 230-40.
   This is exactly the same article that appeared in
Akzente only with a slightly different title and no
footnotes.

Taylor, John Russell. Anger and After. London: Eyre
Methuen, 1962. Pages 143-58.
   Taylor traces the curve of Wesker's popularity as

a playwright, scans Wesker's working-class background and career, and reviews the trilogy and The
Kitchen. Taylor praises the boldness of Wesker's
designs, but questions the authenticity of his characters and language and criticizes the lack of
skilled construction in the trilogy and the muddled
messages.

_____. "Arnold Wesker." The Times, 12 December 1963,
    p. 13.

_____. "British Theatre." In On Contemporary Litera-
    ture. Ed. Richard Kostelanetz. New York: Avon,
    1964. Pages 90-96.
    Taylor only briefly alludes to Wesker as an art-
ist, who along with Delaney, began writing for the
stage directly with no prior experience in other
media.

Temkine, Raymonde. "La Trilogie d'Arnold Wesker."
    Europe, 48 (August-September 1970), 286-88.
    This is a brief description of the Wesker tril-
ogy, its subject matter, and its enthusiastic acceptance by audiences.

Thompson, Dennis. "British Experiment in Art for the
    Masses." New Republic, 21 November 1964, pp. 7-8.
    Thompson mentions the progress of Centre 42 and
Wesker's dream of the government's assuming responsibility for the subsidy of art. Thompson also outlines the contradictions inherent in the idea of a
liberal elite within a democracy attempting to "im-
prove" (and thus dictate) the cultural tastes of the
masses.

Trilling, Ossia. "The Young British Drama." Modern
    Drama, 3 (September 1960), 168-77.
    This is a look at the encouragement offered new
dramatists by such theatres as the Arts Theatre, the
Royal Court Theatre, the Theatre Workshop and provincial repertory theatres. Trilling comments on
the irony that although Wesker's trilogy and The
Kitchen are about working-class people, they do not
attend his plays.

Trussler, Simon. "British Neo-Naturalism." Drama Review,
    13 (Winter 1968), 130-36.
    As a form well-adapted for exploring social prob-
lems, encouraging political commitment, and presenting semi-autobiographical material, naturalism
served as a vehicle for new-wave British dramatists
like Osborne, Wesker, and Bolt. The article briefly
traces this British neo-naturalism from its original
use for revolutionary expression to its present "re-
spectable" use for mild sex comedies.

Tynan, Kenneth. *Tynan Right and Left*. New York: Atheneum, 1967. Pages 19-20, 32-33, 35, 37-39, 81-82,
119-21.
In this collection of reviews and comments on
plays, films, books, and people, Tynan includes reviews of Wesker's trilogy, *The Kitchen*, and *Chips
with Everything*. Tynan commends Wesker's ability to
combine the international and domestic, his living,
sympathetic characters, and his adroit use of language. The review of *The Kitchen* compares this play
to plays of O'Neill.

Wardle, Irving. "New Waves on The British Stage." *Twentieth Century* (Summer 1963); also in *Plays and Players* (October 1963), 12-14.
Wardle explores the impact of "theatrical fashion"
on artists and audiences from 1957-63. Wesker complains about the waning interest in working-class
plays.

_____. "Revolt Against the West End." *Horizon*, 5
(January 1963), 26-33.
Wardle claims "Postwar drama in England has taken
its main impetus from the Royal Court Theatre playwrights, who have encompassed a surprising range of
subject matter and style." Such writers as Osborne,
Simpson, Jellicoe, Arden, Wesker, and Pinter have
brought the theatre to contemporary issues, and have
"broken with old formulas to provide broader definitions of what constitutes an interesting play." The
article only briefly mentions Wesker's background
and his trilogy.

Weightman, J. "Heroes of Our Time." *Encounter*, 27
(August 1966), 45-47.
Weightman compares Wesker's *Their Very Own and
Golden City* and Osborne's *A Bond Honoured*, with emphasis on the opposite attitudes revealed towards
the problem of evil: "Wesker wants to eliminate
evil and has, regretfully, to conclude that it ex-
ists, whereas Osborne needs it to stimulate his
verve and is inclined to invent it, where it is not
already present."

Wellwarth, George. *The Theatre of Protest and Paradox*.
New York: New York University Press, 1964. Pages
52, 197, 221, 234-43, 244, 255, 274.
Wellwarth gives a scathing evaluation of Wesker's
trilogy which he feels is not a true trilogy but a
promotional stunt. Furthermore, the playwright's
communism is not ideological but merely a reaction
to injustice. Wellwarth's final complaint is that
Wesker has "as much feeling for language as a suet
pudding."

"Wesker on 42." The Observer Weekend Review, 14 July
    1963, p. 22.

Williams, Raymond. "Recent English Drama." In The Modern
    Age 7. The Pelican Guide to English Literature.
    Ed. Boris Ford. Baltimore: Pelican Books, 1963.
        Williams gives brief mention of Wesker's treat-
    ment of the "disorganization, restlessness, and
    frustration" of life in the Jewish East End and his
    declarations of rage at the general conditions of
    modern life.

Winegarten Renee. "Arnold Wesker: Is Sincerity Enough."
    Jewish Observer and Middle East Review, 19 April
    1963, pp. 18-19.
        Moved by anger, grief, and pity, Wesker writes
    sincere and emotionally effective plays but fails to
    take into account the complexity of human nature.
    He lays too much blame for human illnesses on the
    capitalist society and paints his "bosses" too black.
    Winegarten also believes that Wesker fails to re-
    lieve the dull, inarticulate language with games,
    songs, dreams, and play-acting.

Woodroofe, K. S. "Mr. Wesker's Kitchen." Hibbert Jour-
    nal, 62 (April 1964), 148-51.
        According to Woodroofe, "Probably no play gives a
    more vivid glimpse of what living in Western indus-
    trial society may mean than Arnold Wesker's The
    Kitchen." He provides a plot summary of the play to
    show, how despite political freedom, the characters
    in Wesker's world are denied human dignity, warmth,
    and pleasure.

II. DISSERTATIONS

Conlon, Patrick O. "Social Commentary in Contemporary
    Great Britain, as Reflected in the Plays of John
    Osborne, Harold Pinter, and Arnold Wesker." Disser-
    tation Abstracts International 29:3713A (Northwest-
    ern, 1969).
        Conlon discusses the literary, historical and
    theatrical influences which led to the British the-
    atre's "wave of new dramatists, largely from the
    working class" in the 1950s. He then examines works,
    with an emphasis on social commentary, by Osborne,
    Pinter, and Wesker, as the three major playwrights
    of the period. He treats Wesker's plays through
    Golden City, finding an increased political complex-
    ity in Chips and Golden City.

McKernie, Grant F. "Politics in Modern British Drama: The Plays of Arnold Wesker and John Arden." Dissertation Abstracts International 33:4580A (Ohio State, 1973).
See Arden above.

III. REVIEWS

CHICKEN SOUP WITH BARLEY

The Times, 9 July 1958, p. 6.

The Times, 15 July 1958, p. 5.

Spectator, 10 June 1960, p. 835.

CHIPS WITH EVERYTHING

The Times, 28 April 1962, p. 4.

Spectator, 11 May 1962, p. 621.

Illustrated London News, 12 May 1962, p. 768.

The Times, 2 August 1962, p. 7.

Drama, no. 65 (Summer 1962), 18.

New York Times, 2 October 1963, p. 49.

Educational Theatre Journal, 15 (December 1963), 358-60.

Hudson Review, 16 (Winter 1963-1964), 585-86.

Partisan Review, 31 (Winter 1964), 98-99.

THE FOUR SEASONS

The Times, 11 September 1965, p. 10.

New Statesman, 17 September 1965, pp. 409-10.

The Times, 23 September 1965, p. 8.

New York Times, 15 March 1968, p. 32.

THE FRIENDS

The Times, 20 May 1970, p. 14.

New York Times, 22 May 1970, p. 41.

New York Times, 24 July 1970, p. 17.

New York Times, 30 August 1970, II:1.

I'M TALKING ABOUT JERUSALEM

The Times, 5 April 1960, p. 7.

Illustrated London News, 16 April 1960, p. 660.

The Times, 28 July 1960, p. 5.

Hudson Review, 14 (Spring 1961), 96-97.

THE KITCHEN

The Times, 7 September 1959, p. 3.

The Times, 18 November 1959, p. 4.

New York Times, 14 June 1966, p. 50.

MENACE

The Times, 9 December 1963, p. 14

THE OLD ONES

The Times, 10 August 1972, p. 10.

New York Times, 26 August 1972, p. 16.

ROOTS

The Times, 1 July 1959, p. 15.

New York Times, 7 March 1961, p. 40.

New York Times, 19 March 1961, II:1.

THEIR VERY OWN AND GOLDEN CITY

The Times, 20 May 1966, p. 8.

New Statesman, 27 May 1966, p. 785.

HEATHCOTE WILLIAMS

Born Helsby, Cheshire, November 15, 1941.

The 1960s provided the perfect milieu for Heathcote
Williams and it will be curious to see if his talents
survive the post-psychedelic age. The Local Stigmatic
and A.C./D.C. are both concerned with the effect of the
media on our lives and the schizophrenic nature of modern
existence. Marshall McLuhan's theories concerning television and civilization, the effects of hallucinogenic
drugs, and the panic over the sexual revolution tie Williams' work to a particular cultural era. The foul language which shocked early English and American audiences
seems rather puerile and affected today. Still, there
are serious issues to be resolved which Williams poses
and a perverse humor and energy that could perhaps be
channeled into a forceful statement at a later time.

PRIMARY SOURCES

I. STAGE

AC/DC. Staged London 1970; New York 1971. Gambit, 5
    (1971), 5-138.

_____. London: Calder and Boyars, 1972.

_____. New York: Viking Press, 1972.

Hancocks Last Half Hour. Staged London 1977.

The Local Stigmatic. Staged Edinburgh 1965; London 1966;
    New York 1968. Published in Traverse Plays. Ed.
    Jim Haynes. London: Penguin, 1965.

_____. Evergreen Review, 11 (1967).

_____. Published in Traverse Plays. Viking Press, 1972.

Remember the Truth Dentist. Staged London 1975.

II. FILM

Malatesta, 1969.

III. FICTION

The Speakers. London: Hutchinson, 1964.

_____. New York: Grove Press, 1967.

IV. INTERVIEW

Wardle Irving. Gambit, 5 (1971), 139-44.
    In the same issue of Gambit in which AC/DC was
    first published, Williams and Irving Wardle discuss
    the play. Wardle says it was written "from the
    point of view of a schizophrenic" and represented "a
    collision between two closed systems of drugs and
    schizophrenia." Williams in astonishingly chaste
    language, considering the raw dialogue of the play,
    confesses he is genuinely concerned about mind-con-
    trolling monolithic institutions and notes that an
    article in Time had alerted him to the dangers of
    electro-magnetic pollution. "Trepannation" is a
    metaphor for what society and the media are trying
    to do to men's minds. A personal friend, Billy
    MacGuiness, now deceased, was the model for Maurice
    in the play.

SECONDARY SOURCES

I. CRITICISM

Marowitz, Charles. "The Importance of Understanding
    Heathcote Williams." New York Times, 21 July 1974,
    II:3.

Taylor, John Russell. The Second Wave. New York: Hill
    and Wang, 1971. Pages 219-22.
    Williams is seen to be a conscious, deliberate
    writer "like Congreve." In both The Local Stigmatic
    and AC/DC all the characters seem mad. His ability
    to evoke the lunatic world of Speaker's Corner, Hyde
    Park, in his book, The Speakers, anticipates his
    ability to capture the language of the wild and an-
    gry denizens of AC/DC. That play is seen as a tour
    de force, often funny, sometimes tedious.

II. REVIEWS

AC/DC

New York Times, 24 February 1971, p. 36.

New York Times, 21 March 1971, II:17.

New York Times, 21 July 1974, II:3.

THE LOCAL STIGMATIC

New York Times, 4 November 1969, p. 55.

CHARLES WOOD

Born Guernsey, Channel Islands, August 6, 1933

Charles Wood's army career has provided him with the
themes, language, and situations for his best plays. He
is bitterly anti-war, and both the tragic and satiric
elements of his plays attest to his essential pacifism.
To find justification in war is only possible through
elaborate self-deception. In a larger sense self-deception is the major theme in Wood's plays. He asks dis-
turbing questions of his audience. The questions his
characters ask are intellectually probing and their dialogue reflects the playwright's considerable verbal gifts.

PRIMARY SOURCES

I. STAGE

"Bill and Ben--The Flower Pot Men: A Short Play in
    Progress." Encore, 11 (March-April 1964), 34-42.

Cockade. (Includes Prisoner and Escort, John Thomas,
    Spare.) Staged London 1963. New English Dramatists
    8. London: Penguin, 1965.

_____. London: Hansom Books, 1967.

_____. New York: Grove Press, 1967.

_____. Plays and Players, 11 (December 1963), 23-30+.
    ["Prisoner and Escort"--Play #1 of the 3 plays en-
    titled Cockade.]

_____. Plays and Players, 11 (January 1964), 23-30+.
    ["John Thomas" and "Spare"--Plays 2 and 3 of the 3
    plays.]

_____. Evergreen Playscript Series, No. 13. New York:
    Grove Press, 1967.

Colliers Wood. Staged Liverpool 1970; London 1971.

<u>Dingo</u>. Staged Bristol and London 1967. London: Penguin, 1969.

_____. New York: Grove Press, 1969.

_____. <u>Plays</u> <u>and</u> <u>Players</u>, 14 (July 1967).

"Don't Make Me Laugh." Presented on the Royal Shakespeare Company's bill <u>Expedition</u> <u>Two</u>: <u>Home</u> <u>and</u> <u>Colonial</u>, 4 February 1965.

<u>Fill</u> <u>the</u> <u>Stage</u> <u>with</u> <u>Happy</u> <u>Hours</u>. Staged Nottingham 1966; London 1967. <u>New</u> <u>English</u> <u>Dramatists</u> <u>11</u>. London: Penguin, 1967.

<u>H</u>: <u>Being</u> <u>Monologues</u> <u>in</u> <u>Front</u> <u>of</u> <u>Burning</u> <u>Cities</u>. Staged London 1969. London: Eyre Methuen, 1970.

<u>Labour</u>. Staged Bristol 1968.

"Meals on Wheels." Staged Royal Court Theatre 19 May 1965.

<u>Tie</u> <u>Up</u> <u>the</u> <u>Ballcock</u>. Staged Bristol 1964. <u>Second</u> <u>Playbill</u> <u>3</u>. Ed. Alan Durband. London: Hutchinson, 1973.

<u>Veterans</u>; <u>or</u>, <u>Hairs</u> <u>in</u> <u>the</u> <u>Gates</u> <u>of</u> <u>the</u> <u>Hellespont</u>. Staged Edinburgh and London 1972. London: Eyre Methuen, 1972.

<u>Welfare</u>. Staged Liverpool 1971. (A triple bill consisting of "Tie Up the Ballcock," "Labour," and a shortened version of "Meals on Wheels.")

II. TELEVISION

"A Bit of a Holiday," 1969.

"A Bit of Family Feeling," Yorkshire TV, 1 June 1971.

"A Bit of Vision," 1972.

"The Drill Pig," 1964.

"Drums Along the Avon," BBC2, 24 May 1964.

"The Emergence of Anthony Purdy, Esq.," 1970.

<u>Not</u> <u>at</u> <u>All</u>, 1962.

"Traitor in a Steel Helmet," 1961.

III. RADIO

Cowheel Jelly, 1962.

Next to Being a Knight, 1972.

Prisoner and Escort, 1962.

IV. FILM

The Adventures of Gerard.   (Based on a novel by Sir
     Arthur Conan Doyle.)

Bed-Sitting Room.   Adaptation of original screenplay by
     John Antrobus and Spike Milligan, 1968.

The Charge of the Light Brigade, 1968.

Hadrian the Seventh.   (Based on the play by Peter Luke
     from the novel by Frederick W. Rolfe [Baron Corvo].)

Help!, 1965.

How I Won the War, 1967.   (Based on a novel by Patrick
     Ryan.)

The Krack, 1965.

The Long Day's Dying, 1967.

Tie Up the Ballcock, 1965.

Wood wrote the English dialogue for Federico Fellini's
     Satyricon, 1969.

V. NON-FICTION

"My Boyhood Life and Work in the Theatre and How I Came
     to Be Obsessed with Sex and Violence." The London
     Magazine, 5 (October 1965), 72-75.

"T.V. Drama." Plays and Players, 18 (August 1971), 56-57.

VI. INTERVIEWS

The Times, 18 February 1967, p. 9.

"The Theatre Outside London." Gambit, 5 (1970), 69-74.
     An interview/discussion between three playwrights
     --Alan Plater, Edward Bond, Charles Wood--and three
     directors--Stuart Burge, Jack Emery, Colin George.

Discussion of the relationship between theatre and locality, the author and the community.

SECONDARY SOURCES

I. CRITICISM

Billington, Michael. "Actor-Writer's Anti-Literary Attitude." The Times, 18 February 1967, p. 9.

Bryden, Ronald. "'Veterans.'" Plays and Players, 19 (April 1972), 30-32.
    Bryden compares Veterans thematically to earlier Wood plays and notes the playwright's obsession with the military and the theme of self-delusion.

Cushman, Robert. "The Impression of Impotence." Plays and Players, 16 (April 1969), 28-31, 73.
    Cushman's article begins with a review of Wood's H but soon develops a thematic analysis of the work. H is concerned with the paradox of the Christian who is also a good soldier, with the Englishman who loved India but was spurned by the natives, and with the psychology of men at war. Cushman finds the facts of the Indian Mutiny of 1857 accurate enough but he feels Wood's long soliloquies are old-fashioned and dull. He contrasts the text of the play as written with the performance he had seen.

Hunt, Albert. "Images of War." New Society, 20 February 1969, p. 290.

Rudlin, John. "Charles Wood--An Actor's Writer?" New Theatre Magazine, 6 (1965), 2-5.
    An analysis of the paradox in Wood's relative unpopularity with audiences and popularity with theatre people. Rudlin finds that Wood is attempting, using techniques from "British popular theatre," to "break down the barrier between actor and spectator, between acting and re-acting."

Taylor, John Russell. "British Dramatists--The New Arrivals: No. 8, Charles Wood." Plays and Players, 18 (November 1970), 16-18, 28.
    Review of Wood's work through A Bit of a Holiday (1969). Taylor feels that, although the military has been a central theme in the major plays, Wood himself "is not simply propagandistically pro or anti" army. He is presenting "an anatomy of military life." Includes brief plot summaries and analyses.

_____. The Second Wave: New British Drama for the Seven-
ties. New York: Hill and Wang, 1971. Pages 59-76.
Reprint (with some revision) of the article
above.

II. REVIEWS

"A BIT OF FAMILY FEELING"

The Times, 25 May 1967, p. 6.

The Times, 2 June 1971, p. 6.

"H"

The Times, 14 February 1969, p. 11.

MEALS ON WHEELS

The Times, 20 May 1965, p. 19.

VETERANS

The Times, 10 March 1972, p. 13.

INDEX

This index includes authors (and co-authors) of secondary sources, including interviews, criticism, dissertations. The entry numbers refer to the page numbers.

115181 WITHDRAWAL